FRENCH MARXISM

Between the

WARS

FRENCH MARXISM

Between the

WARS

Henri Lefebvre
and the "Philosophies"

Bud Burkhard

HB

Humanity
Books

an imprint of Prometheus Books
59 John Glenn Drive, Amherst, New York 14228-2197

Published 2000 by Humanity Books, an imprint of Prometheus Books

French Marxism Between the Wars: Henri Lefebvre and the "Philosophies." Copyright © 2000
Bud Burkhard. All rights reserved. No part of this publication may be reproduced,
stored in a retrieval system, or transmitted in any form or by any means, electronic,
mechanical, photocopying, recording, or otherwise, without prior written permission
of the publisher, except in the case of brief quotations embodied in critical articles
and reviews. Inquiries should be addressed to Humanity Books, 59 John Glenn Drive,
Amherst, New York 14228–2197. VOICE: 716–691–0133, ext. 207. FAX:
716–564–2711.

04 03 02 01 00   5 4 3 2 1

Library of Congress Cataloging-in-Publication Data

Burkhard, Fred, 1956–
     French Marxism between the wars : Henri Lefebvre and the "Philosophies" /
Bud Burkhard.
          p.   cm.
     Includes bibliographical references and index.
     ISBN 1–57392–722–8 (cloth : alk. paper)
     1. Communism—France—History—20th century. 2. Marx, Karl, 1818–1883.
3. Lefebvre, Henri, 1905– I. Title.
HX263 .B87 2000
335.4'0944'09043—dc21   99–054681
                                                                    CIP

Printed in the United States of America on acid-free paper

For my parents,

Ken and Eileen Cobleigh

Contents

Acknowledgments   9

Preface   13

Introduction: La Crise de l'Esprit   19

1. Introducing "Philosophies Morhange" (1924–1925)   35
2. Philosophers of the Spirit (1926–1927)   59
3. Politzer and "The Dramatic Life"   81
4. The *Revue Marxiste* (1929)   105
5. And So Ends the Avant-Garde (?) (1930–1940)   133
6. Friedmann: That Man Might Become Man   169
7. Lefebvre, Guterman, and the Critique of Everyday Life   205

Epilogue   235

Conclusions   245

Bibliography   249

Index   271

Acknowledgments

Numerous professional and personal detours and disruptions delayed the completion of this study, and over the years I've benefited greatly from the encouragement and insights of many friends and colleagues. I hope that those I may have inadvertently forgotten to thank below will forgive my oversight and be aware of how grateful I am. In the end, of course, all errors remain mine. All translations, unless stated otherwise, are my own.

At several key junctures in the progress of this project, Steven Eric Bronner offered invaluable advice, criticism, and support which finally brought it to completion. Fellow researchers pursuing parallel topics— especially Michael S. Roth, Kevin Anderson, and Michel Trebitsch— shared their findings with an openness and a shared joy of exploration. Several portions of the manuscript were offered as conference presentations or appeared as articles or research notes. Much of chapter 4 was first presented at the Society for French Historical Studies meeting in El Paso, Texas, during March 1992, and later appeared as "The *Revue marxiste* Affair: French Marxism and Communism in Transition Between the Wars," in *Historical Reflections/Réflexions historique* (winter 1994). Details of the *Revue marxiste enquête* were presented at the American Historical Association meeting of January 1995 in Chicago, and appeared as "Revealing Thoughts: French Post-War Cultural Diversity and the *Revue marxiste enquête* of 1929," in *Contemporary European History* (November 1993). Highly condensed discussions of chapters 6 and 7 were presented to the Colloque Georges Friedmann, held at the Université Libre de Bruxelles during October 1987, and to the Association for Humanist Sociology meeting held in Washington, D.C., in November 1989. I thank Paul Mazgaj, Jack Roth, Stuart Campbell, and William Logue, along with the anonymous readers of this manuscript and its offshoots, for their useful commentary. The late Tom Blakeley encouraged the publication of some preliminary pieces in *Studies in Soviet Thought*. Maxwell Boverman gave a critical last reading to the first four chapters and helped me avoid several unnecessary mistakes. Support from the American Council of Learned Societies, the National Endowment for the Humanities, and the French Ministre des Affaires Etrangères enabled me to participate in scholarly conferences in Brussels and Paris devoted to Friedmann, and brought me into contact with Pierre Nora, Pascal Ory, Edgar Morin, Alain Touraine, and other colleagues who have offered advice and suggestions over the years.

Like many others who studied at the University of Wisconsin at Madison, I was deeply influenced by the late Edward T. Gargan. His enthusiasm for French history, his love of the profession, his methods of graduate education, and his gentle approach to living are the standards I hope to achieve in my career and life. Equal credit should be given to Bernadette (Bunny) Gargan, who not only put up with Ed and his students, but who shares her warmth, love, and intelligence with all. My colleagues from Madison have time and again been the best of friends as well as colleagues, a blessing I treasure: Steve Kale, Michael Berkowitz, Tom Adams, Kathy Alaimo, David Applebaum, Franca Barracelli, Deborah Buffton, Carol Gold, Robert Good, Keith Gorman, Scott Haine, Robert (Ted) Ingham, Craig Johnson, Esther Kanipe, Rosemary Scullion, Brian Stezenski-Williams, Whitney Walton, and David Wright. In Venita (Vinni) Datta, Andrea Tyndall, and Robin Walz, I have found new friends and colleagues, and their encouragement made finishing this study possible.

The late Norbert Guterman occupies a special place in this project. For three years (1981–1984) he shared his memories with me in numerous letters, in telephone conversations, and in two sets of interviews. His puckish humor disguised his failing health until nearly the end. His daughter, Moira Hyle, and her family made me welcome in their home for a final visit before his passing.

Similarly, Docteur Liliane Boccon-Gibod and her family welcomed me in Paris, and she has shared a wealth of information about her father, Georges Friedmann. I am deeply thankful for the interest she has shown in my work as well as for the personal kindness she and her family extended to me.

My children—Amanda, Rose, and Mike—contributed more to my work than they'll ever know. To those friends and relatives who influenced my efforts, thank you. I am particularly grateful to my sister, my brother, their families, and to my entire extended family—all have encouraged and supported my education and writing (and probably wondered—at least once in a while—if I would ever finish!). Celeste Kolodin's friendship helped me through many difficult moments, and Nina Lafiner tolerated my preoccupation during the final revisions with amusement and patience.

But my greatest appreciation, my real debt, and my deepest thanks belong to my parents, Ken and Eileen Cobleigh. For all their love and understanding I dedicate this book to them.

27 August 1997

Preface

Despite the fact that the Philosophies circle included some of twentieth-century France's most prominent and influential intellectuals, there is no history of the Philosophies. The existence of the Philosophies *équipe* (invoking the images of an artisanal workshop as well as a "gang"), has long been recognized, in part thanks to George Lichtheim, who wrote in 1966 that

> the formation of the first Marxist-Leninist group on France may be said to have occurred between 1929 and 1934. Its members, Georges Politzer, Henri Lefebvre, Norbert Guterman, Georges Friedmann, Pierre Morhange and Paul Nizan, kept out of factional disputes, and hence attracted less attention than the Surrealist literati.[1]

David Caute offered a similar, brief acknowledgment when he claimed "the emergence of a dynamic and advanced school of Marxist philosophy in France may be dated from the mid-twenties and associated with the Philosophies group."[2] Later, in three of those massive, collective histories at which the French excel, the Philosophies were praised and recognized by some of the most respected intellectuals of post-1968 France. In *Histoire des Français*, Pascal Ory noted that Friedmann, Lefebvre, and Politzer were the leaders in introducing theoretical Marxism into French academic and general intellectual discourse.[3] In the *Histoire du Socialisme*, Georges Lefranc agreed that

> more doctrinally oriented [than the Surrealists] was the group formed by six young philosophes: Georges Friedmann, Norbert Guterman, Henri Lefebvre, Pierre Morhange, Paul Nizan, Georges Politzer. In 1929, they founded *La Revue marxiste*. Politzer specialized in political economy, Henri Lefebvre and Paul Nizan in Marxist exegesis.[4]

And in *L'Etat des Sciences sociales en France*, Alain Touraine, Edgar Morin, Jean Duvignaud, Emmanual Terray, and Daniel Lindenberg repeatedly cite Lefebvre, Friedmann, and Politzer as the key twentieth-century French theorists who must be dealt with.[5]

And yet the Philosophies, their history, and their influences have never received more than these brief, general nods of recognition. That simple oddity provoked the initial curiosity leading to this project.

Yes, the postwar writings and influence of Lefebvre have been discussed in a number of studies. And, since the republication of his works began in 1960, Nizan—the most peripheral member of the Philosophies—has been the object of increased scholarly interest, although his image has suffered the predictable ebb and flow of popularity over time. Yet those seeking to discover how and why these young men became Marxists, what their influence was, and more importantly what kind of Marxism they developed will discover next to nothing. Nor has there been any attempt to link this small group to the broader currents of French and European intellectual and polticial life between the wars.

There is no history of the Philosophies because they are an embarrassment.

The Philosophies are an embarrassment because of the path they traveled on their way to Marxism. When they first coalesced as a group in 1924, they were searching for a philosophic and religious solution to the *inquiétude* plaguing French intellectuals after the Great War. Worse still, they embraced mysticism, in an effort to understand the world they lived in, directly, immediately, and totally. They traveled through classical Idealist philosophy, especially Kant, Schelling, and Hegel, before reaching Marx, Engels, and Lenin. Their first project as militants of the Parti Communiste Français (PCF, the French Communist Party) was the *Revue marx-iste*, a short-lived journal which collapsed in semicomic fashion with sev-eral members of the Philosophies being ejected from the PCF, only to be reinstated later.

The Philosophies are an embarrassment because of the type of Marxism they developed. They brought Hegel into their Marxism, and worse still into their Leninism. Among the first in France to read the famous "1844 Economic and Philosophic Manuscripts," they saw in Marx's concept of alienation the key to understanding their own *inquiétude*. When Friedmann, Lefebvre, and Guterman read Lenin, they turned to his *Philo-sophic Notebooks on Hegel's Science of Logic*. And, in committing themselves to the Communist movement, the Philosophies worked to overcome and to dispel the conditions of not just their own personal, cultural, and intellec-tual confusion, but that of their postwar generation as well.

Despite the explosion of interest in alternative theoretical Marxisms since the sixties, the Philosophies remained unstudied. The reasons are to a degree understandable. What self-respecting "Marxist" since 1945, regardless of the particular theoretical or political orthodoxy adhered to, would write a book about a bunch of mystics? How could theorists com-mitted to the notoriously unimaginative Parti Communiste Français write a history about French Marxist thought and deal fully with the develop-ment of their mentors, and especially Lefebvre—the "losers" in the humanist versus scientific Marxism battles associated with Althusser's fraud—mentors who taught them "wrong"? And in a strictly academic context, how can one impose meaning and cohesion onto a trajectory like this, with its slippage from mysticism through Idealist philosophy to Marx?

Still, as Leszek Kolakowski so neatly phrased the situation, each of us has intellectual ancestors whose portraits we would not care to hang in the family dining room, and of whom the neighbors' malicious gossip reminds us.

The project of these young French intellectuals is more than an ignored episode in intellectual history. With their activities during fifteen interwar years alone, by seeking answers in fields as diverse as traditional philosophy, urban and industrial sociology, psychology, political economy, poetry, the novel, and critical literature, the small Philosophies circle cre-ated a montage of investigations rivaling the output of their colleagues of the Frankfurt School. As a group, they—Lefebvre and Guterman, Friedmann and Morhange, Politzer and Nizan—were seeking answers to the basic questions of human existence, those questions that fall into the category of "what really matters." How can the world be understood? How does one act, both effectively and ethically, in the world? These are essential human concerns, and whether one accepts the answers that these men found is, in a sense, less important than the recognition that their questions are our own.

This recreation of the history of the Philosophies offers detailed insight into the responses to inquietude the Philosophies shared with other French intellectuals, the dissemination of Hegelian and Marxist thought in France, and a revisionist examination of the history of French Communism and theory. In the introduction, the postwar cultural crisis is established as a context, as is the immediate contemporary attention that focused on this handful of young men. In chapter 1, the formation and politicization of the Philosophies during 1924–1925 are examined. Their evolution through classical Idealism, through Schelling and Hegel, is recounted in chapter 2. Chapter 3 is devoted to Politzer's writings on philosophy and psychology prior to his joining the French Communist Party, with an examination of his related works of the 1930s. In chapter 4, the importance of *La Revue marxiste* is discussed, along with the context and details of the "scandal" that caused its demise.

Chapter 5 contains a general outline of the dramatically changing personal and broader French contexts during the early and mid-thirties, and also offers an examination of some of the circle's activities and minor writings. Since the life and works of Nizan are well-covered in a number of monographs, only his activities and works connected to the Philosophies project are examined here. The major works of Friedmann during the 1930s are discussed in chapter 6, with particular emphasis on his theoretical evolution and the stormy reaction to his now-classic study of the early Soviet Union. A similar scrutiny is applied in chapter 7 to the major writings produced by Lefebvre, usually in partnership with Guterman, during the same years, along with a closing emphasis on the continuities and developments within Lefebvre's thought after 1945. A brief epilogue outlines the activities of the Philosophies from the summer of 1939 through the remainder of their lives.

NOTES

1. George Lichtheim, *Marxism in Modern France* (New York: Columbia University, 1966), p. 86; note that Lichtheim thanks Guterman as one of his "personal friends and acquaintances" in the preface, p. ix.

2. David Caute, *Communism and the French Intellectuals* (New York: MacMillan, 1964), pp. 263–65. In this work, Caute's erroneous reference to Nodier is derived from Simone de Beauvoir's *Memoirs of a Dutiful Daughter*, trans. J. Kirkip (New York: World, 1959), pp. 249–50.

3. Pascal Ory, "Une Culture nationale à son appogée," in *Histoire des Française XIX-XX siècles*, ed. Y. Lequin, tome 3 (Paris: Armand Colin, 1984), p. 255.

4. Jacques Droz, ed., *Histoire générale du Socialisme*, tome 3, 1919–1945 (Paris: Presses Universitaires de France, 1977), p. 404. There are passing references to Nizan, Politzer, and Lefebvre scattered throughout tomes 3 and 4.

Nearly any work on post-1917 French or "Western" Marxism will mention the Philosophies in passing, usually by paraphrasing Lichtheim's comments. The longest published discussions are Edward Mortimer's *The Rise of the French Communist Party, 1920–1947* (London and Boston: Farber and Farber, 1984) and Daniel Lindenberg's *Le Marxisme introuvable* (Paris: Calmann-Lévy, 1975): Curiously, both examine the groups's history only from 1924 until 1929. Brief biographies for Friedmann, Lefebvre, Nizan, and Politzer appear in Denis Huisman, ed., *Dictionnaire des Philosophes* (Paris: Presses Universitaires de France, 1984) and in the appropriate volumes of *Dictionnaire Biographique du Mouvement ouvrier français, quatriéme partie (1914–1939)*, under the general editorship of the late Jean Maitron (Paris: Editions ouvriéres, n.d.).

5. See Marc Guillaume, ed., *L'État des sciences sociales en France* (Paris: La Déouverte, 1986). Elsewhere, Michelle Perrot has written on Friedmann's influence on the post-1945 Christian "workerist" movement, including the young Jean-Marie Lustiger, future cardinal and archbishop of Paris. See Perrot's "L'Air du Temps," in *Essais d'Ego-Histoire*, ed. Pierre Nora (Paris: Gallimard, 1987).

Introduction

La Crise de l'Esprit

In the wake of the Great War, French intellectuals—indeed intellectuals across Europe—faced a cultural crisis of unprecedented proportions. The underlying intellectual and cultural assumptions of the prewar elites may have been challenged before 1914, but the naive idealism and the arrogant rationalism shared by fin-de-siècle Europeans ultimately disintegrated when confronted with the irrational experience of the trenches. The most treasured European beliefs about rationality and human progress vanished into the muck of the Great War's battlefields even more quickly than the physical debris the fighting left strewn in its wake.

In 1919, this loss of confidence and of cultural cohesion was dubbed "*la crise de l'Esprit*" by Paul Valéry—a crisis of the spirit or soul as much as of the mind. Writing for the leading periodical, *Nouvelle revue française,* Valéry argued that the collapse of intellectual certainty brought with it a new obsession with locating principles for restructuring and reunifying the postwar world. The dissolution of cultural unity set off a desperate search for certainty and meaning, indeed for salvation, Valéry continued:

> Never have so many prayed, nor so profoundly: ask the priests. All the saviors are evoked, all the founders, all the protectors, all the martyrs, all the heros, the fathers of nations, the sainted heroines, the national poets. . . .[1]

19

Valéry believed the chaotic frenzy of the ensuing search for certainty was symptomatic of just how deeply European intellectuals had been shaken:

> And within this same mental disorder, in the name of this same anguish, cultivated Europe has undertaken the rapid resurrection of its innumerable schools of thought: dogmas, heterogeneous idealist philosophies, three hundred ways of explaining the world, one thousand and one nuances of Christianity, two dozen from positivism. The entire spectrum of intellectual illumination displays its incompatible colors, exposing with a strange contradictory flash the agony of the European soul.[2]

Valéry pinpointed the essential yearning of this pell-mell reassimilation and restructuring of all of European cultural history as a search for freedom from the "menacing conspiracy" of an irrational destiny beyond human control. The solution he offered was an acceptance of the crisis and its symptoms:

> Perhaps one creates this freedom while searching for it. But for such an undertaking, one must abandon for a time the considerations of ensembles and study, within the reasoning individual, the struggle of the personal life with the social life.[3]

Yet Valéry could offer no solution to sufferers other than an acceptance, for the moment, of the crisis and an examination of its symptoms through literature and art.

Five years later, Marcel Arland, one of the afflicted, reproached Valéry for not finding a cure for what Arland labeled the "new sickness of the century," "*la nouveau mal du siècle.*" Once again *Nouvelle revue française* provided the forum, as Arland claimed that the real root of their anguish and despair lay in the continuing absence of spiritual and rational certainty, the lack of philosophical Absolutes, in brief, the absence of God,

> ... a spirit within which this destruction of God is accomplished, where the problem of the divine is no longer debated, with what will it fill the void unleashed within itself and what can support the waning strength of centuries and of the instincts? The absence of God is the nonsense of all morality.[4]

Arland argued that without belief in some form of Absolute, be it philo-sophical, scientific, or theological, there could be no certainty, no order to the human or the natural worlds, no ethics or meaning in life. Arland believed a solution could be found, perhaps in a new mysticism or in a mir-acle of revelation. Yet while Arland held out the hope of spiritual and cul-tural reconciliation, he himself was so overwhelmed by frustration and despair that he could offer no better solution than the one already suggested by Valéry, simply to continue to express individual isolation and anguish through literature and art. For Arland and the young men of the 1920s, Valéry's short-term cure had become an inescapable disease in its own right.

Just as the physical and demographic impacts of the Great War lin-gered on throughout the 1920s and 1930s, so too did this chronic cultural anguish. Various individuals and small groups ransacked "the entire spec-trum of intellectual illumination" without reaching a consensus that a cure had been revealed or was even near to discovery. Perhaps some briefly found some certainty to grasp onto, and all certainly would agree with LeCorbusier's 1921 claim that "the primordial physical laws are simple and few in number. The moral laws are simple and few in number."[5] But beyond such sweeping generalities there was never any agreement. Intellectual doubt, psychological confusion, and anguished isolation remained a fixture of French intellectual life until the Nazi occupation. Traces of the "*nou-veau mal du siècle*" are easily identifiable in Jean-Paul Sartre's famous 1938 novel *La Nausée*, of which one reviewer wrote:

> If *La Nausée* had appeared thirty years ago, what excitement in the world of letters, what an uproar probably! Today the novel appears perfectly normal.[6]

Two full decades after the war, Sartre was simply viewed as adding yet another study of individual isolation and anguish to an already moun-tainous collection of despair leading nowhere. An almost schizophrenic fascination with and rejection of "orientalism," "americanization," "bolshe-vism," "munichois culture," various classicisms, and the myriad other ill-defined and contradictory possibilities were inescapable features of the entire era after the war.

*   *   *

But Arland had held out a glimmer of hope, a hope shared by others. Commenting on Arland's arguments in 1925, Georges-Philippe Friedmann wrote that Arland and his compatriots were indeed pursuing "a doctrine, a conception of the world, a mystique which will permit him to build a moral code first, later and by rebound an aesthetic code."[7] While recognizing Arland figured among those searching for an answer, "he says so without overemphasis, on every page," Friedmann found the result less a search for resolution and more a lucid description of Arland's personal suffering and internal disorientation, a continuous description of *inquiétude*'s effects.[8]

Friedmann agreed numerous inquiéts already desperately sought their solutions in a new mysticism. Whether the answers lie with one of the Catholic tendencies or in the aesthetics of sensualism, in the renaissance of Hebraic messianism by the Philosophies or the exploration of the unconscious undertaken by the Surrealists, Friedmann could not say. Yet, like the rest of this "new generation" Friedmann asserted the solution could be found: "To each epoch its mystique. A single mystique is possible today."[9]

Only a month after writing these lines, Friedmann selected just one of the tendencies within his generation as the most likely to transcend the crisis of *inquiétude*. He suggested that if the Philosophies moved beyond their messianic emphasis, ceased being merely destructive of existing culture, and began addressing the basic problems of living in the world, then they would discover the solution all craved. Friedmann thought the Philosophies were already particularly effective in pursuing their goals with an "ardent confidence," but felt they must overcome their "fierce apoliticism" and get involved in daily life.[10] Recalling his own assertion that a single solution in mysticism was possible, Friedmann concluded, "and the young writers who participate in Philosophies will discover it, if they agree to enter into the times with decision and candor."[11]

Nor was Friedmann alone in singling out this one small circle of the tormented for special scrutiny. At the midpoint of the two decades between the world wars, when the French still envisioned themselves as living after the war and not yet between the wars, Henri Daniel-Rops, another sufferer, similarly described the dilemma of his time. By turning away from the search for ensembles and universals, the "new generation" emerged as, in his words, a "generation without souls."[12] This youth, socialized to sacrifice themselves in the war but missing the numbing horrors of battle, remained undisciplined and unwearied, staring at the horrors their fathers had made, and horrified by the normalcy of postwar daily life. Daniel-Rops employed the same vocabulary and listed the same symptoms as had Valéry, Arland, and others earlier in the decade: "a strong opposition between the sentiments that constitute our souls, a marked desire for intellectual, moral and metaphysical suffering, an instability pushed to the point of disequilibrium," resulting in the fragmentation of the generation itself into isolated, anxious, despairing individuals sharing only their fears and their anguish.

Echoing Arland, Daniel-Rops claimed the craving for absolutes required either a forever-uncertain profession of faith in its existence or the direct apprehension and understanding of the Absolute—mysticism. "And the mystics," Daniel-Rops told his readers, "are already here, within Catholicism and within the Philosophies group."[13]

These and other articulate members of the new generation singled out from their own ranks one small circle as representative of the "Crisis of Spirit" and the "illness" shared by all. At the same time, the Philosophies were repeatedly described as somehow distinctive, and possibly the ones who would discover the method of transcending the dilemma of inquietude.

The Philosophies derived their name from the first journal they published. The core of the circle was a handful of Sorbonne students, all born at the turn of the century. The acknowledged leader was Pierre Morhange. A poet, compared by some to the Surrealists Paul Eluard and André Breton, Morhange was born in June 1901 into a secular Parisian Jewish family devoted to music and artistic creation.[14] Without being a Zionist and lacking an education in any specifically "Jewish" culture, Morhange nonetheless identified with a "Jewish sensibility." Engaged in a deeply personal search for religious salvation and for absolute truth, his drive to understand, to express, and to live an ethically based life led him to be what he himself later described as messianic. This element of Morhange's personality is captured in the fact that some of his pieces were signed with the pseudonym of a bogus Oxford scholar, "John Brown," evoking the image of the nineteenth-century mystic and abolitionist of North America.

No one ever disagreed with this self-labeling. Even after years of friendship, Henri Lefebvre wrote of the difficulty of judging and understanding Morhange: "He did not hesitate to use blackmail, to break with you straight away and to publicly denounce you as a traitor if you did not recognize the glory of God."[15] And Georges Friedmann later attributed to Morhange "the ardor of a prophet."[16]

Born just weeks before the beginning of the twentieth century, Norbert Guterman joined a horde of Central European students who arrived in postwar France to pursue their educations and careers in relative calm. Arriving in Paris from Warsaw in 1921, Guterman decided on a French education after reading the essays of Montaigne. Although Guterman's family had a long rabbinical history, his father had become a music teacher and hence a member of the Central European liberal intelligentsia. While Guterman officially "missed" the war, he found himself conscripted as an artilleryman and translator in the battles to defend Warsaw from the Red Army.

With little money and disappointed expectations, ("he imagined that the French all spoke and thought like Montaigne, in his language, with the same finesse and the same lightness," Lefebvre recalled[17]), Guterman took a room on the rue Git-le-Coeur with a childhood friend and fellow student from Warsaw, the mathematician Szolem Mandelbrojt.[18] Henri Lefebvre, his closest friend and collaborator for the next fifteen years, described Guterman as the shrewdest member of the Philosophies, reasonable and moderate despite his personal reserve and cynical debunking of the ideas of others. Lefebvre believed Guterman's irony and realism served as a counterweight for the energy and grandiose exaggerations of Morhange.[19] More importantly, Guterman brought with him a command of ten languages, an ability which later allowed him to become one of the world's leading translators.

Georges Politzer began his direct contribution to the Philosophies with the fourth issue of *Philosophies*. Born in Transylvania during 1903, Politzer reportedly was involved in the Soviet revolutions in Hungary. The son of a physician, Politzer left his homeland to pursue his education, first to Vienna in 1919 (where he would later claim to have worked with Freud himself) and later to Paris in 1921.[20] Another philosophy student at the Sorbonne, he shared the apartment of Guterman and Mandelbrojt. Politzer was the most flamboyant of the collective. Within the diversity of interests contained in the Philosophies, Politzer claimed psychoanalysis as his private preserve and practiced self-analysis "in a slightly peculiar manner."[21] Lefebvre later wrote that Politzer would work himself into a fury, "half-feigned, half-real," and provoke violent arguments with his colleagues. Lefebvre found himself alternately amused and intimidated by Politzer, and suggests the process was one of catharsis. Theoretically inclined, Politzer contributed his intelligence, humor, and taste for practical jokes to the Philosophies.

Describing himself as a young man, Lefebvre wrote that he inherited his massive physical appearance and blond hair from his Breton father, and long face "like a Goya painting" from his mother, a native of the Pyrenees.[22] Similar to many young intellectuals during the interwar years, Lefebvre saw himself as alienated from his family and the values of his parents, an alienation compounded by the respect Lefebvre clearly felt for his humorous, Voltairean, anticlerical father and his staunchly Catholic mother, from whom Lefebvre claims to have received his tenacity and "violent passions curbed by reason." Among the Philosophies he believes he was the most philosophic, "in the technical sense of the word."[23] Lefebvre's conception of his role within the group was to sort out the nebulous ideas and plans generated at the group's sessions and to capture the arguments in a more properly theoretical form. To the task he brought the encouragement and the lessons of his mentor, Maurice Blondel, whose efforts to bridge the chasm between philosophy and theology in his *L'Action* of 1893 discomforted liberal secular Republicans and traditional conservatives and Catholics alike.[24]

As a youth Lefebvre suffered from all the classic symptoms of *inquiétude*, but with an unusual twist. A devoted reader of Nietzsche and Pascal, Lefebvre found himself afflicted with a double infection of disorientation. On the one extreme, he shared the essential problem of his generation: how to replace God, absolute intellectual certainty, the problem posed by Pascal in his famous fragment "The Wager," as well as by Nietzsche's Zarathustra. On the other extreme, Lefebvre also linked his personal and individual anguish to another image, that of Nietzsche's crucified Christ as revolutionary, destroyed for disrupting a stagnant society and threatening those in power, an image capturing the role he and others foresaw for their generation.[25] These two themes are complementary rather than contradictory, although the successful solution to the problems would require Lefebvre fuse several distinct and complementary analytical frameworks.

When he wrote about the Philosophies in 1925, Georges-Philippe

Friedmann was not yet a member of their collective project. Born in 1902, Georges was the fourth of five children in a family headed by the successful financier Adolphe Friedmann. From 1926 on he would provide the funds for the projects of the Philosophies. An indication of the younger Friedmann's personal wealth can be found in the well-circulated but inaccurate tale of Friedmann having once purchased, out of his pocket money, a Monet painting to give to his mother as a birthday gift.[26] After preliminary studies in the more practical fields of industrial chemistry and physics, Friedmann received his father's permission to enroll at the École Normale Supèrieure (ENS). While preparing to enter the ENS as part of the promotion of 1922, Friedmann befriended Paul-Yves Nizan and Raymond Aron, and presumably was acquainted with Nizan's alter ego, Jean-Paul Sartre.

Privileged by family background and by education, Friedmann rejected the complacent enjoyment of life. As early as 1920 he had joined the *Clarté* movement of militant and leftist pacifism associated with Henri Barbusse.[27] He also threw his support into the periodical *Europe*, inspired by the disciple of Gandhian nonviolence, Romain Rolland.[28] By 1923, at the age of twenty-one, he coauthored his first book, an English-language *History of the French People*, prefaced by Barbusse.[29] And at the École Normale, Friedmann founded a "Groupe d'information internationale de l'École Normale Supèrieure," the chair of which he turned over to Nizan in August 1925.[30] At an usually young age, therefore, Friedmann demonstrated both a great deal of talent as well as commitment to the solutions offered by the postwar "Left."

Throughout his life, Friedmann shared the vision of Spinoza, who sought an underlying unity between men, and between Man and Nature, by dissolving the Absolute into everything, making the human universe perfectible. Yet Friedmann also remained fascinated by Leibniz, who described a world of isolated and discrete substances seeking harmonious coexistence and interaction. The problem of simultaneously adopting both these great philosophers is obvious, for how could one bridge the gulfs separating the singular man and Social Man, and those separating Man and Nature? How could absolute unity and irreducible individuality be reconciled?

But this antagonism posed by coupling Spinoza and Leibniz, this chasm dividing the eternal and universal from the finite and singular—are these not, in more philosophic and less poetic language, simply the same thing as *la crise de l'esprit, la mal du siècle, l'inquiétude?* In his very choice of philosophic guides Friedmann revealed himself to be representative of an entire generation.

Paul-Yves Nizan did not begin to share in the activities of the Philosophies until 1928, but his friendship with Friedmann and Nizan's own activities within their common intellectual world made him well aware of their efforts from the start. Born in 1905, *normalien*, Nizan sought to flee his inquietude by taking a position as tutor in the British Crown Colony of Aden during 1926 and 1927, an experience later described in his pamphlet *Aden-Arabie*. In his published correspondence to his fiancée Henriette Alphen, there are two references to Friedmann, Morhange, and the Philosophies. In January 1927, Nizan mused that perhaps only mysticism offered the possibility of a meaningful life:

> That's the opinion of my friend Friedmann and generally of *l'Esprit*: they place [their faith] in the Bolshevik mystique. That direction is good: it's one of my directions.[31]

Shortly after, he flippantly wrote Mlle. Alphen on a postcard: "Sometimes you make me think of what my friend Friedmann wrote by way of eulogy to Pierre Morhange: 'an amoeba delivered to a tropism.' "[32]

Since the revived interest in Nizan's life and works began in 1960, scholars have explored at length his almost desperate search for meaning and community as a solution to the *mal du siècle*. At one point Nizan considered becoming a Protestant minister, and as late as 1927 he was still warning Mlle. Alphen of his attraction to religious life. During the mid-twenties, his anxiety manifested itself as brief and nearly simultaneous flirtations with both Georges Valois's Faisceau and the Parti Communiste. Returning from Aden and marrying, Nizan's definitive step to resolve his personal anguish was to rejoin the Communists in early 1928.[33] Over the next decade Nizan played several important roles in the collective history and development of the Philosophies.

*   *   *

At first glance it is difficult to find anything particularly distinctive or promising about this handful of very young intellectuals. Certainly, the Philosophies shared in the cultural disorientation of the era, and were representative of their generation's experiences. On the other hand, four of the six core members were Jewish by heritage, but while all felt a strong attraction to a generally religious solution to their spiritual crises, none appears to have had a strong religious education or identity. Two members of the Philosophies, Guterman and Politzer, were not even native French. According to Simone de Beauvoir, they were considered as disreputable and violent by other Sorbonne students.[34] And Lefebvre would later admit to their *testism*, the petty and rather adolescent dares with which they challenged themselves. They engaged in gratuitous acts, minor breaches of propriety such as theft, in order to demonstrate their contempt for bourgeois morality. Pilfered items were returned or destroyed to prove their disdain for material comforts.[35] As university students the Philosophies were a "delinquent peer group," a phrase usually reserved for adolescents of lycée age.[36] By any standard, these were rather unlikely candidates for the task of resolving the *inquiétude* of a generation!

However, in several basic aspects, the Philosophies were distinctive from their peers. There were of course other groups, other circles pursuing the same goal. But most of the other circles of disoriented youth shared, as Daniel-Rops noted, mostly their fears and their anguish. These "groups" in a sense were no more than accidental meetings of individuals who remained isolated and disoriented. The Philosophies from the onset emphasized themselves as a collective engaged in a search for a universal answer to the problem, rather than simple and repeated expressions of their internal anxieties. Contemporaries frequently described them as an *équipe*, signifying a work crew or a team as well as a gang. Moreover, in their quest for absolute truth the Philosophies never totally retreated into contemplation and inactivity, but instead always addressed the problem of living and acting in the world, and of the need for an ethics to be implemented. Finally, the collective written products of this project include poetry, sociology and political economics, philosophy, history, novels, literary criticism, and psychology. By pooling their talents, the Philosophies's search resulted in a richly textured expression of *inquiétude* while working toward their goal of discovering a synthetic, totalizing answer.

*   *   *

One of the most astute internal and later external critics of Marxism, Leszek Kolakowski, once reminded us that:

> Twentieth-century thinkers have done everything to keep alive in our minds the main questions that have troubled theologians over the years, though we phrase the questions somewhat differently. Philosophy has never freed itself from its theological heritage, which means that theological questions were merely clumsy formulations of essential enigmas that still hold us in thrall.[37]

The foremost of these is the very possibility of the complete realization of human values and thought, of the resolution of desires in either a divinely ordered heaven or a rationally constructed utopia. This problem of eschatology, Kolakowski adds, presumes a conflict between human essence and human existence, an alienation of some basic human trait that can and will be abolished with the creation of a just, egalitarian, and universal harmony.

For Kolakowski, modern secular philosophy and theology alike must justify and give meaning to individual adversity while awaiting the construction of this harmonious utopia. Pangloss's "best of all possible worlds" requires a teleological grounding in either a divinely ordained plan or a rational "slaughter-bench of history" if life is to be palatable. And the comprehension of this ultimate meaning requires revelation, an insight into the essential order and organization of the chaotic experiences that fill human daily life.

Yet, Kolakowski notes, any conceptualization of the Absolute claiming systemic completeness and closure is doomed to stagnate in sterile immobility:

> So far we know of no completely flexible final method invulnerable to history's threat of petrification. We know only of methods that maintain durable vitality because they have created the tools of self-criticism, even though they may have originally included certain dogmatic premises or a belief in certain absolutes. We believe that these methods have, over a long period of time, devised instruments to overcome their own limitations. In our day Marxism, phenomenology, and psychoanalysis have demonstrated this radicalism.[38]

Thus, human pursuit for knowledge ruptures into a conflict between the endless search for absolute certainty and the rigid maintenance of knowledge already grasped as an Absolute. This philosophical conflict Kolakowski describes as the antagonism of the priest and the jester:

> The priest is the guardian of the absolute; he sustains the cult of the final and the obvious as acknowledged by and contained in tradition. The jester is he who moves in good society without belonging to it, and treats it with impertinence; he who doubts all that appears self-evident. He could not do this if he belonged to good society; he would then be at best a salon scandalmonger. The jester must stand outside good society and observe it from the sidelines in order to unveil the non-obvious behind the obvious, the non-final behind the final; yet he must frequent society so as to know what it holds sacred and to have the opportunity to address it impertinently.[39]

Kolakowski declared himself in favor of the jester, whose antics may amuse good society but contribute to its destruction. The mystical vision of the jester, with its unending quest for the reconciliation of human desires and existence, its ceaseless pursuit of a utopia where alienation is banished, this quixotic project is that of the Philosophies and of their generation. And, as their story will demonstrate, each of the Philosophies chose which of the two roles to play.

NOTES

1. Paul Valéry, "La Crise de l'Esprit," *Nouvelle Revue Française*, no. 71 (August 1919): 323.

2. Ibid., pp. 323–24.

3. Ibid., p. 337.

4. Marcel Arland, "Sur un Nouveau Mal du Siècle," *Nouvelle Revue Française*, no. 127 (February 1924): 157.

5. LeCorbusier, "Les Tracés Régulateurs," *L'Esprit nouveau*, no. 5 (May 1921), as cited in Kenneth E. Silver, *Esprit de Corps* (Princeton: Princeton University Press, 1989), p. 381.

6. André Thérive, "Les Livres. Jean-Paul Sartre, La Nausée," *Temps*, 14–15

July 1938, p. 3, as cited in James Smith Allen, *In the Public Eye: A History of Reading in Modern France* (Princeton: Princeton University Press, 1991), pp. 121–22.

7. Georges-Philippe Friedmann, "L'Inquiétude de Marcel Arland: à propos d'une nouvelle mystique," *Europe*, no. 28 (April 1925): 491.

8. Ibid., p. 492.

9. Ibid., p. 495.

10. Georges-Philippe Friedmann, "Une direction dans la Nouvelle Génération," *Europe*, no. 26 (May 1925): 125.

11. Ibid., p. 126.

12. Henri Daniel-Rops, "Sens et perils d'une inquiétude," *Notre Temps* (July 1928): 38.

13. Henri Daniel-Rops, *Notre Inquiétude* (1927; reprint, Paris: Academie Perrin, 1953), p. 70. All references are from the 1953 edition; other references to mysticism are scattered throughout *Notre Inquiétude*, especially pp. 142–50, and, directly linked to the Philosophies, pp. 145, 148–50, 295.

14. Biographic details of Morhange's life can be found in his interview with Luc Boltanski, "Ce qui m'engage," *Action poétique*, no. 18 (October 1962), and in the introduction by V. Nikiprowetzky to Morhange's *Le Sentiment lui-même*, (Paris: SPDG, 1966).

15. Henri Lefebvre, *La Somme et le Reste* (1959; reprint, Paris: Bélibaste, 1973), p. 392; all references to this autobiography are from the 1959 edition. See also Lefebvre's other autobiographic writings, *L'Existentialisme* (Paris: Editions du Sagittaire, 1946) and *Les Temps du méprises* (Paris: Stock, 1975).

16. Georges-Philippe Friedmann, *La Puissance et la Sagesse* (Paris: Gallimard, 1970), pp. 363, 379; Friedmann's massive intellectual autobiography contains surprisingly few references to the Philosophies, although he does state his warm memories of the comradery he shared with Morhange and the "gang" and the "experience and enrichment they had given."

17. Lefebvre, *L'Existentialisme*, p. 18. Guterman is constantly mentioned in all of Lefebvre's autobiographic writings, including in his interview with Bruno Bernardi, "Une Vie pour penser et porte la lutte de classes à la theorie," *Nouvelle Critique*, no. 306, ns# 125 (June 1979).

18. Mandelbrojt is recognized as a leading mathematician of the twentieth century. I am indebted to James E. Cyphers, Archivist of the Rockefeller Archive Center in North Tarrytown, N.Y., for providing materials from the International Education Board Records, box 54, folder 689. See also Max Jacob's enthusiastic comments on Mandelbrojt in *Collection Correspondance*, ed. F. Garnier (Paris: Editions de Paris, 1955), pp. 315–16. Guterman enjoyed sharing his memories of Man-

delbrojt, beginning with his communication of 8 May 1982 and continuing throughout his correspondence and interviews with the author.

19. Lefebvre, *La Somme et le Reste*, p. 243.

20. Lefebvre has written several slightly differing descriptions of Politzer, reflecting the political contexts during which the pieces were written more than afterthoughts about Politzer. In the years immediately following the Second World War, Lefebvre adhered to the Parti Communiste policy of comparing the Party stalwart and Resistance hero Politzer, who died in 1942 at the hands of the Gestapo, with Paul Nizan, the "traitor" who resigned from the PCF with the Hitler-Stalin Pact of 1939 and died during the German offensive during the following spring. Lefebvre's longest, most detailed accounts of the Philosophies and of Politzer can be found in his *La Somme et le Reste*, written after his rupture with the Communist Party in the late 1950s. In 1986 Viktor Polgar, cultural attache at the Washington, D.C., embassy of what was then the Hungarian Peoples' Republic, kindly provided me with information from *Magyar Eletrajzi Lexikon* (Budapest: Akademiai Kiadó, 1981), pp. 623–24, regarding Politzer (correspondence, 4 March 1986). Gyorgy Ranki, director of the Institute of History of the Academy of Sciences, Budapest, corresponded with me on the state of Politzer studies during the same year. And Béla Szombati, cultural attache of the Republic of Hungary, responded to my inquiries both by telephone and by letter (29 March 1990).

21. Lefebvre, *La Somme et le Reste*, p. 389.

22. Ibid., p. 243.

23. Ibid., p. 392.

24. Ibid., especially tome 2, part 4, chap. 1, "Maurice Blondel et le Catholicisme liberale."

25. Ibid., tome 1, part 3, chap. 1, "Le Soleil Crucifié." On the philosophic combination of Pascal and Nietzsche, see Charles M. Natoli, *Nietzsche and Pascal on Christianity* (New York: Peter Lang, 1985). This Dionysian image of the "Crucified Christ" is a major theme in Kurt Meyer's *Henri Lefebvre, Ein Romantischer Revolutionär* (Vienna: EuropaVerlag, 1973). See Pierre Boudot's discussion of Lefebvre in *Nietzsche et l'au-delà de la liberté* (Paris: Aubier-Montaigne, 1970); as well as Rémi Hess, *Henri Lefebvre et l'aventure du siècle* (Paris: A. M. Métailie, 1988); and Douglas Smith, *Transvaluations: Nietzsche in France 1872–1972* (Oxford: Clarendon Press, 1996). For an overview of the explosion of Nietzsche studies since 1988, see Allan Megill, "Historicizing Nietzsche? Paradoxes and Lessons of a Hard Case," *Journal of Modern History* 68, no. 1 (March 1996). Michel Trebitsch is currently writing a biography of Lefebvre, the first fruits of which include his "Les mésaventures du groupe Philosophies (1924–1933)," *Revue des Revues*, no. 3 (spring 1987); "Le groupe 'Philosophies' de Max

Jacob aux Surréalistes 1924–1925," *Cahiers de l'Institut d'Histoire du Temps Present*, no. 6 (November 1987); "D'Avant-Poste à La Conscience mystifiée," *Communication to the Colloque Henri Lefebvre* (May 1986); and "Le Renouveau philosophique avorté des années trente. Entretien avec Henri Lefebvre," *Europe*, no. 683 (March 1986).

26. Guterman repeated this anecdote during our interviews. Annie Cohen-Solal and Henriette Nizan suggest the painting was a Renoir, not a Monet, in *Paul Nizan, Communiste impossible* (Paris: Grasset, 1980), pp. 75–76. However, Docteur Liliane Boccon-Gibod (personal communication, 4 October 1986), has informed me that the tale is "pure legend" and "part of a myth" circulated to discredit Friedmann by the orthodox Communists. My thanks for her corrections and the precise biographical information she has provided about her father. See also Friedmann, *La Puissance et la Sagesse*, for other details.

27. Friedmann had short reviews in *Clarté*, no. 59 and no. 65 during 1924, and in no. 70 (January 1925). His longest contributions were "Quelques jeunes," *Clarté*, no. 65 (1924) and "Sur une Ethique des nations," *Clarté*, no. 71 (1925).

28. On the Barbusse-Rolland debates, embodied in *Clarté* and *Europe*, see David James Fisher, *Romain Rolland and the Politics of Intellectual Engagement*, (Berkeley and Los Angeles: University of California, 1988).

29. Georges-Philippe Friedmann with Guy de la Batut, *A History of the French People* (London: Methuen, 1923). Reviewed for *Europe* by Léon Bazalgette, no. 17 (May 1924).

30. The friendship between Friedmann and Nizan is gaining increasing attention. See Pascal Ory, *Nizan: Destin d'un révolte* (Paris: Ramsay, 1980) and especially Cohen-Solal with Nizan, *Paul Nizan, Communiste impossible.* Curiously, Raymond Aron, in his *Memoires* (Paris: Julliard, 1983), does not mention Friedmann at all until the post-1945 era. Yet Robert Colquhoun, in the first volume of his *Raymond Aron* (London: Sage, 1986), pp. 29–30, notes that Friedmann and Aron were tennis doubles partners at the ENS.

31. Paul Nizan, "Correspondance d'Aden," in *Paul Nizan, intellectuel communiste*, ed. J. J. Brochier (Paris: Maspero, 1970), tome 1, p. 105.

32. Ibid., p. 107. Nizan's reference is to Friedmann's letter to Morhange, published as a preface to Friedmann's "Ils ont perdu la partie éternelle d'eux-mêmes," *Esprit*, no. 1 (May 1926): 120.

33. For Nizan, one should begin with Sartre's preface to the 1960 Maspero edition of *Aden-Arabie*. Major studies include A. King, *Paul Nizan* (Paris: Editions Universitaires, 1966); Jacqueline Leiner, *Le Destin Littéraire de Paul Nizan* (Paris: Klincksieck, 1970); W. D. Redfern, *Paul Nizan: Committed Literature in a Conspiratorial World* (Princeton: Princeton University, 1972); Youssef Ishashpour, *Paul Nizan,*

Une figure mythique et son temps (Paris: Sycomore, 1980). Most recent and useful are Ory, *Nizan: Destin d'un révolte*; and Cohen-Solal with Nizan, *Paul Nizan, Communiste impossible*. With the assistance of Marie-José Jaubert, Mme. Nizan completed her *Libres Mémoires* (Paris: Editions Robert Laffont, 1989) before her death.

34. Simone de Beauvoir, *Memoirs of a Dutiful Daughter*, trans. J. Kirkup (New York: World, 1959), pp. 249–50. For another memoir by a contemporary at the Sorbonne, see Janine Bouissounouse, *La Nuit d'Autun* (Paris: Calmann-Lévy, 1977), especially pp. 15–20, 25–28, 42, 60, 121, and 215.

35. Lefebvre, *La Somme et le Reste*, p. 385–86.

36. See the discussion of French adolescent "delinquent peer groups" in Jesse Pitts, "Continuity and Change in Bourgeois France," in *In Search of France*, ed. S. Hoffman et al. (New York: Harper, 1965), pp. 254–59. See also David Schalk, *The Spectrum of Political Engagement* (Princeton: Princeton University, 1979).

37. Leszek Kolakowski, "The Priest and The Jester," in *Toward a Marxist Humanism*, trans. J. Z. Peel (New York: Grove, 1968), p. 9.

38. Ibid., p. 33.

39. Ibid., pp. 33–34. Kolakowski has written extensively about the political and philosophic need for utopia. See his "The Concept of the Left" in the same collection; "Need of Utopia, Fear of Utopia," in *Radicalism in the Contemporary Age*, vol. 2: Radicalism, Visions of the Future (Boulder: Westview, 1977); and his *L'Esprit révolutionnaire/Marxisme—utopie et anti-utopie*, trans. J. Dewitte (Paris: Presses Universitaires de France, 1978). One should also recall Karl Mannheim's *Ideology and Utopia*, and the writings of Ernst Bloch on the subject of Utopia. J. P. Nettl's "Ideas, Intellectuals and the Structures of Dissent," in *On Intellectuals: Theoretical Studies and Case Studies*, ed. Philip Rieff (Garden City, N.Y.: Doubleday, 1969), remains a provocative study. An applicable alternative analytic framework would be Michel Löwy's concept of "revolutionary romanticism," as set out in his *George Lukács—From Romanticism to Bolshevism*, trans. P. Camiller (London: NLB, 1979) and *Dialectique et Révolution* (Paris: Editions Anthropos, 1973). After all, Lefebvre himself wrote an important essay on just this topic: "Vers une Romanticisme révolutionnaire," *Nouvelle Revue Française*, no. 58 (October 1957), followed by a roundtable discussion with L. Goldmann, T. Tzara, and others, published as *Le Romanticisme révolutionnaire* (Paris: La Nef de Paris, 1958). This theme is evident in Meyer's biography of Lefebvre cited above, and is employed with remarkable success by Mitchell Cohen in his *The Wager of Lucien Goldmann: Tragedy, Dialectics, and a Hidden God* (Princeton: Princeton University Press, 1994).

Chapter 1

Introducing "Philosophies Morhange"

(1924–1925)

Elbowing its way into the horde of periodicals saturating French intellectual life during March 1924, *Philosophies*, with its implication of a hodgepodge of ideas and enthusiasms thrown haphazardly together, encapsulated the cultural confusion of the postwar years. The Cubist poet Max Jacob penned the opening pages, and Jean Cocteau's playful parody of the itinerary of an admiral jostled Pierre Drieu la Rochelle's gloomy meditations on the stifling complexities of modern life. The Surrealists René Crevel and Philippe Soupault found their writings wedged in with Paul Lotte's prayer for divine aid, while Jean Grenier (using the pseudonym "Jean Caves") mused on the decadence of western Europe. The closing page of the journal declared "the first characteristic of *Philosophies* is to juxtapose the works of poets, essayists and philosophers." By self-definition *Philosophies* embodied Paul Valéry's "*crise de l'Esprit,*" with its disorderly coexistence of the most contradictory ideas and opposed principles of life and art.

Pierre Morhange, the young director of *Philosophies*, contributed several reviews and five "Fragments," prose poems interspersed with verse, to the issue. In these "Fragments" Morhange switched constantly back and forth between the first- and third-person pronouns, leaving the impression that he was examining himself from a variety of angles. All of the actors portrayed in Morhange's "Fragments" were preoccupied by their own searches for internal peace:

> My personality is a psychological debate. One day, it will be known. I am,
> by dabs. . . . An important point: I am or I was accursed. I am a little
> accursed. That's indispensable. . . .[1]

"God has promised me his ingratitude," one of Morhange's sufferers
brooded, expressing the poet's bitter confusion and that of an entire generation of *inquiéts*.

Yet Morhange did not extend this bond of shared anxiety to all,
restricting this comradery to those few "touched by grace" who displayed
originality and strength. Badly disguised as "John Brown," Morhange
expressed disdain for

> those men who work for audiences of the third rank because, having been
> at school since they were five and going there until they're thirty, they
> write worse than notaries, because they write for impoverished men. I
> leave aside those who fart like horses to flatter the prowesses of people,
> if I am not to feel a great pleasure for their errors and if I do not wish to
> express my pain for that which we take to be the junkroom of France.
> What joy to pull them, at all costs, under my blessed fool's feet! I always
> will discover, me, what goes to heaven. [2]

By simply obtaining so many contributions from so many notorious
and violently opposed writers, Morhange demonstrated an unusual ability
to carry out audacious and high-profile projects. Morhange's success was
particularly impressive given the general hostility existing between the
individual authors. The only common characteristics most of these writers
shared were a relative newness to literary notoriety and their isolated, individual searches for a subjective or idealistic philosophy to replace the
values and beliefs bankrupted by the war.

Morhange's energy also led to his efforts to gather signatures on a petition supporting the Spanish philosopher Miguel Unamuno, recently exiled
by the dictatorship of Primo de Rivera. Fellow students from the Sorbonne
added their names to an impressive list which included the prestigious signatures of Henri Barbusse, militant pacifist and founding editor of *Clarté*,
and Leon Brunschvicg, the prominent Sorbonne philosopher. The manifesto itself was brief, describing *Philosophies* as a "new group of poets,

essayists and philosophers" who wished to express to Unamuno their respectful sympathy and their admiration. "Youth is a tyranny more cruel and more certain" than political tyranny, the petition read, and Unamuno's message to youth would endure when tyrants were forgotten.[3] The petition apparently circulated to other periodicals, for *Nouvelle Revue Française* carried a notice associating itself with the protests against Unamuno's exile "which have arisen in all the French press."[4] In March and May, another new journal, *Europe*, carried its own protests.[5] But the independent leftist review *Clarté*, despite (or perhaps because of) the presence of its former editor, Barbusse, among the fifty-two signatories, savagely criticized the *Philosophies* declaration, sneering at "the ridiculous gesture" of the petition, and demanding an explanation why these same men did not protest on behalf of the workers and militants who bore the brunt of the dictatorship's repressions.[6] The sharp *Clarté* editorial must have shocked some of the well-meaning if politically naive signatories, and forced some, particularly Morhange, to begin confronting their personal beliefs regarding the proper roles of intellectuals in politics.

In a separate review, *Clarté* reviewer Georges Michael continued the assault by decrying the issue as a pompous collection of representative avant-garde writers. Contributors were criticized one after another for illogical organization, apolitical themes, and preoccupations with sensuality. For example, Robert Honnert's piece on the physical maturation of an adolescent was dismissed with a curt "it's as if the body doesn't exist before puberty!" Morhange, the literary newcomer, had the dubious honor of being selected for this ridicule along with Jacob, Cocteau, and Drieu la Rochelle (the last had over half the review devoted to his "petite bourgeois fatalism"): Morhange's "Fragments" were "long enough already," and his style no better than a bad imitation of Cocteau.[7]

Other reviewers viewed the first issue with mixed reactions. *Nouvelle Revue Française* thought the contributions very uneven in quality, and the combination of poetry, essays, and philosophy confused. However the reviewer believed *Philosophies* contained some "hidden, but profound, thought," and hoped future issues would fulfill expectations. In *Accords*, another journal launched in March 1924, André Desson and André Harlaire jointly heralded *Philosophies* as a sister project of "authentic youth."[9] The problem with *Philosophies* they attributed to the fact that "right now they agree upon the ends to be attained but not upon the means to employ," the common dilemma of the postwar generation. If Morhange had not garnered instant immortality, he least attracted the attention of the Parisian literary and political avant-garde.

With the second issue of *Philosophies,* released two months later, a distinct program began to be evident. *Philosophies* now proclaimed itself "the review of the new literary generation, the movement devoted to poetry, analysis and the renaissance of philosophy." Although the diversity of writers who published in *Philosophies* no. 1 was not maintained, many younger writers filled their place. The lesser members of the Surrealist movement, such as Soupault and Gérard Rosenthal (using the pseudonym "Francis Gérard") were welcomed. Max Jacob, who had been introduced to Morhange during the fall of 1923 by Jean Grenier, continued to submit his writings and exerted considerable influence on Morhange. Grenier, always under the alias of Jean Caves, contributed several more pieces, as did another protégé of Jacob, Marcel Jouhandeau.[10]

The type of renaissance *Philosophies* represented was quickly established in this second issue of May 1924. Edgard Forti took to task the venerable literary critic of *Nouvelle Revue Française,* Albert Thibaudet, for ignoring Henri Bergson's efforts to establish a "positive metaphysics in science" in his just-released *Bergsonisme.*[11] Worse still for Forti was Thibaudet's silence on the purpose of pursuing Bergson's path: the immediate apprehension of data from experience, the understanding of the direction history flowed in, and self-immersion into that current. The great philosopher himself fared no better, for Jean Weber peeled back the "verbal elegance" of *Essai sur les Données immédiates de la conscience* to expose Bergson's side-step around the issues of individual free will and action. Grenier continued his examination of the decline of the West, and found the resurgent East—Russia, India, China, and Japan—was profoundly altering the way Europeans thought.[13] And Henri Jourdan applauded the critically disdained *Nietzsche* by Ernst Bertram for its lively reconstruction of the philosopher's multifaceted personality and thought.[14]

Two other young students continued Morhange's task of sorting out those writers touched by grace from those to be ignored. Henri Lefebvre's first contributions to *Philosophies* were reviews of current literature. Of Marcel Lesvignes's *Ordor di Femina,* Lefebvre wrote only two terse lines:

M. Marcel Lesvignes brags he has made love in ten capital cities. We are persuaded that he has never left Paris, chastity or boredom.[15]

Lefebvre's second piece was a lengthy defense of Marcel Proust's *Recherche du Temps perdu* against the criticisms of Ramon Fernandez, a young but established commentator for *Nouvelle Revue Française*. Lefebvre claimed that the novel represented far more than the simple "psychological study" Fernandez suggested, since Proust provided a subtle, harmonious, and original masterpiece, documenting an individual's search for universal spiritual meanings in life, in short, a solution to the pervasive "*mal du siècle.*"[16]

Norbert Guterman continued this defense of Proust, arguing he had not simply created a work of psychology, or merely attempted to link some psychic manifestations to their causes. Instead Guterman compared Proust's novel to a painting, since his characters were somewhat detached and overdrawn. Proust's failure to locate a passage to the universal was far less important than his attempt, Guterman thought, and Proust's work reflected his effort to determine the contents of his consciousness.[17]

Philosophies became the review of those seeking to throw off the tutelage of the established norms of art, literature, and thought. The literary critics, the renowned philosophers who taught them, the entire edifice of fin-de-siècle culture debased in the Great War was being shoved aside as insufficient and tainted. The problem facing the young iconoclasts was where to find a replacement. Lefebvre and Guterman underscored Proust's attempt to uncover universal meanings. Grenier and other contributors pointed East. Morhange looked heavenward:

> Où aller maintenant?
> O Dieu, où revenir, où retourner?
> Mon lieu de naissance.
> O Dieu, ma colonne vertébrale. Me pousse, dure et
> belle.
> Mon dos.
> Mon os.
> Je viens à la suite, dieu des Armées.
> Dieu le Seul.
> O que ta volonté est fait.[18]

In a closing note, *Philosophies* announced that John Brown would soon arrive in Paris, where he would live near Max Jacob and prepare a "Grand Pamphlet" for *La Revue des Pamphletaires*.[19] This new journal was another of Morhange's projects, although only the first pamphlet, the American expatriate Julien Green's *Pamphlet contre les catholiques de France*, appeared in October 1924.[20]

The critics were not terribly impressed. Thibaudet waited a year before deigning to reply to Forti, and even *Clarté* did not bother to grumble. *Accords* suggested sending "some old farts" to Oxford in exchange for Brown, "who surely must be afflicted by some handicap preventing him from laughing at himself." Part of the problem, Dessan and Harlaire thought, lay in the "invisible and omnipresent" hand of Jean Cocteau.[21]

Cocteau was not, however, the behind-the-scenes mentor of *Philosophies*. True, Guterman became friendly with Cocteau after reviewing *Thomas l'Imposteur* in *Philosophies* no. 1.[22] But the real influence was that of Max Jacob, the Cubist poet who converted from Judaism to Catholicism after a mystical vision and who was then rather uneasily residing in the monastery St. Benoît-sur-Loire. Jacob had several attractions for the frequent visitors he described as "Philosophies Morhange."[23] Like Morhange, Guterman, and others connected to the review, he was Jewish by birth, and espoused mysticism as the method of discovering universal truths, even if he turned to Catholicism for the certainty he craved. And, more important for Morhange at least, he used poetry as the vehicle for capturing and expressing those truths he found. For Jacob, poetic inspiration and insight became mystical revelation, unifying the individual and the cosmos.[24]

"Morhange and I are good friends," Jacob wrote Jean Grenier in May 1924:

> He visits here frequently. . . . He is surrounded with interesting friends, notably Fèvre or Lefèvre and Guterman, who pleases me, and others who guard a secret that must be divined, like Forti. In taking the road of philosophy these young men have taken the best.[25]

Jacob thought Morhange and the others had the potential to become writers of the first rank, and played the role of mentor and prophet thrust upon him. In return, Morhange provided an outlet for Jacob's writings and served as defender against those younger writers who, like the Surrealists, refused to acknowledge their debts to this master poet and attacked him with a "ferocious ingratitude."[26]

Yet there were differences of personality, of purpose, and simply of age that made the relationship between "Philosophies Morhange" and Jacob tense. "Morhange disturbs me," Jacob wrote in July 1924; he found Morhange too demanding of perfection, too intent, and too "poodle-like" in his attempt to model himself after his chosen master.[27] When *Philosophies* ceased publication Morhange procrastinated the return of one of Jacob's manuscripts, leading to an exchange of letters and quarrels born of misunderstanding before matters were cleared up. Afterward, a perplexed and rather bitter Max Jacob summed the situation up: simple men (like Jacob) are men of character, Morhange is complicated.[28]

Morhange dominated the circle of students and young writers gathering around his *Philosophies*. Others took note of his antics and his occasionally bombastic proclamations, and forgot if his comrade's name was Fèvre or Lefebvre! In much the same manner, the first lengthy articles of Guterman and Lefebvre in *Philosophies* no. 3 of September 1924 (essays on Brunschvicg and Lavelle, respectively) were overshadowed by the "Billet de John Brown: où l'on donne le «la»." This piece may have been the promised "Grand Pamphlet" mentioned in the previous issue. Morhange certainly attached great importance to the piece, even dubbing it "Premier Manifeste de *Philosophies*" and circulating handbills in an effort to sell an expensive deluxe printing of the issue.

The "Billet" was the last major piece signed "Brown" to appear. According to Morhange/Brown, the project of *Philosophies* was to search for eternal, absolute truths in the Aristotelian tradition. To critics pressuring the Philosophies into social and political actions, Morhange offered instead their dedication to the "pure acts" of literature and contemplation. *Philosophies* heralded a "great philosophic renaissance" in preparation for "a great human revolution," the "triumph" of which would be ensured by the "warrior spirit" and "monastic discipline" of the Philosophies.[29] Morhange/Brown claimed this militancy was exemplified by the lives of "Szolem, Norbert, and Georges," whose austere lives revolved around philosophical and mathematical debates.[30] The manifesto rambled from philosophy to literature, and Morhange even offered space to his anticipated critics, as in asides like "A voice as in theaters of old—My dear John

Brown, if this is a manifesto which you have written, I pity you, because it is very poor, and you have much to learn."[31]

Were it not for one very brief section of the manifesto, Morhange's own words probably sufficed as a generalization for most readers' reactions. However, in a section entitled "Petite Note sur le Surréalisme," Morhange wrote:

> Surrealism is just an art, or even a process—of forsaking a movement already begun and jumping aside without crying "Station," followed by the exploitation of the little corner conquered. This art, invented by the genial Max Jacob, pleases me less when used by Louis Aragon, who uses it very coldly (is it—goodness—for us that he wears himself out?). Surrealism is only beautiful when performed by a living, lyrical scrawler, or in other words, instinctive, natural.—Surrealism contents itself by making crude sweeps of detail, while failing to be humorous. And nothing is as ugly as lyricism which mocks itself.[32]

The reaction of the Surrealists was characteristic of the violent challenges that movement was famous for. *Nouvelle Revue Française* published without comment the following "curious exchange of letters."[33] The Surrealist note was succinct:

To M. Pierre Morhange:

Monsieur, We are warning you once and for all that, if you permit yourself to write the word "Surrealism," spontaneously and without our consent, slightly more than fifteen of us will correct you with severity. Adhere to this warning!

The note was signed by Paul Eluard, Louis Aragon, André Breton, Roger Vitrac, and "etc." for the other members of the Bureau de Recherches surréalistes. Morhange's reply occupied the entire following page. He acknowledged receiving their "nasty letter," and taunted the Surrealists to carry out their threat, which "will be received by an efficient and implacable defense, have no doubts about it. . . . My friends and I, I know it well, are the last defenders of human liberty." Much of the letter was filled with predictions of divine wrath against the Surrealists, proclaimed the vision of "the new Spirit, Love and the Fate of Man" seen by Morhange, and welcomed "persecution." Morhange swore to combat the "unhappy men" of Surrealism, and worse still, promised to convert them! Titillated by the promise of a prolonged disagreement, the literary reviews gave wide coverage to the impending scandal.

The incident was indeed curious. Surrealists continued to contribute to every issue of *Philosophies*, despite the exchange and the escalation of the quarrel in *Philosophies* no. 4 of November 1924. Guterman and Lefebvre openly sided with Morhange in irritating the Surrealists. Guterman described Surrealism as the "impotence of being intolerant," as capable of surviving only as a parasite, and as "a method of speaking with nothing to say."[34] Lefebvre sympathetically reviewed Tristan Tzara's *7 Manifeste Dada* and suggested the spirit of Dada be judged alongside the "outrages of certain innovators," open insults to Breton, who initially welcomed Tzara at Paris with the enthusiasm of a disciple and later broke with him angrily.[35] Furthermore, *Philosophies* no. 4 contained an announcement that Morhange would comment on specific works by Breton, Aragon, Crevel, Eluard, Soupault, Delteil, and other Surrealists in the following issues. (In fact, Morhange only reviewed Eluard in the final issue of *Philosophies*, which closed with the note that the other pieces were already written and omitted only because space was lacking).[36]

Beyond the quarrel with the Surrealists lay a more important point. Breton and the Surrealists addressed their protest to Morhange directly, indicating that the true author of the "John Brown" selections was no secret. Yet Morhange had written of the Philosophies in his manifesto, and specifically mentioned "Szolem, Norbert, and Georges." The fact is that Morhange now saw *Philosophies* as a group project, as emphasized by his use of "my friends and I" in his reply to the Surrealists. Guterman and Lefebvre's reviews in *Philosophies* no. 4 indicate their support of Morhange and their participation in what began as his quarrel. The transition from "Philosophies Morhange" to "the Philosophies" was well under way.

This fourth issue of *Philosophies* is noteworthy for several reasons. Most noticeable was the complete absence of anything written by Morhange himself, and only a few scattered and short pieces in which he obviously participated in the cooperative writing. But *Philosophies* no. 4 also contained a collective meditation on God, an annoying topic to the militant atheists of Surrealism.[37] The declared intention of the *enquête* was to attempt to locate, within the spirit (*esprit*) of readers, that portion corresponding to the word "God," but the questions that followed probed at the religious sensibilities of individuals, how each separately felt about the roles of God and eternity in an inquiet age. The Philosophies circle was still working within the framework outlined by Arland in *Nouvelle Revue Française.*

But the appearance of Georges Politzer as a collaborator with *Philosophies* marked an important change. His contributions, critiques of recent writings on psychoanalysis and on Kant, were symptoms of an increasing seriousness for *Philosophies.* Equally important was the emphasis on the intellectual traditions and innovations of Central Europe Politzer wove into discussions of French philosophy.[38]

The major indication of a serious new direction for *Philosophies* was Henri Lefebvre's "Critique de la Qualité et de l'Etre," a fragment of a lengthy manuscript on being, identity, and consciousness that Leon Brunschvicg, as Lefebvre's academic advisor, had the good sense to turn down as a thesis topic.[39] The publication of Lefebvre's effort was continued in *Philosophies* no. 5/6 of March 1925, and later in the journal which superseded it, *Esprit.* Lefebvre began by attempting to reclarify a key concept commonly used in the postwar discourse about *inquiétude,* the definition of that "Self" or "*Moi*" which Arland and others so fruitlessly and desperately pursued. The problem, Lefebvre asserted, was that one should not begin with the individual Self and then seek its affirmation in external reality, but instead first seek the external sources of the elements constituting the individual, in a process of comprehending and integrating similar to the reconstruction of the ego in psychoanalysis.[40] Lefebvre argued for the acceptance of an inescapable duality of universal and finite elements within individual Being, a tension requiring self-conscious action if those disparate fragments were to be reunified.[41] But throwing resolution of the schism between individual and universal back into Being and Action, Lefebvre admitted, raised another question: How, then, does one act? Lefebvre acknowledged that traditional resolutions of the problem of how to act either accepted the extreme relativism of individual choice or presupposed an internal unity already preexisting within Being. Breaking off his effort at this point, he conceded that the first solution became a matter of faith, and the latter a vicious circle as one tried to create a unity already there.[42]

The belatedly published *Philosophies* no. 5/6, dated March 1925, was unremarkable except for Lefebvre's continuation of his efforts in "Positions d'attaque et de defense de nouveau mysticisme." Lefebvre claimed the solution to inquietude could be discovered in those "certain privileged moments" when mysticism provided insight into "a reality knowable, definable, perceptible even to the heart or the mind (*esprit*)."[43] Yet Lefebvre found traditional mysticisms trapped in a contradiction since, if total knowledge of the Absolute was obtained, then neither the individual nor the search for absolutes needed to exist. Moreover, Lefebvre faulted traditional mysticisms for attributing the status of absolutes to idealized human concepts in the attempt to transcend the human condition.[44] He suggested a solution might be found in the conception of an internally divided mysticism where one part was the restricted and isolated insight available to individuals, while the second was pure, absolute, and only partially comprehensible by the first.[45] And moreover "*L'esprit n'est pas donné à lui-même...*"; knowledge of itself was denied to the abstract spiritual side of Lefebvre's dialectic as well as to individual consciousness.[46]

Lefebvre posited the necessity of the "Total Act" to achieve a progressive unification of the individual and the universal fragments of consciousness. In seeking to create itself, the individual selected and pursued a path which it believed would effectively transform itself and the external reality confronting it, a transformative element Lefebvre believed would prevent a pure and simple negation—that is, the total but static comprehension—of the Absolute. The "Total Act" that Lefebvre conceived would be

> truly decisive and inaugural. It introduces us into a total activity, entirely creative, because it does not rely on perceptive support from any known given in the manner of the ancient mystics. It is not obviously or abstractly determined, but uniquely as "perception of the Other, impetus toward the Other."[47]

Thus, Lefebvre's individual engaged in a self-creative adventure requiring faith in one's choices. Moreover, the project was ceaseless, since the brief glimpse of universal and essential unity gained by the unique individual was quickly lost. Then the individual must gamble again on another choice in its efforts to fleetingly grasp the "Self" and a portion of the Absolute.[48]

In his first, awkward philosophic effort, Lefebvre had posed the postwar problem of inquietude in precisely the same terms as Valéry and Arland: how to bridge the gap between the essential and universal on one hand, and the individual and transitory on the other. Strongly influenced by Schelling, but drawing inspiration from Nietzsche and Pascal as well, Lefebvre began to explore themes that would fascinate him for the next half century. As stumbling and problematic as this attempt was, Lefebvre's fragments represented the first efforts to move beyond literary pranks and schoolboy critiques to the serious project of creating a method for understanding and transforming the world.

The greatest interest in this new theme within *Philosophies* came from an unexpected quarter. Georges Michael, one of the animators of *Clarté*, extensively reviewed Lefebvre's "Critique." Michael thought Lefebvre at the point of articulating an original doctrine, one capable of brushing aside Bergson as well as the whinings of the sufferers of the *mal du siècle*. He insisted that the "Critique" was just a beginning, since Lefebvre's method contained internal contradictions and required considerable development. Michael's most serious concern was the confusion of consciousness and action, and in particular the danger of substituting discussion about action for action itself. Still, Michael concluded that "when the editors of *Philosophies* better express and define themselves, the moment will arrive to expound on their optimism, which contrasts in such a singular fashion with the fundamental pessimism of the Surrealists."[49]

When reviewing *Philosophies* no. 5/6, Michael devoted his entire lengthy discussion to Lefebvre's "Positions d'attaque et de defense du nouveau mysticisme." Now Michael knew Lefebvre and the Philosophies for what they really were: bourgeois anarchists! Michael contended Lefebvre had taken the Cartesian *cogito* and, as feared, substituted action for thought, and therefore blundered in a manner typical of bourgeois philosophy: his spontaneous metaphysical adventure lacked any grounding in reality as actually constituted. The real world was not defined by individual consciousness, Michael underscored, but by classes.[50] Yet, a major shift was evident here. Michael and *Clarté* had totally disdained *Philosophies* when it first appeared, but Lefebvre's stumbling attempt to weave a theory of self-conscious action appealed to the *Clartéistes* who found their inspirations in Marx and Sorel. Michael took Lefebvre's ideas, even if incomplete and "wrong," seriously, in a sense simultaneously political and philosophic.

With this combined issue *Philosophies* ceased publication.[51] But as a group the Philosophies solidified around Lefebvre's project of self-definition through action. And they arrogantly began to see themselves as Daniel-Rops and others thought they might be: They were the ones with the answer to *inquiétude*. Their assurance was so great that they planned a series of open forums at the Atelier Theater, with the first billed as "Ouverture de votre Testament" in the endpage of *Philosophies* no. 5/6. Here occurred the most striking example of their self-confident posturing, a confrontation between Politzer and a member of the audience:

> Politzer: We affirm that...
> Listener: (violently) We? Who is that, "we"?
> Politzer: We? νους *l'Esprit*, monsieur![52]

Politzer's grandiose claim to be spokesman for the Absolute was thrown into the surely startled face of Henri Massis, one of those who had claimed to be the spokesman of pre-1914 youth![53] The Philosophies had chosen a truth as theirs and were intent on shouldering aside anyone who obstructed their search.

However, the Philosophies began to find themselves increasingly entangled with the projects of others. The relations between *Philosophies* and the Surrealists had improved, and the Philosophies joined in some of the notorious scandals of that group. After the "John Brown Affair," Breton himself, in *Révolution Surréaliste* of January 1925, requested "certain of my friends not to fight the activities, possibly entirely exterior to Surrealism, but highly changeable, of Pierre Morhange."[54] The same issue of *Révolution Surréaliste* also contained without commentary excerpts of Guterman's sarcasms from *Philosophies* no. 4.

These shifts are most evident from the differing receptions of the Philosophies' initial "Ouverture." In his *Clarté* review, Georges Michael denounced the constant evocation of revolution and action, and rhetorically asked, quite simply, when were the Philosophies going to stop talking and do something. Moreover, he warned against those who applauded when the Philosophies spoke of revolution and action: "But when you try to give these words their real and actual class meaning, everyone will hate you like they hate us."[55]

Conversely, the Surrealist Paul Eluard thought their mysticism and call for a total revolution was misunderstood by most in the hall. Yet rather than berate the Philosophies, he spent the bulk of his short discussion attacking the

> optimism of the gentlemen of *Clarté* in spreading, while glorying under the grand sunshine of hammers and sickles, a mediocre regime relying on, like the capitalist system, the accommodating and repugnant order of labor.[56]

The revolution, Eluard claimed, would not come from disciplined militancy or cold rationality, but from intuition and passion.

Ironically, at the very moment when their periodical vanished, the Philosophies suddenly found themselves the center of a great deal of interest. One of the foremost leftist theorists in France had taken them seriously enough to attack them, but in such a way as to suggest that their errors were correctable. One of the most prominent new poets defended them, despite his dislike for the smugness of their mysticism.

Others became interested in their project as well. René Crevel wrote a long summary of the Philosophies' development and their project for *Nouvelles Littéraires*.[57] And within the space of several months, the prestigious *Nouvelle Revue Française* printed more mentions of *Philosophies* than it had published during the life of the journal. *Nouvelle Revue Française*'s literary commentator, Albert Thibaudet, mentioned them twice in his column, although once only to lump them together with the Surrealists and *Cahiers du mois*.[58] In his other mention Thibaudet "rejoiced" in the announcement that *Philosophies* would publish a translation of Ernest Curtis's study of Balzac.[59] In May 1925, *Nouvelle Revue Française* printed a short "recognition" of "three young reviews founded in France during 1924: *Philosophies, Les Cahiers du mois, Accords* are equally directed by young philosophers, Spinozists for the most part, mystics or preoccupied by mysticism."[60] The following issue contained a brief statement from the rather baffled *Nouvelle Revue Française* editors, who acknowledged receiving a note from

Morhange claiming that "*Philosophies* is the only one of the young French reviews which freely and honestly declared itself mystical."[61]

This interest was the applause Georges Michael had warned them of. And the Philosophies believed he was right. They decided to cease talking and to act.

Events in the "real world" Michael kept telling them about provided the opportunity. Rebelling Rif tribesmen of Spanish Morocco smashed the Spanish colonial forces and, under their leader Abd-el-Krim, spilled over into the French Moroccan Protectorate in April 1925, leading to joint military action by the two European governments. In June, *Clarté* carried two articles announcing a new program for the journal and the movement it represented. First, in "Crise et reorganization de *Clarté*," Georges Michael outlined the "broad cultural front" tactics that the group henceforth would pursue in the hope of working with like-minded intellectuals.[62] Second, the initial step in building such an alliance was taken with *Clarté*'s "Lettre Ouverte aux Intellectuels pacifistes, anciens combattants, revoltes," and the editorial "Ce que nous en pensons...," and posing this simple question: What do you think of the war in Morocco?[63]

The response to *Clarté*'s question was immense. The squabbling groups of Parisian intellectuals finally had a common focus. An initial protest against the French government's plans to intervene in the crisis was printed in *L'Humanité*, the daily organ of the Parti Communiste Française, on 2 July, and reprinted in *Clarté* of 15 July, bearing almost a hundred signatures. The same issue of *Clarté* also contained the individual responses to its *enquête*. Morhange's printed response read simply: "My friends and I totally protest against the war in Morocco. We give you our reasons below."[64] The *Clarté* editors added a footnote indicating that, for reasons of space (and, one wonders, of content?), the response could not be printed in full.

This first manifesto was quickly followed by a second, in which the Surrealists, *Clartéists*, Philosophies, and Belgian Surrealists clustered around the journal *Correspondance* began to pool their resources and energies. "La Révolution d'abord et toujours" appeared in *Clarté* during August, in *L'Humanité* on 21 September, and in the October issue of *Révolution Surréaliste*.[65] The rather late publication of the manifesto in *L'Humanité* can be traced to the content of the document itself. The groups enthusiastically called for revolution, one embracing Marx, Nietzsche, and Rimbaud, along with other intellectual guides. They proclaimed "we have need of liberty, but a liberty calculated according to our most profound spiritual needs. . . ." It is not surprising that the Communist daily hesitated to print such a muddle of materialism, spiritualism, and overenthusiasm.

During the first week of July, the PCF set up a Comité d'Action contre la guerre du Moroc, directed by the future General Secretary of the PCF, Maurice Thorez.[66] This appointment was crucial for both Thorez and the Philosophies, for it provided the young party militant with experience in working in broad coalitions and direct contact with left-wing intellectuals, while the Philosophies would later benefit from his protection and patronage during the thirties. Throughout August 1925, *L'Humanité* published a steady avalanche of declarations from the new Surrealist/Philosophies/*Clarté* alliance. During September, only "La Révolution d'abord et toujours" was carried by *L'Humanité*, although it may be assumed that the "alliance" participated in a series of PCF-sponsored protests held that month. Although a sharp decline in the number of declarations is evident after August, October was the month when political tensions reached their peak.

Appointed head of the Sureté Générale in June, Jean Chiappe received instructions to curb the outburst of antimilitarism in early autumn, apparently because of government worries about a recurrence of the wave of PCF activity that accompanied French occupation of the Ruhr several years earlier. Chiappe quickly established himself as the implacable enemy of the Left for the next decade. Numerous Communist Party militants were jailed. In October 1925, *Cahiers du Bolchévisme*, the Party's theoretical organ, had to advise militants on the basic formalities of conspiratorial behavior: Don't carry Party papers on your person, don't talk about Party matters in public, don't get followed to Party meetings. . . .[67] Thorez and his future rival, Jacques Doriot (then head of the Communist Party Youth Section), were imprisoned. In all, 165 militants were imprisoned, and 263 prosecuted. Nonetheless, the long-postponed "general strike for peace" of 12 October was an impressive display of support for the Party and its antimilitarist program. But it was neither massive enough to meet the Party's expectations nor effective enough to influence government policy.[68]

At this point the alliance published on its own responsibility the manifesto "«*Clarté*», «*Philosophies*», «*La Révolution Surréaliste*» solidares du Comité Central d'Action," carried prominently in *L'Humanité* on 16

October. Given the political atmosphere during the fall of 1925, this blatant defiance of the police invited trouble. Curiously, none was evident.[69]

After having survived this period without any devastating consequences, the alliance disintegrated by the end of November. The Philosophies figure among the signatories of the declaration "Les Intellectuels et la Révolution," published in *L'Humanité* on 8 November, not only declaring solidarity with the jailed militants but also calling for French military personnel to fraternize with the Rif tribesmen. But the alliance had clearly fractured when the *Clarté* issue dated 30 November went to press. Jean Bernier, in his "Où nous en sommes," briefly snarled at the Philosophies and others "who filed out when they envisioned themselves at the foot of the wall," suggesting fear of police intervention was the primary motive for the Philosophies' departure.[70] Yet the Philosophies had not been laggards during the worst days, and by November the worst of the police repressions were over.

It is more probable that the desire of each of the three partners to maintain its organizational distinctiveness and as much of its "program" as possible led to the breakdown of relations. Unraveling the conflicting versions of the breakdown suggests that the three groups had worked well together, and logically the next step would have been a fusion of their organizations and resources. This move was contemplated and discussed. Without providing a specific date, Lefebvre later described a fusion talk between just the Philosophies and Surrealists. As the Philosophies spokesman, Lefebvre was instructed to stall the discussion by taunting the Surrealists with the Philosophies' belief in God.[71] The Philosophies departed from the coalition, and the projected fusion of *Clarté* and the Surrealists failed during January 1926, just as the trimmed alliance was preparing to launch a new periodical entitled *La Guerre Civile*. The root cause was the Surrealists' refusal to give up either their organizational independence or their review *La Révolution Surréaliste*. Relations between the *Clarté* and Surrealist groups remained close for some time after the joint project fell through.[73] Years later, the quarrel between Philosophies and their onetime partners still simmered. While the Philosophies came under immediate attack from the new editorial board of *Clarté* during 1926, the response of the Surrealists would not come until 1929, and would play a role in the *Revue marxiste* affair.

The Philosophies emerged from the alliance in a new alignment. The literary figures and the school friends vanished during the summer's introduction to political activism, leaving a tightly knit core of Morhange, Politzer, Guterman, and Lefebvre. Georges Friedmann joined this small circle, possibly due as much to increasing discomfort with the policies of the new *Clarté* editors as to agreement with the Philosophies project. With the loss of peripheral supporters and the addition of Friedmann, the Philosophies took the form they retained well into the thirties.

Morhange's journal, *Philosophies*, changed drastically from March 1924 through January 1926, evolving from a one-man forum to a clearly identifiable collective project, supported by a larger circle of like-minded but less active young men. The consolidation of Philosophies can be attributed to two inseparable developments: the sketching of a distinctive program of "philosophical mysticism" and the self-definition of the collective in opposition to other movements, particularly the Surrealists and *Clarté*. But with the apparent failure of a mysticism centered on action, the Philosophies needed to reappraise their positions before tackling the problem of *inquiétude* again.

NOTES

1. Pierre Morhange, "Cinq Fragments," *Philosophies*, no. 1 (March 1924): 31. Publishing information regarding *Philosophies* can be found in J.-M. Place and A. Vasseur, *Bibliographie des Revues et Journaux littéraires des XIXe et XXe Siècle* (Paris: Editions J.-M. Place, 1977), tome 3. As an indication of the relative diffusion of *Philosophies*, one should note that the printing run for no. 3 was 250 copies; in comparison, the Belgian review *Disque Verte* released a mere fifty copies of its issues on Chaplin and Freud during 1924. Morhange provided a response to the "enquête sur les rêves" in *Disque Verte* 3, no. 2 (1925): 41.

2. "John Brown" [Pierre Morhange], "Billet," *Philosophies*, no. 1 (March 1924): 80.

3. "A Miguel de Unamuno," *Philosophies*, no. 1 (March 1924): 78.

4. *Nouvelle Revue Française*, no. 128 (March 1924): 516.

5. *Europe*, no. 15 (May 1924): 1, 378–80.

6. "Unamuno et ses généreux defenseurs," *Clarté*, no. 55 (1924): 125–26.

7. Georges Michael, "Les Revues: *Philosophies*," *Clarté*, no. 56 (1924): 171–72.

8. *Nouvelle Revue Française,* no. 129 (April 1924): 771.

9. "D. H." [A. Desson and A. Harlaire], "Revues: *Philosophies,*" *Accords,* no. 1 (May 1924): 18.

10. Max Jacob, *Lettres à un amie. Correspondance avec Jean Grenier 1922–1937* (Cognac: Les Temps qu'il fait/Monti, 1982), letter of 18 May 1924, p. 27. Moreover, "cette revue sera tres utile pour lui [Morhange]; elle a attiré attention." Jacob therefore urges Grenier to submit his writings as well.

11. Edgard Forti, "Sur le Bergsonisme de M. Thibaudet," *Philosophies,* no. 2, (May 1924).

12. Jean Weber, "Rétrospection: «Essai sur les Données immédiates de la Conscience» de Henri Bergson," *Philosophies,* no. 2 (May 1924).

13. "Jean Caves" [Jean Grenier], "Le Nihilisme européen et les Appels de l'Orient, (2)," *Philosophies,* no. 2 (May 1924).

14. Henri Jourdan, "Le Nietzsche de Bertram," *Philosophies,* no. 2 (May 1924).

15. Henri Lefebvre, "Odor di femina," *Philosophies,* no. 2 (May 1924): 224.

16. Henri Lefebvre, "Sur une note de M. Ramon Fernandez «les intermittences du coeur»," *Philosophies,* no. 2 (May 1924): 225–27.

17. Norbert Guterman, "La Prisonniere, Sodome et Gomorrhe III: Marcel Proust," *Philosophies,* no. 2 (May 1924): 206–207.

18. Pierre Morhange, "Julius Fabius," *Philosophies,* no. 2 (May 1924): 157.

19. *Philosophies,* no. 2 (May 1924): 231.

20. "Theophile Delaporte" [Julien Green], "Pamphlet contre les catholiques de France," *Revue des Pamphletaires,* no. 1 (October 1924); contained in Green's *Oeuvres Completes* (Paris: Gallimard, 1972), tome 1, pp. 877–916, with notes on pp. 1227–41; includes Green's preface from the 1963 Plon edition. Reviews can be found in *Revue Européenne,* no. 21 (November 1924); in Henri Daniel-Rops, *Notre Inquiétude,* (1927; reprint, Paris: Academic Perrin, 1953) p. 281; and by Joseph Delteil in *Philosophies,* no. 4 (November 1924). The second issue of *Revue des Pamphletaires* was to be written by Delteil.

21. *Accords,* no. 2 (June 1924): 50–51.

22. Guterman's review of Cocteau caught the eye of the German poet Rilke, then visiting Paris. (Rilke himself had been reviewed by Emile Benveniste, later a famed linguist, in the first issue as well). Rilke asked Guterman to arrange a meeting with Cocteau, which led to a friendship between Guterman and Cocteau (Guterman, personal communications). Lefebvre's review of Tzara led to a similar, lifelong friendship. Note that the Philosophies were establishing friendships with major avant-garde poets who preceded and influenced the Surrealists.

23. Max Jacob, "Lettre à Nino Frank" (15 June 1924), *Collection Correspondance*, ed. F. Garnier (Paris: Editions de Paris, 1955), p. 299, and pp. 315, 334, 336, 345, and 349 for scattered comments. See Pierre Morhange's 1924 poem "Max Jacob" in *Le Sentiment lui-même* (Honfleur: Pierre Jean Oswald, 1966), originally published in Morhange's *L'Estafette dans le vestibule*, and see also Lefebvre's *Temps des Méprises*, pp. 40–43.

24. A revival of interest in Max Jacob during the past two decades has led to the appearance of additional volumes of correspondence as well as increased critical attention. In particular see G. Kamber, *Max Jacob and the Poetics of Cubism* (Baltimore: Johns Hopkins, 1971) and Judith M. Schneider, *Clown at the Alter* (Chapel Hill: University of North Carolina, 1978). Contemporary evaluations include pieces by Marcel Arland wrote for *Nouvelle Revue Française* during 1923 and 1924, *Disque Verte*'s November 1923 issue, and numerous pieces in *NRF* during July and August 1934. And Lefebvre's comment is worth noting: "Max Jacob n'était qu'un petit bouffon, un petit fou de Dieu," *Temps des Méprises*, p. 53.

25. Max Jacob, *Lettres à un amie, Correspondence avec Jean Grenier 1922–1937* (Cognac: Le Temps qu'il fait/Monti, 1982), 18 May 1924, p. 27.

26. Pierre Morhange, "Max Jacob: Visions Infernales," *Philosophies*, no. 3 (September 1924): 338.

27. Max Jacob, *Lettres à Marcel Jouhandeau*, ed. Anne S. Kimball, (Geneva: Droz, 1979), letter 27, dated as early July 1924, p. 120.

28. Ibid., Letter 62, 3 July 1925, pp. 199–200; see correspondence and editor's notes pp. 148–55, 164–68, and especially 178–95.

29. "John Brown" [Pierre Morhange], "Billet: où l'on donne le «la»," *Philosophies*, no. 3 (September 1924): 253.

30. Ibid., pp. 275–76.

31. Ibid., pp. 276–77.

32. Ibid., pp. 271–72.

33. *Nouvelle Revue Française*, no. 134 (November 1924): 643–44, also printed in *Journal Littéraire*, 18 October 1924. See François Berge, "A propos du «Billet de John Brown»," *Cahiers du Mois*, no. 8 (January 1925): 61–63, for an example of contemporary reaction.

34. Norbert Guterman, "La Fin d'une Histoire—Quelques notes sur le 'Surréalisme' dans le sens qui lui donne M. Breton," *Philosophies*, no. 4 (November 1924): 445–46. Excerpts in *Révolution Surréaliste*, no. 2 (January 1925): 29.

35. Henri Lefebvre, "7 Manifestes Dada," *Philosophies*, no. 4 (November 1924): 443–45. See André Breton's "Pour Dada," *Nouvelle Revue Française*, no. 83 (August

1922): 208–15; Robert Short, "Paris Dada and Surrealism," *Journal of European Studies* 9, no. 1/2 (March/June 1972); Michel Sanouillet, *Dada à Paris* (Paris: Pauvert, 1965).

36. *Philosophies*, no. 5/6 (January–March 1925): 651, and Pierre Morhange's "Mourir de ne pas mourir par P. Eluard," pp. 622–25 in the same issue. The rather good relationship between Eluard and the Philosophies is evident here, for Morhange refrained from being obnoxious to the point of provoking a break with the Surrealist.

37. "Votre meditation sur Dieu," *Philosophies*, no. 4 (November 1924): 464–66. Responses included Max Jacob, "Le Clef des Songes, etc.," and the pieces collected as "Votre meditation sur Dieu," in *Philosophies*, no. 5/6 (January–March 1925). This latter included responses from Maurice Blondel, Henri Barbusse, Paul Eluard, Gabriel Marcel, Lucie Schwob, Ernst Robert Curtis, Mathias Lubeck, Fernand Divorse, and René Chalput, with more promised for future issues.

38. Georges Politzer, "Médecine ou philosophie?" "L'idée critique et le systeme Kantiene," "L'Experience intense chez Kant," and "Contributions à l'histoire de l'évolution philosophique de Kant," all *Philosophies*, no. 4 (November 1924); all can be found in Politzer's *Ecrits I: La Philosophie et Les Mythes* (Paris: Editions Sociales, 1969).

39. Lefebvre, *La Somme et le Reste*, p. 407–409, and *L'Existentialisme*, pp. 25–34.

40. Henri Lefebvre, "Critique de l'Qualité et de l'Etre: Fragment," *Philosophies*, no. 4 (November 1924): 414–15.

41. Ibid., p. 420.

42. Ibid., pp. 420–21.

43. Henri Lefebvre, "Positions d'attaque et de defense du nouveau mysticisme," *Philosophies*, no. 5/6 (March 1925): 472.

44. Ibid., p. 478.

45. Ibid., pp. 481–82.

46. Ibid., p. 484.

47. Ibid., p. 495.

48. Ibid., p. 500.

49. Georges Michael, "*Philosophies* no. 4," *Clarté*, no. 71 (1925): 86.

50. Georges Michael, "*Philosophies* no. 5/6," *Clarté*, no. 74 (1925): 38–39. On the Sorelian influence on Michael and the *Clarté* editors, see Jack Roth, *The Cult of Violence: Sorel and the Sorelians* (Berkeley and Los Angeles: University of California, 1980).

51. Future issues had been announced, including a combined special num-

bered 9, 10, and 11 dedicated to Henri Bergson. This special issue, announced for autumn 1925, was to contain only three hundred pages, instead of the nearly five hundred pages it should have had, although three hundred copies were to be released. While Norbert Guterman indicated that *Philosophies* was receiving more contributions than it could print (personal communication 8 May 1982), problems had become evident with the third issue, which appeared two months late, and by the shrinking size of each succeeding issue. It is highly probable that, given the belated appearance of no. 5/6, and the reduced format of the Bergson issue, *Philosophies* found itself in financial problems by the end of 1924. This impression is given substance if one considers the cost of the full and double page advertisements for *Philosophies* in *Europe* during the fall of 1924 and the winter of 1925. Simone de Beauvoir's comment (in *Memoirs of a Dutiful Daughter*, trans. J. Kirkup [New York: World, 1959] p. 249) that the banker supporting the periodical withdrew funds because of the group's antimilitarism, may be partially true: Friedmann's father was the financial supporter she incorrectly had in mind, but it is not improbable that Morhange's father, a musician, would have taken a similar stance.

52. Lefebvre, *La Somme et le Reste*, p. 394.

53. Lefebvre, *L'Existentialisme*, p. 41. On Massis and *les Jeunes gens d'aujourd'hui*, see Robert Wohl's *Generation of 1914* (Cambridge: Harvard University, 1979). During this period, Lefebvre presented a "Declaration des Droits de l'Esprit" before the Société des Amis de la Sorbonne; see *La Somme et le Reste*, tome 1, p. 299, and tome 2, p. 387, and *L'Existentialisme*, p. 42 and 55.

54. André Breton, "La Vie: Bouquet Sans Fleurs," *Révolution Surréaliste*, no. 2 (January 1925): 25.

55. Georges Michael, "Une rectification. Une Constatation," *Clarté*, no. 75 (1925): 38.

56. Paul Eluard, "Manifestation Philosophies du 18 mai 1925," *Révolution Surréaliste*, no. 4 (15 July 1925): 32.

57. René Crevel, "Voici Pierre Morhange et Philosophies," *Nouvelles Littéraires* (16 May 1925).

58. Albert Thibaudet, "Réflexions sur la littérature: Du Surréalisme," *Nouvelle Revue Française*, no. 138 (March 1925): 334. On Thibaudet, see René Wellek, "Albert Thibaudet," in *Modern French Criticism*, ed. J. K. Simon (Chicago: University of Chicago, 1972).

59. Albert Thibaudet, "Réflexions sur la littérature: Critique française et critique allemande," *Nouvelle Revue Française*, no. 143 (August 1925): 231.

60. "Les Revues," *Nouvelle Revue Française*, no. 140 (May 1925): 958.

61. "Notes," *Nouvelle Revue Française*, no. 141 (June 1925): 1080.

62. *Clarté*, no. 75 (June 1925): 5–10.

63. Ibid., pp. 1–4.

64. *Clarté*, no. 76 (July 1925): 23.

65. This manifesto, along with many others, can be found in Jose Pierre, ed., *Tracts surréalistes et declarations collectives* (Paris: Terrain Vague, 1979[?]) tome 1 (1922–1939). The "Révolution d'abord" carries the names of ten "Philosophies" adherents, although the previous "Appel" bore only the names of Morhange, Guterman, Lefebvre, and Politzer —that is, of the core group. The other six were Gabriel Beauroy, Emile Benveniste, Henri Jourdan, Maurice Muller, Jean-Paul Zimmerman, and Andre Barsalou. The latter did not contribute to *Philosophies*. Their inclusion as Philosophies to the July manifesto indicates that the group extended beyond the obvious core to a larger circle of Parisian students.

66. There is substantial disagreement regarding this period in the history of the French Communist Party, and I believe that Thorez's "initiation" to what amounted to Popular Front circumstances has been underestimated in the historiography. The materials I have found most useful are the materials contained in *Commune*, no. 4 (December 1933): 379–88; Robert S. Short, "The Politics of Surrealism. 1920-1936," *Journal of Contemporary History* 1, no. 2 (April 1966), and his full thesis "The Political History of the Surrealist Movement in France, 1918–1940," University of Sussex, 1965; Nicole Racine, "Une revue d'intellectuelle communiste dans les années vingt: *Clarté*," *Revue Française de Science Politique* 17, no. 3 (June 1967), and her full thesis "Les Ecrivains communistes en France (1920–1936)," Université de Paris, 1963; Nicole Le Guennec, "Le Parti Communiste Française et la guerre du Rif," *Mouvement Sociale*, no. 78 (January–March 1972). For a chronologically precise but far narrower view of the Surrealist and *Clarté* alliance, see Alan Rose, *Surrealism and Communism: The Early Years* (New York: Peter Lang, 1991).

67. "Vie du Parti," *Cahiers du Bolchévisme*, no. 28 (1 October 1925): 1908.

68. Le Guennec, "Parti Communiste française et guerre du Rif," p. 47. Jacques Fauvert notes that during this period, French Communists often awaited their arrests patiently, with bags packed, in *Histoire du Parti Communiste* (Paris: Fayard, 1977), p. 73.

69. Robert Short succinctly noted that "it was an act of some recklessness on the part of the Surrealists, *Clarté* and 'Philosophies,' at the height of the repression, to declare their solidarity..." in his "Political History," p. 164.

70. Jean Bernier, "Où nous en sommes," *Clarté*, no. 78 (30 November 1925): 4. Short also suggests the Philosophies "beat a hasty retreat" in his "Political History," pp. 165, 238.

71. Lefebvre, *La Somme et le Reste*, p. 395. André Breton substantiates the story in *Entretiens 1913–1952* (Paris: Gallimard, 1952), p. 123. In an essay written to commemorate Breton's death, Lefebvre indicated that a series of meetings had in fact taken place, "1925," *Nouvelle Revue Française*, no. 172 (April 1967). Lefebvre's accounts lack any mention of the *Clarté* group. The account of André Thirion, a Surrealist and PCF member (and future Gaullist), discusses the alliance of the Surrealists and *Clarté* but leaves out the Philosophies. See *Revolutionaries without Revolution*, trans. J. Neugroschel (London: Cassell, 1975), pp. 118, 166–68, 208. Friedmann, in a note to his "Ils ont perdu la partie éternelle d'eux-mêmes," *Esprit*, no. 1 (1926): 134, indicated that the break came in October 1925.

The development and trajectory of the Philosophies is strikingly similar to that of the Surrealists. However, it should be recognized the Philosophies coalesced later than the Surrealists and yet emerged as adherents of the PCF almost simultaneously, which suggests the politicalization of the Philosophies core was more rapid and intense. Short makes the interesting suggestion that Breton and Morhange had similar personalities, a factor which precluded a relationship of either equality or discipleship.

72. Short, "The Politics of Surrealism," p. 166. Besides the excellent works by Short, on the *Guerre Civile* project see the résumé of the Bureau politique du PCF, meeting 18 February 1926, in *Cahiers d'Histoire d'Institute Maurice Thorez*, no. 43, ns# 15 (January–March 1976). On the relations between Surrealists and the Communists, Jean-Pierre A. Bernard's *Le Parti Communiste française et la question littéraire 1921–1939* (Grenoble: Presses universitaires, 1972), pp. 81–112, remains a most useful guide.

73. The result of the Philosophies's stalling tactics was, as Robert Short put it, "not the abandonment of the plans for a closer alliance; it was the exclusion of Philosophies," in "The Politics of Surrealism," p. 10. Perhaps, but since the Surrealist/*Clarté* alliance collapsed on the issue of organizational independence, it seems likely that the schism with the Philosophies stemmed from the same problem. Moreover, Lefebvre and his friends obviously did not want to be included.

Chapter 2

Philosophers of the Spirit
(1926–1928)

T he three years following the break with the Surrealists marked an important transitional phase for the Philosophies. Their initial attempt to merge philosophy, politics, and poetry rebuffed, they withdrew into a comparative, contemplative isolation. During the period 1926 through 1928 they reevaluated their positions and goals by turning back to their academic training in search of a guide for their efforts.

The disputes of 1925 infused the Philosophies with a greater collective identity and left them more zealous than ever in pursuing their convictions. Before switching his allegiance to the Philosophies, Georges Friedmann had written that, more than any other tendency within the *nouvelle génération*, they were on the path to the only possible solution. And the Philosophies, joined by Friedmann, remained confident that they were in the process of finding the solution they proclaimed possible. Moreover, this handful of young philosophes continued to convince many others to take them just as seriously. For example, Henri Daniel-Rops consistently listed the Philosophies among those suffering from the postwar lack of certainty, but thought this group somewhat different because

not wishing to boast of their anxiety, these young men are, without any doubt, on the road where they will discover divine peace. . . .they preserve, in the midst of their search, an equilibrium assuring that they have escaped the influence of the neurosis of anguish. They may play, within their generation and especially within that part of it which will never be catholic, a role analogous to that of neo-thomism. They display . . . an impassioned watchfulness.[1]

Confidence and impassioned watchfulness alone could not solve all of their problems, and the responsibilities of adult life interfered with their collective search for intellectual certainty. The completion of academic studies also meant the beginning of military service, at least for those who were French citizens. Pierre Morhange's term of service was commemorated by a forty-page poem by Norbert Guterman, only a fraction of which was belatedly published in *Cahiers du Sud*.[2] Meanwhile, Guterman himself did research on paranoia at a Parisian insane asylum while translating the writings of Dostoyevsky and other Russian authors into French and Spanish. Henri Lefebvre turned his conscription into an opportunity for philosophic contemplation. Several days in military prison aided in his reflections, a circumstance brought about by an officer who knew of his activities against the Rif War and his status as "a dangerous and subversive element."[3] Slightly younger the others, after completing his *agrégation*, Friedmann began his service as well, although with much less excitement. Georges Politzer appeared launched on a brilliant academic career, appointed in 1925 to the lycée of Moulins and, after his *agrégation* in 1926, nominated to the lycée of Cherbourg.[4] Such a rapid posting to a teaching position followed by promotion indicates that Politzer was highly regarded within the educational system. But Paris remained the center of Politzer's universe, and he regularly commuted between lycée and capital.

These enforced separations, combined with the need to reassess and redefine their program, led to a great deal of confusion and failed projects. *Philosophies* was replaced by *Esprit*, financed primarily by Friedmann.[5] Scheduled to appear three times annually, only two issues were ultimately released, separated by a full year and with several changes of planned contents. The fact that they saw themselves in a transitional period was captured in the choice of the subtitle for their new journal, *Cahiers*, implying notebooks for jotting down ideas or rough drafts. The title itself, like the German *geist*, evokes both "Mind" and "Spirit," a duality capturing the ambiguity with which the Philosophies imagined their own projects.

Unfortunately it also highlights the very real confusions they felt and suffered.

For example, Morhange's long-promised pamphlet "J'appelle à poétes" originally had been scheduled as part of the *Revue des Pamphletaires* series, and was later announced as forthcoming in the *Cahiers du Sud* series "Poétes." Finally, "J'appelle à poétes" was to appear in the second issue of *Esprit*, due for release in October 1926. The pamphlet, along with half of the originally announced contributions to that issue, never appeared. Indeed, this last issue underwent several revisions of content and date of release before finally appearing in March 1927, with numerous blank pages, and shortened length.[6]

Morhange's difficulties were shared by the Philosophies as a group. He, Lefebvre, and Politzer were to collaborate on a multivolume *Voici ce qu'il y a* as part of their "Collection Philosophie" (later renamed "Collection Esprit"), published through Editions Rieder. Neither this project nor Guterman's *La Vie est Unique* ever appeared. However, those volumes that did reach completion were of excellent quality and received substantial critical attention. The release of William Blake's *Premiers Livres Prophetiques* as an early part of the series attested to the Philosophies' continued equivocation between direct mystic knowledge and rationalist philosophy. Schelling's *Recherches philosophique sur l'essence de la liberté humaine* was released in 1926, with Politzer translating the work from German and Lefebvre providing a lengthy introduction to be discussed below. Jean Wahl contributed his highly respected works, *Etude sur la Parmenide de Platon* (1926) and *La Malheur de la conscience dans la philosophie de Hegel* (1929). The first volume of Politzer's own *Critique des fondements de la Psychologie* was published in 1928, although other titles planned for that series were never released.

This rapid outline of the Philosophies' publishing achievements during 1926–1928 indicates three complementary trends. Most obviously, the bulk of their published writings appeared in 1926, before teaching, military obligations, and later, families interfered with their efforts. Second, the works left unfinished were those in which the Philosophies promised to set out a definitive program, a program they clearly were unable to articulate. Last, the two translations and Wahl's two contributions indicate a turn toward classical idealist philosophy in search of direction and an analytical framework. This search was summarized by Lefebvre's recollection that in these years Politzer once remarked: "We are searching for a spiritual father."[7]

The first real indication of a major shift toward a philosophical system came with Politzer's translation of Schelling's *La Liberté Humaine*, which strongly influenced the group's *Esprit* writings. Like many of his contemporaries, Schelling was preoccupied with the problem of resolving the contradictions between human consciousness and perception of external reality. Schelling achieved this resolution by necessitating the extraction of concepts from the material world as the means of enriching consciousness. For Schelling—as for his friend and rival Hegel—this dialectical process broke down the distinctions between concepts and created a unity within consciousness. Necessity lay in the need for knowledge by the consciousness, a need best described as Passion and Desire, to become more than it was at a given moment, creating perpetual and necessary movement toward perfection and reconciliation. For Schelling, freedom of consciousness not only implied the necessity of free will but also was equated with Absolute knowledge, or God.[8] Schelling's system retained the idealist concerns so dear to Morhange and his friends, while setting out a justification for action in the world in the name of the universal value of Freedom.

In his introduction, Lefebvre praised Schelling, the *métaphysician concrète*, who took the data of human experience as transmitted and sought to unify that knowledge without abolishing contradiction and without privileging any element. Schelling offered "a new life, free, active, divine," created by the will of a self-liberating Humanity.[9] Lefebvre acknowledged that Schelling wove a speculative philosophy in which the unification of experience was an artificial creation imposed by the will to know, and accepted the fact that in practice Schelling left isolated individuals pursuing their independent conceptions of the Absolute—in essence, contemplating their own private divinities. What remained useful in Schelling's system, Lefebvre argued, was his emphasis on the human will to know fused with an act of knowing as the basis of logical synthesis.[10]

The influence of Schelling and of his framework was amply demonstrated in those writings the Philosophies did publish during 1926 and 1927. For the first issue of *Esprit*, dated May 1926, most of the pieces had been written during the preceding twelve months and reflected a shift away from literary and political disputes to philosophic inquiry. The unsigned introduction, ". . . Y," was clearly attributable to Morhange because of its religious imagery and poetic style. None of the others could write lines like

> . . . I, your appetite which flowers, fresh and white, from which you satisfy yourself, I your next hunger when you hunger again. . . [11]

Morhange's ". . . Y" was the monologue of an omnipresent source of spiritual nourishment, one requiring the reader to embrace it in order to attain its own fulfillment. A "return to the true" for Morhange could only be attained through a return to the beginning:

> I am the seed, you are the stem, later, I will be the fruit. It should be said: Thus before all else, the word. . . .[12]

An earthly apocalypse was needed to resolve the separation of individual and universal, and "the truth drowned in the soul" could only emerge through "the flames of the forge." For Morhange, the material manifestation of this apocalypse now lay, as it did for many others, in the East: "O les Russes à nous!"[13]

Morhange's second contribution to the issue emphasized the same points, in language less poetic if only slightly less cryptic. "La Presence" was the first half of a longer essay, the continuation of which, once again, was repeatedly promised but never fulfilled. Morhange defined philosophic research as the pursuit of a pure state of internal happiness in which the reason and soul were reconciled:

> Joy is the moment in which one finds the principles of life, the knowledge of life, the greatest reconciliation of life completely unified; a place within the total life, within the solitude of the eternal life. It is Spirit: because it is the place where life goes to its final, best and most true reconciliation. . . .[14]

For Morhange, until the resolution of individual and universal, of eternal and transient, was complete, reason—*l'Esprit*—derived its nourishment from the material world while patiently separating the "true" from the imperfect. The final unity of mind and soul would be achieved through a total revolution that stripped away the variable, the individual, and the false while leaving the true and the essential.[15] Although this "revolution" was not here specifically linked to the advance of the Red Army, Morhange did deny Reason the ability to achieve its own resolution without a grounding in material being.[16] Morhange's unfinished essay had affinities with at least a half-dozen major philosophies and religions, but was distinct from most theories of existential action since Morhange insisted on a total and collective "revolution" as a qualitative leap. Moreover, this "revolution" somehow was to be fixed in material life and find its expression there, although Morhange never clearly delineated the reciprocal relations between individual mind and material existence. In fact, Morhange never defined his major categories of "soul," "spirit," "material being," and so forth at all, leaving them as abstract concepts without connection. And the crucial question of how a "revolution" of the consciousness could achieve itself by drawing from material reality was the one Morhange and his colleagues desperately needed to answer.

The other Philosophies continued this search for intellectual and spiritual reunion, and made similar ambiguous connections between that reunion and the material world. "Spiritual life has need of a substance in order to nourish itself," Politzer wrote, in almost the exact wording Morhange had used, and "philosophy has need of a genuine substance to be valuable before Spirit."[17] Politzer's introduction to the first issue of *Esprit* was more rigorous in its philosophical language and in the structure of its arguments, but conveyed the same sense of groping toward a solution found in Morhange's writings. For Politzer, the solution to be found in a spiritual renaissance would be part of a greater movement

> corresponding to the discovery of a new substance. This discovery follows
> a period without substance, a period of unconscious convulsions . . . in a
> word: scholastic.[18]

Politzer claimed the manifestations of this unfolding fulfillment of *esprit* were found in philosophy, or more properly in the history of philosophy. Yet Politzer saw academic philosophy in the twenties as stagnant, reduced to tedious seminar exercises, and sunk into simple retrieval as indicated by the sectarian divisions of neo-Kantians, neo-Hegelians, neo-Realists, and so forth. Unconsciously echoing Valéry's diagnosis of the symptoms of the postwar cultural crisis, Politzer rejected all these schools as equally trapped within a sterile academic discourse despite their apparent differences.

Moreover, Politzer continued, since Descartes' thought and existence had taken isolated, individual forms, "the discovery of the solitude of thought is therefore also the discovery of the solitude of Man. Man is alone with his thought."[19] Politzer argued it was necessary to abstract from thinking and living individuals to *le genre Homme* as a concrete and universal reality. Thus it would be Humanity serving as its own subject and object, acting upon the material world in order to achieve its potential, providing the new substance Politzer claimed philosophy required. For Politzer, this process required the destruction of material constraints preventing the realization of "liberty." In a word, it required revolution.

Politzer accepted Idealism as providing half of the framework necessary for this revolution, as embodied in Schelling's concept of freedom or liberty. For an analytic framework of the material world he turned to Marxism for its explanatory value of the conditions that held humanity in bondage. Still, despite the descriptive powers he attributed to Marxism, Politzer refused to accept wholeheartedly the doctrine and in fact displayed little knowledge of Marxist theory. For Politzer in 1926, the Marxist class struggle was only part of the revolution he envisioned, but not part of the truth to which his humanity aspired.

Politzer thus continued to posit the ultimate goal of human existence as an ideal resolution of the mind or spirit. He did see, however, a role for Marxism as a tool for destroying the material constraints preventing that resolution. His reference to Marx was interesting, not the least because Politzer linked Marx to his Idealist predecessors. Since the early writings of Marx exposing this link were not yet generally known or available, Politzer drew upon his own knowledge of German Idealist philosophy to make the connection. At the same time, his acceptance of Marxism relegated it to a subordinate role. Such a position could not have endeared Politzer to the comparatively orthodox Marxists of the Communist Party or of *Clarté*. However, by suggesting Marxism as the framework linking the material world to the abstracted essential world of thought, Politzer alone among the Philosophies sought to avoid vagueness in delineating a field for purposeful action.

In his first contribution to the collective, Friedmann set the Philosophies distinctly apart from those suffering *la mal du siècle* with the very title of his essay, "Ils ont perdu la partie eternelle d'eux-mêmes."[20] Friedmann described the twentieth century as the age in which machines were equated with human progress, and both were manipulated by indifferent technocrats of a *saint-simonien* stamp. Under the cloak of science these *saint-simoniens* directed social and economic life while separating themselves from the implications of their actions, imposing the machine around the globe in the name of progress. Most intellectuals contributed to this imposition by assuming a stance of individualism or of indifference, ignoring their critical duties by irresponsibly losing themselves in quarrels about style and form couched in academic jargon. Equally guilty in Friedmann's eyes were writers like Gide, Barres, Arland, and those suffering from individual and isolated *inquiétude*, for they ignored universal values for the examination of interior individual life. Such intimate explorations were indifferent to the external world and its problems, Friedmann argued, and could not lead toward constructive action since there was no goal to achieve.[21]

Friedmann advocated, but did not work out, a return to ethics and a search for moral guidelines for action in the world. Although his personal preference as guide was Spinoza, the advocate of moral acts in the "here and now," Friedmann championed all thinkers who carried through the implications of their ideas into social acts: Socrates, Jesus, Lenin, and so on.[22] Friedmann saw Spinoza himself as a great revolutionary who taught the necessity of fusing comprehension, action, and freedom. To follow Spinoza's example, Friedmann concluded, it was necessary to turn from individualism's miserable passions and recognize the *inquiétude* of the modern world as a symptom of its preoccupation with individuality. From individual variation must be extrapolated the universal essences of humanity, and from these an ethical code for worldly action created.

Morhange, Politzer, and Friedmann each emphasized that the essence of human existence lay in the realm of the mind and spirit. Each also recognized that this essence had to work through, yet be liberated from, the material world, with only Politzer accepting a framework for analyzing and achieving that liberation by his granting of a subservient role to Marxism. Finally, each presented an essay reflecting a widely scattered knowledge of philosophy, and the extraction of concepts from different sources only partially reintegrated into a novel presentation.

This chaotic assimilation and presentation of ideas were best illustrated by the writings of Lefebvre during 1925 and 1926. More of Lefebvre's writings appeared than of the others during these years, although the manner of presentation was often fragmentary and confused, and the prose and logic tortured. Yet in these pieces set out the basic problems that would preoccupy him through six decades and nearly eighty monographs.

The starting points of this project lie in two pieces reflecting Lefebvre's rejection of Christianity as a solution. In the first issue of *Esprit*, Lefebvre rejected Jacques Maritain as a spiritual guide because of the Catholic writer's acceptance of the religious projection of universal harmony into an abstract otherworld.[23] Of more interest was the forward Lefebvre had prepared for a larger work, "Notes pour le procès de la Chrétiente," hastily written during the summer of 1925 as part of yet another unpublished monograph, and which was to include a critique by Jean Wahl.[24] For Lefebvre, Christianity failed to resolve human yearnings for expression because it had become a church. Universal values, perfection, and even the meaning of Christ's actions were displaced from concrete existence and attributed to the will of God, while the actions and aspirations of human beings in the world were doomed to inevitable failure.[25] The authority of the church Lefebvre saw as based on ritualized obligations, political dominance, and a cosmology based on mysteries forever beyond human comprehension. Therefore, Lefebvre argued that human consciousness could only destroy the constraints imposed by Christianity and especially by the churches through mysticism.[26] Lefebvre's account was drawn heavily from the critiques of Christianity provided by Pascal and Nietzsche, a sign of his continuing interest in these philosophers.

Yet this initial rejection of Christianity required that Lefebvre search for a new definition of human potential and existence. Portions of this "equisse d'une philosophie de la conscience" already had appeared in *Philosophies*, and two further segments were carried as "La Pensée et l'Esprit" in *Esprit* no. 1, and as "Reconnaisance de l'Unique" in *Esprit*, no. 2.

Lefebvre rewrote these last two parts prior to publication, certainly with the criticisms and experiences of 1925 in mind. Still, by the time the final portion was published Lefebvre was embarrassed by the whole project and added a note to the 1927 "Reconnaisance de l'Unique" stating that the "article" would not have been released at all if it did not represent a stage, now transcended, in his development.

His discomfort was understandable, for Lefebvre maintained the same dichotomy between a search for an abstracted universal consciousness through a confrontation with the material world that Morhange, Politzer, and Friedmann had. Lefebvre added a new complication by continuing to argue that resolution might be achievable through action alone, a concept almost certainly borrowed from Maurice Blondel. Consciousness could only impose definition onto external objects without fully comprehending the nature of the material world. At the same time, thought in itself could create only unrealizable ideas of itself, and hence required an external reality in order to define itself. Lefebvre thus found the resolution between the ideal and the material to be located in a *lutte mystique* and an *aventure métaphysique*. But Lefebvre unintentionally destroyed this resolution on two grounds. The first, as Georges Michael had pointed out, was that he never defined where or how these actions should be undertaken.[27] Second, Lefebvre recognized that acts themselves cannot be abstracted by thought to provide "a common measure and a communication between men," since the result would be, at best, a false unity similar to the definitions imposed onto objects.[28] The major dilemma, Lefebvre acknowledged, was that the part of human existence constituting thought or consciousness was ultimately individual and unique.[29] Each of these individual essences was, for Lefebvre, self-developing "*pour soi.*"[30] These self-realizing individual subjects sought their own truths through acts of will and the proclamation of their desires.[31] In an effort to use its physical embodiment in the material world, each individual consciousness necessarily confronted other subjects seeking to realize their own individual wills. But for each individual, unique, and self-fulfilling consciousness, the "other" "is defeat, satiation, finality, death, that is to say Nothingness."[32]

Thus, in rejecting religion as his guide for moral action, Lefebvre at this time retreated into a theory of individualism and existential action, precisely the combination Friedmann rejected. Moreover, he lacked the ethical guide required by Friedmann, as well as a theory with which to analyze the material world, such as Politzer conceded to Marxism. The final result of Lefebvre's early attempt to create a theory of Consciousness and Action was simply a circular theoretical justification for isolated and individual searches to transcend *inquiétude*!

These fragmentary writings need to be evaluated in the light of post-1945 French political thought. In his 1946 autocritique, *L'Existentialisme*, Lefebvre repudiated his youthful conception of action supposedly because of an alleged resemblance to elements of Heidegger's thought, a problem stemming in part from Lefebvre's lack of ethical and material groundings in his earliest writings. Despite the alleged similarities to Heidegger, there were in fact no direct connections between the future Marxist theorist and the future supporter of National Socialism: *Being and Time* appeared in 1927, while Lefebvre's manuscript was composed during 1925 and 1926. Lefebvre then turned around and, in a critique paralleling that of Georg Lukács, bludgeoned Jean-Paul Sartre with the same stick.[33] Lefebvre's early emphasis on the uniqueness of individual consciousness and its conflict with a negating Other has affinities with Sartre's *Being and Nothingness*. And Lefebvre's search for identity through action alone was as flawed as Sartre's effort to comprehend revolutions in *Critique of Dialectical Reason*. Still, the apparent similarities between the two allowed Lefebvre to claim he had stumbled on the fundamentals of existentialism and moved beyond them to Marxism. These were my *youthful* writings, Lefebvre could then taunt Sartre, what is your excuse? However, a major distinction is evident, for while Lefebvre's process was repetitive in that each individual continually searched to establish its self-consciousness, Sartre's literary works, particularly his early plays and his unfinished series of novels, *Chemins de la Liberté*, suggest that a final resolution followed a Sartrean existential act: death.

Lefebvre's fragments capture the central problems the Philosophies confronted in 1926 and 1927. Their search for universal values, for ethics and meaning, had led them into mysticism, the direct, immediate comprehension of Absolute knowledge. But this strictly cerebral exercise conflicted with the necessities of physical and social existence, and with their desire to act in the world. They sought a more strictly philosophical framework within which to express themselves, yet drew on such disparate sources that their efforts suffered from lack of coherence. All gave priority

to *esprit*, playing with its meanings of soul, spirit, and mind rather indis-
criminately. Adopting Schelling as a guide helped them organize and
express their ideas in a more rigorous fashion, but could not provide the
detailed, synthetic methodology they needed. For all the Philosophies, the
material world was relegated to a subservient position, with only Politzer
even allowing room for specific links between the ideas of the mind,
action, and the material world. The solution seemed obvious. "*Nous nous
cherchons un Père*," Politzer supposedly said, but the question was which to
accept. Although the letters of Friedrich Engels published in the second
issue of *Esprit* gave a hint of the Philosophies' growing interest in
Marxism, they had not yet found their answers there. In fact, the letters
were about superficial problems with publishers and quarrels among the
different leftist groups in 1847, quarrels like those the Philosophies participated in!

     From *La Liberté Humaine* it was simply a short step to the works of
Schelling's contemporary, Hegel, since *The Phenomenology of Mind*
employed many of the same concepts and methods as Schelling outlined,
but with greater detail and historical application. Moreover, Hegel's rela-
tion to Marx was strongly suspected if not well defined, and the transition
from Schelling to Hegel would carry an understanding of Marx with it.

     Breton and the Surrealists suggested Hegel to the Philosophies during
the fusion talks of 1924–1925.[34] Yet the first systematic introduction they
received came from Jean Wahl, whose reading of Hegel was tinged with
Kierkegaardian religious overtones. With Maurice Boucher, Wahl translated a segment of the *Phenomenology* for *Esprit* no. 1.[35] This segment, "La
conscience malheureuse," or "Unhappy Consciousness," had a particular
relevance for the Philosophies at this stage of their development. In
Hegel's tracing of the progress of self-consciousness, the "unhappy consciousness" marked the retreat of the conscious mind from the material
world. This stage was one of "unhappiness" because consciousness remained internally divided. One half identified itself with the universal, the
unchanging, the infinite, and the true. Conversely, the other half equated
itself with the unique, the variable, and the unessential. This contradictory
coexistence of both notions within the same self-consciousness was
resolved only when both states were recognized as parts of an unified consciousness. First, however, the divided consciousness tried to repudiate its

variable and material attributes and to embrace only universal content. Intellectual mysticism and physical asceticism—paths explored by the Philosophies themselves—were the extreme limits of the "unhappy consciousness," before the two extremes were reunited as a higher stage of consciousness, that of Reason. In publishing Wahl's important translation, the Philosophies were endorsing a logic of mysticism that, rather perversely, required that they abandon mysticism.

This breakthrough was followed by the 1929 publication of Wahl's commentary, *Le Malheur de la conscience dans la philosophie de Hegel,* a study with strong attractions for the Idealist side of the Philosophies' search for knowledge. But Wahl's reading of Hegel was at variance with almost any other. The Lord-Bondsman relationship pivotal for the Marxist reading of the *Phenomenology* as well as that of Alexandre Kojéve is usually assumed to concern social relations in the material world. Wahl turned this relationship into one between God and individual. And while Hegel's section on the development of self-consciousness was explicitly a history of philosophic stages, Wahl transformed these stages into a history of the Judeo-Christian religions. In fact Wahl's reading of the *Phenomenology* reflected the influence of Kierkegaard as well as of Hegel's early writings on theology, particularly the unfinished essay on the "Positivity of the Christian Religion," available since the turn of the century.[36]

Wahl's *Malheur de la conscience* was part of a Hegel revival of the 1920s, one traceable in the academic journals of the day but generally overlooked by scholars, who frequently emphasize the "Hegelian Renaissance" of the 1930s associated with Alexandre Kojéve and Jean Hyppolite, or focus primarily on the post-1945 French absorption of Hegel and Marx. In part this periodization is due to Alexandre Koyré's 1931 "Rapport sur l'état des études Hegeliennes en France."[37] Koyré's opening lamentations about the lack of serious interest in Hegel among his countrymen appeared so authoritative that his lengthy discussion of Wahl in the same essay tends to be ignored. For scholars studying post-1945 French thought, Koyré's article provides a convenient starting point, with the lectures of Kojéve and the translations of Hyppolite assuming heroic dimensions instead of being recognized as part of a larger, continuous tradition.[38]

Initially, the Philosophies found in Hegel a system of logic and a language for expressing their mysticism. Yet their absorption of Hegel also marked the end of their search for a rigorous theoretical guide, for the implications of the "unhappy consciousness" section pushed them beyond their purely idealist search. Hegel and Schelling became bridges by which the Philosophies approached Marx. Their preoccupation with the abstracted universal consciousness was transformed but retained as an analytic focus on social alienation, then a barely articulated or defined concept within Marxist theoretical frameworks. The path of the Philosophies to and within Marxism was unusual and distinctive, and made without knowledge of their contemporaries Georg Lukács, Karl Korsch, and Antonio Gramsci.[39]

Yet the critics were surprisingly receptive to the new Philosophies project. That is, with the exception of the *Clartéistes*. A new series of *Clarté* began in June 1926, after a hiatus of five months, with an editorial board dominated by Pierre Naville, a Surrealist and former editor of *Révolution Surréaliste* who had entered the PCF earlier than most other Surrealists and was now on his way out of the Party while the others were moving toward it. In May 1928, Naville would be expelled by the PCF for publishing Lenin's "Personal Testament," harshly critical of the Soviet leadership and particularly of Stalin. Naville had sharp words for Surrealists who became Communists, denouncing them as "naive idealists," but he heaped abuse upon the Philosophies and *Esprit*. In a long, harsh review, Naville tackled the Philosophies one by one, rejected their writings out of hand as "petite bourgeois idealism," and repeatedly argued that their "jargon judeo-philosophique" had no place among revolutionary realities. Naville drove home his point by placing a large-type quote from Engels at the end of his review: "REVOLUTION IS THE ACT BY WHICH A PART OF THE POPULATION IMPOSES ITS WILL ON THE OTHER WITH THE AID OF RIFLES, BAYONETS, AND CANNONS."[40] After Naville's treatment, in which the politest comments were "juvenile" and "ridiculous," the group was probably relieved to receive only sarcastic comments about "masters of the Sorbonne," "pawnbrokers of the spirit," and other puns on the title of their new journal from Victor Crastre when he reviewed the second issue of *Esprit* for *Clarté*.[41]

Other reviewers also observed the Philosophies' evolution, occasionally with trepidation. *Nouvelles Littéraires* took note of the first issue of *Esprit* soon after its release:

If we have the courage to absorb the ponderous articles which compose these bulky cahiers, we will speak of them again in a future Review of Reviews.[42]

Apparently the contents of the first issue were too daunting since no more was heard about the matter. Notice was taken of Lefebvre's "Reconnaissance de l'Unique" from the second issue. Unfortunately, the reviewer lamented, Lefebvre's ideas were more passionate than logical, leaving one wondering exactly what he meant.[43] Lefebvre and *Esprit* fared only slightly better in *Etudes*, where Lucien Roure bemoaned the revolutionary intent of the Philosophies, and felt *Esprit* was merely "the presentation of the doctrine of the intellectuals who have gone over to Bolshevism."[44] And, writing in 1926, Benjamin Crémieux saw in *Esprit* "the aspirations and doctrines of a part of the [new] generation expressed in a form simultaneously dogmatic and polemical," as well as a fierce appetite for life leading to Marxism and to a mystical, revolutionary creed.[45] The Philosophies, Crémieux emphasized, have chosen: "they have overcome one of the terms of the contradiction [of our times], and transcended the anxiety [*inquiétude*] of irresponsibility."[46]

But the prominence that the Philosophies had achieved was evident in the increasing attention that the leading intellectual periodical, *Nouvelle Revue Française*, continued to give to their efforts. In reviewing the first issue of *Esprit*, Gabriel Marcel thought the original essays were as important as their translations, acknowledged Lefebvre's efforts, and claimed Friedmann's "Ils ont perdu," with its rejection of hypocrisy and irresponsibility, the most effective contribution. But he was uncertain what the entire issue signaled:

No one may contest the importance and the timeliness of a critique: it remains to be learned if the young directors of *Esprit* actually can provide the dialectical and verbal machinery which will be indispensable to give this critique a positive and substantial counterpart. It is doubtful. The perpetually aggressive tone that they adopt does not suffice to mask the uncertainties of a thought which strikes out, if one may say so, blindly.[47]

Nouvelle Revue Française commentator Albert Thibaudet was no longer confused about who the Philosophies were and what they represented when he devoted one of his columns entirely to their new venture. They represented the infusion of professional academic philosophy into literature, an intrusion to the detriment of literature.[48] In their search, Thibaudet maintained, they still resembled the Surrealists, and both resembled the romantic revolutionaries of 1830. Yet Thibaudet acknowledged that their mixture of youthful excesses with culture and philosophy were enough to justify an interest in their seemingly frenzied movements and manifestos.[49] Thibaudet was not surprised that the circle was beginning to explore German philosophic romanticism, since their rejection of Bergson left no other frameworks for unifying all of fragmented experience. Thibaudet was not above mixing sarcasm with his critical praise. To Politzer's assertion that the individual who was not alone and isolated was incapable of being a revolutionary, Thibaudet countered with Aristotle: To live alone was the sign of a brute or of a god, and the Philosophies were not likely to become the latter. And he thought the Philosophies would do well to recognize their relationship to the parallel movements of Catholic thinkers and reconsider that path, since a real revolution was not where they could fit in: Surely, Thibaudet mused, Friedmann was as incapable of stubbing out a cigarette on a Gobelin tapestry as Thibaudet himself![50]

A third *Nouvelle Revue Française* review appeared when *Esprit* no. 2 was released. Jean Grenier, the friend of Max Jacob and contributor to *Philosophies*, chose to ignore the weaknesses and imprecisions of Lefebvre's "Reconnaissance" by emphasizing that the piece encapsulated the *Esprit* project:

> This reseizing of all the living forces that constitute *l'esprit*, this union of contemplation, of action and of love within an indissoluble mystical cluster, this exaltation of the ONE as the end of the spiritual path, all this nobleness returns to the singular things which brave the pain of living and of thinking merits for the author our greatest recognition. What already unified the collaborators of *Philosophies* was the will to return the intellect, with its "products," to its place, which is to say at least to the second rank, and that, something new and surprising, in order to better exalt *l'esprit*.[51]

Believing this unifying attempt would sooner or later fail, Grenier wondered how the group would fracture in the future, and decided Lefebvre
and Morhange would opt for "action," with the rest retreating into contemplation.

Marcel and the other critics were correct to wonder if the Philosophies were not just striking out blindly in their search. Of course they
were—just like everyone else in the "new generation." The Philosophies'
search for a unifying Absolute was representative, but the methods by
which they searched were distinctive.

Those reviewers of 1926 and 1927 who saw the Philosophies as intellectuals gone over to Bolshevism were correct as prophets. However there
is no evidence that the group even considered such a step until 1928.
Politzer's few references to Marxism, including those he made in his writings of 1928, restricted it to a subordinate position within their conception
of the revolutionary project. It was not until the spring of 1928 that the
Philosophies seriously began to consider that the resolution of their search
lie within Marxism and the Parti Communiste Français.

The Philosophies' inclination toward philosophic aloofness finally cul-
minated in 1929 with their "Ilse du Sagesse" project. Lefebvre was sent to
the Gulf of Morbihan on the south coast of Brittany in order to arrange
the purchase of an island, where Friedmann's generosity would fund a
sanctuary for persecuted intellectuals. The first visitor they hoped to
entertain was Leon Trotsky, just exiled from the Soviet Union.[52] The project proved unfulfillable, leaving one to speculate about exactly what
Trotsky and Morhange would, or perhaps could, have spoken.

The final step of the transformation of the Philosophies was, like every
stage of their adventure, a public spectacle. An advertisement in the March
1928 issue of *Europe* announced a series of conferences at the Atelier Theater. The *soirées*, all moderated by Morhange, were to be on "L'Appel au
Proletariate juif de Paris" and "Rendez-vous à la fameuse jeunesse intellectuelle." By June the program had been altered, and *Europe* again
announced a meeting for the twenty-third on "La Traite des ouvriers en
Palestine."[53] The major change lay in the list of speakers, now given as "G.
Péri, P. Morhange, P. Vaillant-Couturier du PCF." Morhange naturally
took center stage, but flanked himself with a leading militant of the PCF
(Péri) and the editor-in-chief of *L'Humanité* (Vaillant-Couturier), with all

described as "du PCF." For a young poet and mystic philosopher lacking political experience, Péri and Vaillant-Couturier were prestigious company. Yet their presence indicated that Morhange and the Philosophies found some sympathy within the highest reaches of the same Party suspicious of anyone even slightly connected with the Surrealists. The June announcement also publicized yet another issue of *Esprit*, now subtitled "*revue des poètes et critiques communistes*," due out in July. One wonders whether the failure of this revived *Esprit* to appear should be seen as an appropriate end to the entire transition the journal represented or as a warning about the future of the Philosophies within the PCF.

By the end of 1928, the circle had adhered to the French Communist Party. Politzer delayed his entry until 1929, while both Guterman and Friedmann later would claim that they never became official members at all. Yet all became so identified with the Party and its activities that everyone assumed they were militants like any other. The reasons for this apparently sudden commitment were rather straightforward. Once the Philosophies accepted the position that *l'esprit* and philosophy needed material substance in order to realize itself, the options were few. The extreme Right movements, whether the Action Française or its splinters, looked to the past for universal harmony. The parties forming the Cartel des Gauches were not only part of the established system, but also part of the problem confronting the "new generation." Only the Communists had a demonstrated history of opposition to France as it was then established. As the embodiment of the "revolutionary proletariat," the Party offered the substance, *le genre Homme*, Politzer wrote of. Especially compelling was the Party's new "Class-versus-Class" policy, for its proclamation of the imminent failure of capitalism and the coming of "the Revolution" paralleled the apocalyptic vision of the Philosophies. Moreover, by 1928 the Philosophies had adopted Marx, the "heir" of Schelling and Hegel, as their spiritual and revolutionary guide. The logical extension of their intellectual commitment was their adhesion to the Party appearing to best embody Marx's ideas. Finally, it will be recalled that the Philosophies had already had experience in working with the Party, and in particular with Thorez, providing a smoother basis for entering the Party's ranks.

Before exploring the initial fate of the Philosophies within the French Communist Party, it is necessary to complete the examination of their existence outside of the Party. The last member of the Philosophies to join the Communist Party, Georges Politzer, published his critiques of Bergsonism and of psychoanalysis during 1928 and 1929. Combined with his writings in the short-lived *Revue de la Psychologie concrète*, these works demonstrate Politzer's distinctive trajectory at this stage in the Philosophies' development. These same texts also provide eloquent evidence of the sudden intellectual and political conversion which transformed the course of Politzer's life.

NOTES

1. Henri Daniel-Rops, *Notre Temps* (1927; reprint, Paris: Perrin, 1953), pp. 148–50; see also his "Sens et périls d'une inquiétude," *Notre Temps* (July 1928, August 1928, and September 1928).

2. Norbert Guterman, "L'Ile de Bitche," *Cahiers du Sud*, no. 121 (May 1930). According to Guterman, the original manuscript ended up in the possession of Henri Lefebvre.

3. Henri Lefebvre, *La Somme et le Reste* (1959; reprint, Paris: Bélibaste, 1973), pp. 425–29. Apparently Lefebvre and Morhange seriously considered deserting as a way of creating a political scandal, but were talked out of the idea by the "good sense" of Friedmann; see Henri Lefebvre, *L'Existentialisme* (Paris: Editions du Sagittaire, 1946), p. 44.

4. For Politzer to have received a post at all would have required French citizenship, perhaps obtained through marriage. Guterman suggested Politzer married the daughter of one of his instructors. However, the point lacks substantiation. Also, I can find no record of Politzer performing military service during the 1920s, as he would have been required. Pierre Naville, in "Itinéraire de Georges Politzer," in *Psychologie, Marxisme, Matérialisme* (Paris: Marcel Rivière, 1948), p. 285, credited Politzer with writing almost all of a thesis by one Mlle. V. Arnold, "La psychologie de réaction en Amérique," in 1926. This mysterious link might account for Politzer's use of the pseudonym "Félix Arnold" during 1929.

5. *Esprit: Cahiers*, no. 1 (May 1926): 1–274; no. 2 (March 1927): 1–158. Advertisements for *Esprit*, "Collection Philosophies," and "Collection Esprit" ran periodically in *Europe* from February 1926 (5 pages) through June 1928.

6. Compare the prepublication announcements found in *Europe*, no. 43 (July 1926), with the contents actually published in *Esprit* no. 2. Also, Morhange's reply

to the *enquête* on "Anti-poésie" launched by *Les Cahiers Idealistes*, no. 14 (June 1926): 23, was to be carried in the second issue.

7. Lefebvre, *La Somme et le Reste*, p. 415.

8. F. W. J. Schelling, *Of Human Freedom*, trans. J. Gutman (Chicago: Open Court, 1936). In his introduction, Gutman noted the German "Schelling revival" of the twenties and added "that this interest was not limited to Germany might be implied by the publication, in 1926, of a French translation." (pp. v–vi) Jean Prévost reviewed the Schelling in *Europe*, no. 51 (March 1927) and Félicien Challaye gave both translation and introduction honorable mention in *Europe*, no. 60 (December 1927): 568.

9. Henri Lefebvre, introduction to *Recherches philosophique sur l'essence de la liberté humaine* (Paris: Rieder, 1926), pp. 8–9, 12. See also Lefebvre *La Somme et le Reste*, tome 2, part 4, chap. 5, "Schelling."

10. Lefebvre, introduction to "Recerces philosophique," pp. 51–52.

11. Pierre Morhange, ". . . Y," *Esprit*, no. 1 (May 1926): 79.

12. Ibid., p. 9.

13. Ibid., pp. 10, 12–13; Morhange expands on this theme of salvation from the East in his response to the *enquête* "Appels de l'Orient" in *Cahiers du Mois*, no. 9/10 (February–March 1925): 309–10—"The populations of Europe will be invaded, or, after an invasion, led away into captivity. . . . There will come an unheralded prophet from the extreme west. . . ." Recall here Jean Grenier's fascination with the East in *Philosophies* no. 1 and no. 2, and see also the "Les Appels de l'Orient," in *Navire d'Argent*, no. 1 (June 1925).

14. Pierre Morhange, "La Presence," *Esprit*, no. 1 (May 1926): 220.

15. Ibid., p. 222.

16. Ibid., p. 223.

17. Georges Politzer, "Introduction," *Esprit*, no. 1 (1926): 70; also in *Ecrits I: La Philosophie et les Mythes* (Paris: Editions Sociales, 1969).

18. Ibid., p. 71.

19. Ibid., p. 97.

20. Georges-Philippe Friedmann, "Ils ont perdu la partie éternelle d'eux-mêmes," *Esprit*, no. 1 (May 1926): 115–73.

21. Ibid., p. 137, and further elaboration pp. 144–47.

22. Ibid., p. 156, with discussion of his search for "Sagesse total" on pp. 127, 147, 156–57, 171–73.

23. Henri Lefebvre, "Description de ces temps, misere de Jacques Maritain," *Esprit*, no. 1 (May 1926): 258–71.

24. Lefebvre, *La Somme et le Reste*, p. 254–55.

25. Henri Lefebvre, "Notes pour le procès de la chretiente," *Esprit*, no. 2 (March 1927): pp. 125–28, 132–33.

26. Ibid., pp. 136–38.

27. Henri Lefebvre, "La pensée et l'esprit," *Esprit*, no. 1 (May 1926): 28–29, 30.

28. Ibid., pp. 35, 37.

29. Ibid., p. 49.

30. Ibid., pp. 68–69.

31. Henri Lefebvre, "Reconnaissance de l'unique," *Esprit*, no. 2 (March 1927): 8–9, 16–20.

32. Ibid., p. 22.

33. Lefebvre, *La Somme et le Reste*, pp. 407–409, and *L'Existentialisme*, pp. 25–34.

34. See Lefebvre, "1925," and *Les Temps des Mèprises* (Paris: Stock, 1975,), pp. 48–50. In the latter work, Lefebvre wrote that Breton confronted him with Vera's translation of Hegel's *Logic* and demanded, "Haven't you even read this?" Soon thereafter, Lefebvre continued, he began to read Hegel, "who led me to Marx."

35. *The Phenomenology* was not available in French until Jean Hyppolite's translation of 1939–1941. The sections translated by Wahl and Boucher correspond to paragraphs 206–230, pp. 126–38 of A. V. Miller's English translation (New York: Oxford, 1977).

36. Jean Wahl, *La Malheur de la conscience dans la philosophie de Hegel* (Paris: Rieder, "Collection Esprit," 1928). See also Pierre Morhange's poem "A Jean Wahl," in *La Vie est Unique* (Paris: Gallimard, 1933), reprinted in *Sentiment lui-même*. Jean Grenier reviewed both of Wahl's studies, the *Parménide* in *Nouvelle Revue Française*, no. 164 (May 1927) and the *Malheur* in *Europe*, no. 81 (September 1929). Jean Prévost reviewed the former work for *Europe*, no. 53 (May 1927). A late review of *Malheur* was written by Claude Estève for *Nouvelle Revue Française*, no. 206 (November 1930).

37. Alexandre Koyré, "Rapport sur l'état des études hégéliennes en France," *Revue d'Histoire de la Philosophie* 5, no. 2 (April–June 1931).

38. See Michael Kelly, "Hegel in France to 1940," *Journal of European Studies* 11, no. 1 (March 1981), and his *Marxism in Modern France* (Baltimore: Johns Hopkins, 1982); Michael S. Roth, *Knowing and History: Appropriations of Hegel in Twentieth-Century France* (Ithaca: Cornell University Press, 1988); Laurence Pitkelthy, "Hegel in Modern France (1900–1950)," Ph.D. thesis, University of London, 1979(?); Paul E. McLaughlin, "Alexander Kojéve and the Hegelian Revival in

France Between the Wars," Ph.D. thesis, Harvard University, 1982; and Mark Poster, *Existential Marxism in Post-war France* (Princeton: Princeton University, 1975), chap. 1.

39. By the late 1920s, Lukács had been forced to disown his *History and Class Consciousness*, Korsch had been shoved to the periphery of German political and intellectual life, and Gramsci languished in a fascist jail.

40. Pierre Naville, "Les tendences confusionistes du group «L'Esprit»," *Clarté*, no. 3: 84–88.

41. Victor Crastre, "Chronique de la vie bourgeoise: Ruines," *Clarté*, no. 5: 153–54. Pierre Unik continued the assault in "Les Philosophies de «L'Esprit»," *L'Etudiant de l'Avant-Garde*, no. 3 (January 1927).

42. *Nouvelles Littéraires* (12 June 1926).

43. Ibid. (26 March 1927): 6.

44. Lucien Roure, "Esprit," *Etudes*, tome 194 (January–March 1928): 370–71.

45. Benjamin Crémieux, "Examens de Conscience" in *Inquiétude et Reconstruction* (Paris: Corrêa, 1931), p. 125 (essay dated 1926).

46. Ibid., p. 139.

47. Gabriel Marcel, "L'Esprit," *Nouvelle Revue Française*, no. 154 (July 1926): 126–27.

48. Albert Thibaudet, "Réflexions sur la littérature: Cahiers," *Nouvelle Revue Française*, no. 156 (September 1926): 353. Like Daniel-Rops, Thibaudet comments on the comparatively Jewish composition of Philosophies. Surprisingly, no one really cared that Guterman and Politzer were not native French.

49. Ibid., p. 356. Moreover, "Les jeunes gens de l'Esprit mépriseraient une philosophie qui ne serait pas une révolution philosophique, et peut-être une révolution philosophique qui ne serait pas accompagnée d'une révolution politique." (p. 357.)

50. Ibid., p. 360.

51. Jean Grenier, "L'Esprit," *Nouvelle Revue Française*, no. 164 (May 1927): 706–707.

52. Lefebvre, *La Somme et le Reste*, p. 431.

53. While the meeting topics suggest a link to the creation of a PCF "Jewish Section" in June 1927, direct evidence is nonexistent, nor did the Philosophies ever act as "Jewish Communists." See Maurice Rajsfus, *L'An prochain, La Révolution: Les Communistes Juifs immigrés dans la Tourmente Stalinienne 1930–1935* (Paris: Mazarine, 1985).

Chapter 3

Politzer and "The Dramatic Life"

(1928–1929)

Politzer's rapid entry into and promotions within the French lycée system suggest that major critical and constructive theoretical work was expected from him. In fact, he appeared to quickly establish himself as an innovative scholar with the publication of two major monographs and the launching of a professional periodical within a two-year span. In *Fin d'une parade philosophique*, Politzer focused his attack on Henri Bergson's *Essai sur les données immediates de la conscience*, and, by extension, against Bergson's entire effort to systemize the apparently distinct realms of psychology, philosophy, and physics. At root Politzer claimed to respect and sympathize with Bergson's project, which he believed was inspired by an attempt to grasp the "concrete." (This term, *concrète*, was widely used throughout Politzer's writings during this period, and was defined by him as "the singular individual, conceptualized as a conscious actor within social reality.")[1] Politzer's deference in practice took less obvious forms: He harassed the aging Nobel laureate, planting himself at the same work table at the Bibliotheque Victor Cousin in order to read aloud extracts of his tract, to munch noisily on ham sandwiches, and to "race" a tortoise named "Creative Evolution" from one end to the other.[2] Politzer's respect for Bergson should be measured by the fact that he alone of French philosophers was worth singling out as deserving refutation. And perhaps

Politzer expressed his respect by using the pseudonym François Arouet, the proper name of another irreverent writer better known as Voltaire.

The vast influence of Henri Bergson is generally forgotten today, mostly because his works are so plainly a product of the late nineteenth and early twentieth centuries. In brief, Bergson sought to undermine the mechanistic tendency within French philosophy stretching from Descartes to the prevalent positivist scientism of the late nineteenth century. He did not revolutionize philosophy as he and his supporters hoped, but rather reformulated the traditions of idealist philosophy stretching back to the Greeks. Instead of accepting the broad categories philosophical logic imposed on consciousness, such as sensation, will, and emotion, Bergson attempted to implant those categories into time. This concept of duration (*durée*) as experience-in-time, a concept distinct from the scientific division of time, provided Bergson with a link between the isolated fragments of individual experience. Furthermore, each specific experience was, according to Bergson, to be grasped in its entirety, through intuition and not through artificial pseudoscientific categories.

By privileging sentiment and intuition over science, Bergson's message was one of mystical optimism. To the increasingly mechanized and atomized society of fin-de-siècle industrial France, Bergson announced the value of the individual, the validity of feelings and sensation against the perceived sterility of Reason, and the belief that, despite the rapidity of change within the modern world, individuals and their experiences were just as valuable and just as meaningful as time itself.[3]

Part of Politzer's criticism was historical: Bergson simply took the broad categories of traditional mysticism and idealism, reducing them to specific moments within the *durée*. The categories remained abstract and formal, without reference to external reality: "the concrete for Bergson resided within essence and authenticity," not the everyday, real life of singular individuals.[4] However, Politzer objected, Bergson essentially argued that each individual was qualitatively unique, as was each specific experience of life. Hence, Politzer concluded, there could be no continuity of experience even within the individual life and consciousness, only the intuitive and immediate grasping of isolated moments. What remained were isolated individuals confronting each other with equal and relativized "authenticities."[5] All Bergson contributed to the classic categories of psychology and philosophy were the *durée mouvement* and *vécu* ("authenticity"), which simply appeared to animate the pure abstractions of previous thinkers.[6] This *morcelage* within Bergson's system, Politzer declared, underlined the paradox of Bergson: By fragmenting human experience into discontinuous individual events, Bergson simply repeated the categorical divisions of scientific thought![7] Politzer failed to note that his critique of Bergson also implied that his system gave philosophic form to the very *inquiétude* underlying Politzer's search for a guide.

For Politzer, Bergson failed to confront the relations of individual to collective, and of both to external reality. Bergson's attempt to unite the diversity of individual human experience with the quasi-biological notion of "creative evolution" simply inserted a spiritualist notion of causality into history. More important, the *durée* itself became an abstraction equivalent to progress: Individual moments were serialized and ordered within time, homogenizing the diversity of human experience and, implicitly, allowing for the mutual interpenetration of the supposedly unique moments by one another. This abstraction from isolated minds to Absolute unity made Bergson's *durée* unknowable, since it obeyed its own laws and dominated the individual.[8]

Politzer, the sufferer of *inquiétude* and searcher for absolutes, disdained Bergson's philosophy as a "liberty of indifference." Politzer declared the ultimate relativity of meaning and a disregard for specific, concrete sociohistorical context reduced Bergson to an apologist for bourgeois society. Politzer drove this point home sharply: By divorcing reality and meaning, and by abstracting both, Bergson created a justification of society as it existed.[9]

For Politzer, the essential purposes and meanings of Bergson were political: He justified the status quo and with it social inequalities. Bergson offered consistent public and theoretical support for French nationalism. Bergson was Politzer's "Anti-Marx," a servant of the bourgeoisie. Since the end of the Great War, neither he nor his ideas served any useful function, and both were rapidly falling by the wayside, leading Politzer to conclude that "M. Bergson is not yet dead, but Bergsonism is in fact dead."[10]

Yet in his 1928 *La Fin d'une parade philosophique*, Politzer's own transition to Marxism was clearly incomplete, despite his praises:

Only Marx has denounced the pact giving heaven to philosophers in exchange for the earth, logic in exchange for Man, principles in exchange for institutions, since it was truly he who has revealed the secret of the age-old sleight of hand.[11]

Although Politzer employed violent language in the opening and closing pages to denounce Bergson's political utilization by the bourgeoisie, it was to confront Bergson with Kant or Nietzsche rather than Marx. Politzer's "bourgeoisie" was synonymous with the "establishment" of recent times, and "petite bourgeoisie" with Nietzsche's "cultural philistines." And his scathing remarks regarding the use of Kant for purposes of universal reaction cannot disguise the fact that his polemic barely covered a Kantian critique of Bergson's categories of analysis. Thus Politzer's vehement assertion of civil war permeating daily life and his linking of fascism to the decay of bourgeois society reflect a personal stance and the general politicization of French intellectual debate, but not yet Politzer's adhesion to even a rudimentary form of Marxism or Communism.

With his *Critique des fondements de la psychologie* Politzer launched what promised to be a much more creative and positive line of discussion. Originally, this work was to be the first of several volumes, the second of which would deal with Gestalt psychology and the third, with behaviorism. Hence, Politzer cautioned his readers that all the conclusions he drew in his attempt to further psychoanalytic theory should be regarded as provisional.[12] While his express purpose was not to simply present Freudian thought but to reflect on it and push it beyond its current limits, Politzer also provided an adequate defense of Freud's work against the "psychologues" of France, those heirs of nineteenth-century French psychology, a hybrid of biology and philosophy. To locate the number and exact origin of ideas, they counted brain cells; to conceptualize human emotion and aspirations, they used categories like "the soul" and *la vie interieure*, resulting, Politzer thought, in the reduction of human life to the level of things, mere objects of detached and ethereal scrutiny.[13]

Politzer claimed that Freud's development of the *Traumdeutung*, the method of interpreting dreams, relegated all the petty domestic quarrels of these "psychologues" to the trash basket. For Politzer, the Freudian method of dream interpretation was the most concrete and most central contribution of psychoanalysis. For the first time, psychology had a specific object to investigate: the unconscious. The psychoanalytic interpretation of consciously mediated significations (dreams, images, words, and so on) provided the key for understanding the unconscious. Language and other forms of signification provided the necessary link between the individual and society within the theory, and the specific individual being analyzed was considered as the still incomplete product of a particular historical process.[14]

Nevertheless, Politzer found Freudian psychoanalysis flawed in two crucial aspects. Politzer recognized that Freud retained elements of nineteenth-century psychology in his system. In a related problem, Politzer noted that in Freudian analysis the individual was studied by an external interpreter of signification, and hence remained an object of scrutiny. Moreover, to provide a dynamism to the individual psychological processes, Freud relied on the hypothesis of libidinal energy constantly disrupting the psychic infrastructure of all individuals. Politzer's critique of Bergson's *durée* was exactly paralleled here, as Politzer himself noted: Fascination with electricity and the movements of physical energy was common to many thinkers active at the end of the century. Generally, Politzer stated his willingness to temporarily accept the necessity of the inclusion of these faults within psychoanalysis, arguing that it was still a young science in the process of development.[15]

On the second point Politzer proved less flexible and more critical. Freud's contributions were certainly the most concrete to date, Politzer asserted, but they rested entirely on a series of abstractions. The unconscious evaded direct scrutiny and could be approached only through the interpretation of significations. However, by definition, these same significations were distorted, and the creation of an interpretation from this basis produced a misleading as well as abstract conception of the unconscious. The "actual reality" of latent unconscious meaning could never in fact be known, but only interpreted according to a contradictory set of formalized positions held by the analyst. Psychoanalysis claimed, on the one hand, that libidinal energy originating in a mechanistic fashion created unfulfillable desires and led to individual neuroses; on the other hand, in psychoanalysis, these neuroses could only be treated through the reconstruction of the individual's specific history through an unraveling of significations.

At this point, Politzer argued, a third major abstraction was brought in: From the isolated and specific moments presented to the analyst for interpretation, the entire psychological history of the individual was reconstituted. In approaching the internal operations of human intelligence and consciousness, Freud let the concrete slip away.[16]

The solutions Politzer offered were as brief and provisionary as he warned. Politzer suggested the solution lay in a turn away from the unconscious to a study of *la vie dramatique de l'homme*, a phrase he emphatically denied contained any romantic connotations. Within the concept of *vie dramatique* Politzer sought to capture both biological existence and social interaction.[17] Politzer asserted that his concept avoided abstractions by focusing on the events of human existence, both in singular, individual and collective, social terms. This *vie dramatique* provided, in Politzer's interpretation, an ensemble of events, of external and internal conflicts which constituted *le moi de la vie quotidienne*—the self of daily life.[18] Politzer attempted to shift emphasis from the distorted significations of individuals to that of societies, arguing that this solution would lead to a "true synthesis of subjective psychology and of objective psychology." By focusing on human social activity (*comportement humain*), with the inherent conflict between the social environment in which human life was played out and the individual living subject, Politzer proclaimed his concept of *vie dramatique* was a project of self-creative human liberation. Further elements of this system, along with a methodology, Politzer promised, would be provided in the later volumes.[19]

Despite the appearance of dialectical thought, implied by Politzer's use of terminology and imagery borrowed from Hegel and Schelling, the *Critique* duplicated the form of Kant's *Critique of Pure Reason*, to which Politzer appealed at the beginning and the end of the study. The approach Politzer took toward Freudian theory was a Kantian critical reexamination of the categories from which the system was constructed. Politzer implied the opening of a vast panorama, encompassing not only individual consciousness and unconsciousness and experiences, but all of the progress and conflict of human social liberation as well. How he hoped to achieve this fusion without relying on Bergsonian "intuition," *elan vital* and *durée*, or the "Transcendental Idea" and "Absolute consciousness" of German Idealism, cannot be reconstructed.

Perhaps he himself did not have a solution while preparing the *Critique*. One has the suspicion that his results may have looked quite similar to Kenneth Burke's "symbol clusters" and "drama of moments."[20] Conversely, he might have adopted a position espoused by some members of the Frankfurt School, particularly Fromm, and sought to link a Marxist theory of social development to a Freudian examination of the impact of that development upon individual psychological structure.[21] This latter trajectory seemed the most likely possibility as Politzer continued to develop his concept of *vie dramatique* in *Revue de la Psychologie concrète*.

As part of the Philosophies collective swing toward the Parti Communiste Français, they undertook a new, bolder publishing venture. With Friedmann's money they put together a small company, Les Revues, to publish a series of periodicals and inexpensive books, the first of which was "Arouet's" assault on Bergson. While Morhange and the others poured their energies into *La Revue marxiste*, Politzer received a share of the funds for his own periodical, *Revue de la Psychologie concrète*.

In his opening editorial, Politzer announced that psychology, in all its forms, was in a state of crisis, and therefore

> alongside theoretical work, this publication must attempt as well the material organization of the new unified psychology, and constitute a center around which the *forces psychologiques* now enchained may regroup themselves. . . .[22]

Politzer's *Revue* claimed to adhere to no tendency, and was open to all seeking a synthetic transcendence of the schools of psychology.

Both the first issue of February 1929 and the second of July 1929 carried an impressive number of pieces from major foreign theorists. From the United States, J. R. Kantor sent in two pieces, a previously published article by Alfred Adler was translated from the German, and from Great Britain, Charles Meyers wrote on industrial psychology. In two German theorists, Fritz Giese and particularly Hans Prinzhorn, Politzer found collaborators willing to submit materials and provide theoretical support. Giese supplied a pair of articles, while Prinzhorn sent several reviews, a response to Politzer's *enquête*, and a reply to one of Politzer's critics.

Some of the more interesting pieces concerned an *enquête* Politzer circulated prior to publication. Psychoanalysis, Politzer wrote, was in a period of stagnation, due in part to the inadequacies of some of its concepts. Psychologists were witnessing a "crisis of psychoanalysis" as younger practitioners began to push beyond the problems and answers that had satisfied their mentors.[23] This debate Politzer linked to a second *enquête*, regarding the possibility of exploring the relationships between industrial psychology and psychotechnics in an effort to forge a general psychology without abstraction.[24] Not surprisingly, several respondents conflated the two questions.

In the first issue, Fritz Giese suggested a division into two fields of study, cultural psychology and practical psychology. The former would be devoted to knowledge of psychic facts, while the latter concerned the study of Man in a given situation, in order to adapt the environment "to the biological particularities of Man." Combining the two would result, Giese hoped, in an applied psychology allowing for a better understanding of and control over daily life.[25] Hans Prinzhorn agreed with Politzer that Freudian psychoanalysis needed to be pushed further still. He offered suggestions covering a wide range of solutions, primarily a metaphysics of expression and values.[26]

Otto Rank's response appeared in the second issue. "Crisis is something inherent to psychoanalysis," Rank claimed, "because it represents the tendency to unify two incompatible spheres: the soul (*âme*) and the natural sciences in general, the theory and the technical in particular." After providing a pocket history of the schisms within the Freudian movement, Rank concluded that the crisis that concerned Politzer and Prinzhorn was "less a crisis of psychoanalysis, which has reached the point of death, than of psychiatrists."[27]

The real quarrel came from André Hesnard, in "Á Propos d'une Prétendue «Crise» de la Psychanalyse." The French psychoanalytic movement was just finding itself and gathering its forces despite numerous obstacles, Hesnard blasted, and no crisis existed. Concrete psychoanalysis already existed in the works of orthodox Freudians, Hesnard argued, who provided effective applied psychology in everyday practice. Hesnard made it clear that he and the French Freudians saw no point in attempting to bridge the chasm separating the different schools of psychology: "We confine ourselves to purely and simply confronting the oeuvre of P. Janet to that of

Freud, in order to point out all the consequences of anti-sexualist preju-
dice."[28] For Hesnard, Politzer and Prinzhorn simply raised an "old cry of
alarm." In a comparatively mild conclusion to a strongly written essay,
Hesnard pointedly addressed Politzer: "The curtain is raised, and we await,
eagerly, the drama."[29]

Politzer himself tried to delineate the project of unification he thought
desirable and possible in a major essay in each issue. In "Psychologie
mythologique et psychologie scientifique" in the February issue, Politzer
continued to explore the possibility of a new psychology constructed
around *la vie dramatique*. All other critiques, Politzer noted, have been
reduced to extreme simplification in the course of partisan debates, so
that, for example, behaviorism appeared to lose sight of the individual
while exploring the social. The "best" results thus far, Politzer added, were
only partial reexaminations of the entire foundation upon which psychological theory rested, or perhaps a conciliatory professional agreement.
But the need for a thorough reexamination of the values of the different
criticisms and the lacunas within psychological theory had not yet been
addressed.

Politzer wrote that the time had come to stop pretending "to render
justice to the positive aspects of each tendency."[30] Instead, the time for partial reforms or a supposedly sharp division between classical psychology
and Freudian psychoanalysis was past. The question must be shifted to a
reexamination of the scientific content of psychology in general, and the
prescientific elements weeded out. The proper focus of study should be *la
vie humaine*, constituting a drama. Politzer specified exactly what he had in
mind in three paragraphs:

> It is incontestable that it is within "the drama" that we first place our
> daily experience. The events happening to us are dramatic events: we
> play such and such a role, etc. The vision we have of ourselves is a dra-
> matic vision: we know ourselves to have been the actor or the witness of
> such and such scenes or actions. We remember having made a trip,
> having seen men fighting in the street, of having made a speech. Dra-
> matic also are our intentions: we want to marry, to go to the movies, etc.
> We think of ourselves in dramatic terms.
>
> It is on the dramatic plane that the contact with our fellow-creatures

is also found. An entrepreneur hires a worker, we play tennis with our friends, etc. Dramatic is also the comprehension that we have with one another. Someone invites me to tea, I accept or I refuse. Someone expresses his political opinions to me, I disagree with him violently, but we are having a discussion, living within the significations which touch us in one sense or another, but at no moment can we leave the plane of drama.

It is also on the dramatic plane that we understand one another. The dramatic side is, moreover, the only one which interests us in daily life: what we want to know is the manner in which such and such requires us to behave in a determined situation, and why it is necessary to act in one manner rather than in another. What is it we recite to one another? "M. de . . . , young, handsome, intelligent and rich, has married, Mlle. . . . , old, homely, unintelligent and poor." This is what we seek to comprehend.[31]

This psychology of everyday life, Politzer insisted, could not be based on theories of individual egoism, an abstracted concept of Man-in-general struggling against Nature-in-general, derived from philosophy. Instead, economic life, classes, and class interests must be substituted for the old abstractions.[32] Fusing the subjective and objective psychologies together, Politzer argued, could illuminate the unique and individual as well as the general and common.

These statements were the fullest exposition of *la vie dramatique* as Politzer originally conceived it. By the second issue of *Revue de la Psychologie concrète* in July, Politzer had totally shifted his stance. The crisis of psychology was entirely due to its idealist origins, he wrote then, while claiming that

> concrete psychology truly is that psychology abolishing every trace of idealism in psychology. It is a materialist psychology, adopting therefore the only attitude that is capable of assuring to psychology a scientific future. But it is to contemporary materialism that it re-attaches itself, to that issuing from Marx and Engels and designated by the name dialectical materialism. Psychology has need of a complete materialism, and dialectical materialism alone is complete.[33]

Politzer now equated his *psychologie concrète* with *psychologie materialiste.* All other versions of psychology became simply "spiritualism," seeking merely to develop "the theological-scholastic systemization of the soul," and Politzer relabeled psychoanalysis as the "science of the soul."[34] For Politzer, the entire debate between "classical" and "new" psychology, between "abstract" and "concrete," boiled down to idealism versus materialism. "Idealist psychology," according to Politzer, explained reality through significations, "materialist psychology" explained realities with realities.[35] "Où va la psychologie concrète?," Politzer's second lengthy essay of 1929, failed to develop the concepts he introduced in his earlier writings and marked Politzer's sudden, intense conversion to French Communism and Marxism.

Politzer's *Revue de la Psychologie concrète* vanished abruptly after its second issue, in part due to short-term financial and personal problems that disrupted the Philosophies and their publishing efforts. Even without these difficulties, it is unlikely that *Revue de la Psychologie concrète* could have continued for long. Along with Politzer's sudden rejection of psychoanalysis, two other major factors—the reception of critics and the place of Politzer and his writings within the specific context of the French psychoanalytic movement of the 1920s—combined to wreck the *psychologie concrète* Politzer advocated.

The confused and cool reception of Politzer's writings and of the *Revue* indicated some of the divisions of opinion he confronted. In a major discussion of Politzer's writings that appeared as a "Chroniques des Idées" column in *Europe*, Jean Prévost tied Politzer's critiques of Bergson and of psychology to the development of the collective project of the Philosophies, and provided a fairly generous review. For Prévost, Politzer might be dogmatic at times, yet the number of original ideas made the reader's efforts well spent. In particular Prévost thought Politzer's discussion of the unconscious the best section of the *Critique*. Prévost compared his own recently published *Essai sur l'introspection* to the *Critique*, describing the resemblance as that of a yacht to a dreadnought. Overall, Politzer had written a profession of faith without offering any resolutions for the problems he found. Prévost noted an essential point in closing: Whether Politzer wished it or not, his fusion of philosophy and psychology would only find an audience in the most specialized of professional reviews.

Prévost's review was the most detailed and earliest of the reviews to appear and certainly the most balanced. Happily, no one yet knew what the professionals would write.[36]

In *Nouvelle Littéraires*, Henri Gouhier wrote a short, withering critique of *Le Fin d'une parade philosophique*.[37] Gouhier did not object to the violent language Politzer employed in attacking Bergson, since "violence is a sign of intellectual good health, and there are no true philosophers without passions." But, Gouhier continued, when passion and violent language substitute for thought and substance, then one must conclude that the author is playing the clown.

The newest project of Henri Barbusse, *Monde*, carried a long review signed "Metenie." "Finally, a serious book against Bergson," Metenie proclaimed, one he thought unmasked the contradictory mythological psychology of the philosopher. The review was less an examination of Politzer's writing and more of a gleeful participation in his political denunciation of Bergson:

> And what is the concrete man, the singular who is named Bergson? A philosopher allied to the state and to the class of which that state is the expression, a man who marched exhaustively during the last war, who practiced songs of patriotism in the name of the concrete and of life (14 million dead)....
>
> But Arouet and his friends must persevere in their work of public health, in denouncing traitors and puppets. And thus, as they desire, they will assist the proletariat, all the more as they set themselves—and this is the grand conclusion of the book—on the terrain of dialectical materialism, since the bourgeoisie, despite all its wishes, has not found the anti-Marx which it requires.[38]

In these two reviews, Politzer, like Bergson, was caught in an ongoing political discourse: What either really meant or had to offer in terms of theoretical contribution was secondary. What mattered was which side they were on. Equally obvious was the fact that the identity of François Arouet was as well-kept a secret as that of John Brown had been.

Then the professionals had their say. One of the first reviews appeared in the periodical of the Parisian Psychoanalytic Society, *Revue Française de*

Psychanalyse, soon after Politzer's *Critique des fondements de la psychologie* appeared. Roldolphe Loewenstein underscored the Kantian element within Politzer's work, and in particular Politzer's desire to author a Copernican revolution of his own, but felt the result was a scholastic exercise. Loewenstein argued that much of Politzer's criticism is based upon an inexact knowledge of psychoanalytic theory. Still, he believed that many of Politzer's ideas had a real methodological value and would eventually become part of the psychoanalytic edifice.[39]

Henri Piéron was sympathetic but not supportive toward Politzer's efforts in reviewing *La Critique des fondements de la psychologie* for *L'Année Psychologique.*[40] The *Critique* was a work of frankly revolutionary intent, Piéron thought, meriting attention if only because in the sciences, unlike literature or art, revolutions were rare. But intentions would not suffice, Piéron added quickly: Had a revolution really taken place, or was one being heralded? Probably neither, Piéron answered, since Politzer turned from inner psychological motivations to the study of signification within societies, a shift of focus more in common with literature than scientific procedures: "There may be a revolution if our science progresses forcefully enough thanks to this point of view. I wish it strongly enough, but, at bottom, I doubt it." The study of human drama was too utopian to be scientific, Piéron argued, but could supplement the intuition of novelists.

W. Bischler reiterated the same points in a more condensed form for *Les Archives de Psychologie.* Although original and proclaiming a total revolution, he found that Politzer's *Critique* signified the development of major new ideas which would contribute to the growth of psychology as a science. But Bischler suggested that neither he nor Politzer had any idea how a psychology of real or concrete life could be worked out.[41] And *Archives de Philosophie* did not get around to reviewing the *Critique* until 1930, when a lengthy critique by Etienne Pialat appeared. After devoting the bulk of his review to presenting Politzer's major points, Pialat offered one criticism: The demand for the psychoanalytic study of human drama relied in the end on abstraction as much as the "traditional" psychology Politzer assaulted so vigorously.[42]

La Revue de la Psychologie concrète fared no better than the *Critique.* The orthodox *Revue Française de Psychanalyse* never mentioned the new effort at all. Henri Piéron did review it for *L'Année psychologique* in 1929, by curiously breaking the contributions apart into a series of extremely short notices with little or no commentary. To Politzer's major essays, "Psychologie mythologique et psychologie scientifique" and "Où va la psychologie concrète," Piéron devoted just less than three pages, an indication of interest if not accord. Piéron found the essays full of "interesting and original ideas" presented with "violent enthusiasm" and "mystical fervor," exaggerated beyond necessity and logical acceptability. He dismissed Politzer's idea of drama as an artificial construction, ultimately verifiable only by the reduction of human experience to the correlations of statistics. Piéron again argued that concrete psychology already existed in orthodox Freudianism, focused on the real problems of individuals rather than deriving individual experience from abstracted social categories. Perhaps, Piéron concluded, Politzer's works would improve with experience and the decline of "philosophical freshness."[43]

J. C. Flügel reviewed the *Critique* in the *International Journal of Psycho-Analysis*, the official international periodical of the Freudian movement. His words were comparatively encouraging, at the cost of ignoring the sharpness of Politzer's assault on Freudian theory. Flügel thought a distinct tendency toward behaviorism was evident in Politzer's work, but reserved judgment until the complete series appeared, an achievement he anticipated with polite interest.[44]

The reaction of professional psychologists, with Piéron in the lead, was unenthusiastic if not discouraging. The reception within literary periodicals, despite Gouhier, was slightly better but equally limited. *Nouvelles Littéraires* mentioned the appearance of *Revue de la Psychologie concrète* in passing, but particularly recommended only Meyer's article on industrial psychology in Britain.[45] Jean Wahl provided some brief comments carried in *Nouvelle Revue Française*, praising Politzer's vigorous writing and thought in "Psychologie mythologique et psychologie scientifique," but by restricting himself to rather general praise, Wahl left the impression of trying to fill up space while sparking enough audience reaction to benefit the subscription list of *Revue de la Psychologie concrète*.[46]

And Lucien Roure was now convinced that he was correct in seeing Bolshevism in *Esprit*. Again reviewing for *Etudes*, he boiled Politzer's entire project down to a single essential point: the rejection of "inner life," or soul, and with it Christianity. *"Nous sommes en plein bolchevisme intellectuel,"* Roure concluded in disgust.[47]

Appearing in the July 1929 issue of *Europe*, a full year after Prévost's discussion of *La Fin d'une parade philosophique*, Leon Pierre-Quint's "Les caractères religeux du communisme" highlighted the rapid shift in critical perception, as well as the evolution of Politzer and the Philosophies. Writing in the early summer of 1929, Pierre-Quint already knew where Politzer and the other Philosophies had evolved to, and denounced them for renouncing their earlier mysticism, or rather for submerging it into the new faith of Communism. For Pierre-Quint, all of Politzer's writings were reducible to the opposition of Marx versus Bergson. Politzer and his colleagues had simply abandoned all individuality, along with a sizable portion of their critical faculties, by recognizing only economic facts and Marxist collective discipline. For Pierre-Quint, a past contributor to *Philosophies*, true individuality, true psychological knowledge, was to be found in the philosophy of Bergson, and not the countersystem of Marx.[48]

The critical reception indicates that the failure of *Revue de la Psychologie concrète* as originally conceived cannot be attributed to Politzer's personal evolution alone. Politzer correctly claimed that his *Revue* found itself almost completely isolated within France, although wrong to attribute that isolation to the inevitable confrontation with some preexisting and monolithic profession.[49] Politzer's comments to this effect were particularly idiosyncratic since they were part of his introduction to an essay on the history of the French psychoanalytic movement prepared by André Hesnard and Edouard Pichon, which appeared in the February issue. Even allowing for the probability that Hesnard and Pichon overstated their arguments in order to enhance their own positions, their brief history offered a very different portrait of the development of French psychology and psychoanalysis.

Hesnard and Pichon's outline traced the rapid development and fusion of different psychoanalytic tendencies during the twenties. They divided the penetration of Freudian thought into France into four stages. The first, a period of invasion and resistance, occurred from 1913 to 1920. The second was a period of literary and fashionable popularization from 1921 to 1923, followed by professional control and scientific acceptance during 1923 to 1926, with formal institutional organization beginning only in 1926.[50] Thus, Politzer can be seen as not attacking some Freudian establishment but rather a still-forming and internally divided coalition. Hesnard's staunch refusal to admit there was any crisis internal to psychoanalysis was clearly the result of years of personal struggle against professional ostracism.

The process of merging isolated individuals and quarrelsome groupings into a "Freudian" movement was itself made in the face of opposition of a still older, pre-Freudian, and equally divided psychology profession. The Report of the Paris Psychoanalytic Society for 1925–1927 listed only seven full members, three associate members, and three "permanent guests of the Society."[51] By the first quarter of 1930, the numbers had swelled to eighteen full and twelve associate members.[52] One of the associate members resigned within the next three months.[53]

The Freudians were themselves excluded. Not one member of the Society was invited to contribute to the volume on psychology in the series *Philosophes et Savants Français du XXᵉ Siècle*. The Freudians were equally conspicuous for their absence in the 1933 *Courants de la Philosophie contemporaine en France*. Yet Piéron was not only director of the psychology laboratory at the Sorbonne (accounting for the comparative mildness of his critique of Politzer, one of his students), but editor in chief of *Année Psychologique* as well. And Pichon, considered a compromiser within the professional community to which he belonged, was attracted to Maurras and the Action française![54] By pitting himself against both old and new orthodoxies simultaneously, Politzer effectively isolated himself.

Not one of the reviewers caught Politzer's essential, original project to create a synthesis between internal and external reality, between individual and society. The Freudians, blocked professionally from without and belabored by schisms within, saw Politzer on the road to behaviorism. The Catholic Roure and Bergsonian Pierre-Quint believed, in their different ways, that Politzer had forsaken any hope of salvation. Some of the critics, especially Roure, proved correct in predicting Politzer would adhere exclusively to an explanation of social reality, but his specific, published comments demonstrate that in 1928 and early 1929 he had not yet done so. Only with the second issue of *Revue de la Psychologie concrète* was a definite and even violent shift present.

Why, then, did Politzer suddenly reject the field he had devoted himself to? What wrenched Politzer out of his academic studies between writing the articles that appeared in the February issue of *Revue de la Psy-*

chologie concrète and his "Où va la psychologie concrète" of July? While there is evidence of several personal crises, the intellectual cause underlying Politzer's total abandonment of psychoanalysis can be traced with precision to his reading of Lenin's *Materialism and Empirio-criticism*, newly available in French translation in early 1929.

This 1908 excursion into philosophic debate by Lenin was a thrashing aimed at the Capri School Marxists, who included Maksim Gorky, Anatole Lunacharsky, and A. A. Bogdanov. Lenin derided the religious sentiments being smuggled into theoretical Marxism by his erring comrades, and he attempted to demolish in detail the theories of Ernst Mach and others in vogue during the fin-de-siècle. Politzer found in Lenin a harsh polemical assault on the common intellectual background shared by central Europeans at the turn of the century, a background underlying all of Freud's work and one Politzer himself not only shared but had begun to critique. From Lenin, Politzer derived his violent denunciations of "spiritualism" and of the idealist "sciences of the soul" that peppered "Où va la psychologie concrète." Politzer echoed the famous section of *Materialism and Empirio-criticism*, "Parties in Philosophy and Philosophical Blockheads," in his reduction of all philosophy to the opposition of idealism and materialism. And, most obviously, Politzer did not have to search far for a contemporary example of the Capri School, of others sneaking idealist spiritualism and religious sentiments into Marxism!

None of this tremendous impact was evident in Politzer's review of *Materialism and Empirio-criticism* in the first issue of *Revue Marxiste* in February.[55] Not until "Où va la psychologie concrète" of July, and in Politzer's review of Henri de Man's "Au-delà du marxisme" in the April issue, did the enduring imprint of *Materialism and Empirio-criticism* become evident.[56] In the latter review, Politzer savaged de Man's attempt to broaden Marxist theory through the incorporation of contemporary thought, especially psychoanalysis. In repeated references, Freud was no longer the pioneer of Politzer's new science, but "Freud, the doctor of integral eroticism," and "M. Freud, the theorist of universal eroticism or of love everywhere."[57]

Politzer's reading of Lenin was decisive for his intellectual trajectory. From 1929 *Materialism and Empirio-criticism* served as the ultimate standard of philosophic judgment for Politzer, to the extent that his most important works of the late thirties contain frequent quotes and paraphrases of

Lenin's arguments of 1908. The very terms of condemnation Lenin had hurled at his adversaries were taken up and elevated into theoretical categories by Politzer. Thus, while the remainder of the Philosophies were absorbing Marx's "1844 Manuscripts" and would move on to Lenin's *Philosophic Notebooks* on Hegel, Politzer's intellectual evolution remained grounded in the debates and terms of Lenin's least-sophisticated foray into philosophy. The handful of weeks between Politzer's writings published in February 1929 and those writings appearing just two to five months later were the crucial days of Politzer's intellectual and political development.

*   *   *

The last of the Philosophies to join the Parti Communiste Français, Politzer became a devoted militant immediately. Yet after 1929, Politzer only twice again wrote about psychoanalysis, pieces better discussed within the context of Politzer's own critical efforts in that field than in the discussion of his other writings to be found in the following chapters.

In his "Psychanalyse et marxisme: un faux contre-revolutionnaire, le Freudo-Marxisme," Politzer denied any common meeting ground for Marxism and psychoanalysis. This essay appeared in *Commune*, a newly founded periodical of the slowly forming Popular Front movement, in late 1933.[58] Nominally a thrashing delivered to a young theorist, Jean Audard, the piece was in many ways Politzer's autocritique. Politzer argued that Marxist materialism had nothing at all in common with the sham materialism of Freud, and that the attempt to smuggle psychoanalysis into Marxism inevitably carried with it the taint of idealist revisionism. For the militant Politzer, Audard erred in viewing Marxism as only an economic determinism, unconcerned with the individual and the specific. He also argued that Audard confused psychoanalytic methods for materialist practice, instead of recognizing them for the professions of faith they really were. The struggle of classes became abstracted and internalized as a dialectic of pleasure and reality principles, creating an impression, Politzer suggested, that the "real" struggle went on only in the heads of psychoanalysts. Lenin had foreseen Audard and his kind years before when writing *Materialism and Empirio-criticism*, Politzer concluded, and therefore it was possible to know an enemy by his words.

In this vicious and rather extraordinary piece (*Commune*, after all, was a periodical designed to attract, not scare away, sympathizers from the antifascist movements that would become the backbone of the Popular Front), Politzer demolished his own arguments of 1925–1929. Some of his phrases recalled those used by the reviewers of his own writings. Not once did he mention his own name, or use his personal example as a model for Audard to imitate. But Politzer did make a passing reference to Wilhelm Reich, just expelled from the German Communist Party and soon to be purged for his heresies from the organization of Freudian orthodoxy, the International Psycho-Analytic Association, in the following year. Politzer's reference to Lenin reconfirms the importance of *Materialism and Empirio-criticism* as the key text influencing his thought.

In 1939, "La fin de la psychanalyse" appeared under the pseudonym "Th. W. Morris" in the third (and last) prewar issue of *Pensée*.[59] By now, Politzer argued, psychoanalysis had been institutionalized as a science and begun to decay rapidly. Freud had just died, but his disciples perpetuated his errors. Politzer ridiculed the Freudians for combining mechanistic materialism (to account for individual behavior) with idealism (to explain larger, historical events), and then insisting dogmatically that the impossibility of such a fusion did not exist. Worse still, psychoanalysis could not possibly explain history, and especially not Nazism:

> Nonetheless, even if it may have the rigor to explain what causes Nazi X more than Nazi Y to be more willing to play the role of concentration camp torturer, that does not explain Nazism as a historical phenomena.[60]

Tragically, Politzer, the former advocate of psychoanalysis, would be able to pose the question more directly.

Notes

1. Georges Politzer, *La Fin d'une parade philosophique: le bergsonisme* (1929; reprint, Paris: J.-J. Pauvert, 1968), pp. 15, 24. All citations are from the 1968 edition. Originally published under the pseudonym "François Arouet."

2. Henri Lefebvre, *La Somme et le Reste* (1959; reprint, Paris: Bélibaste, 1973), tome 2, pp. 384–85; *L'Existentialisme* (Paris: Editions du Sagittaire, 1946) pp. 22–23.

3. Such a condensed discussion of Bergson cannot adequately cover his importance and his ideas. There is an increasing need for a historical reevaluation of Bergson and the entire generation of philosophers who came of age in the decade 1890–1900: Boutroux, Brunschvicg, Blondel, and so on.

4. Politzer, *La Fin*, discussion pp. 23–29, quote p. 29.

5. Ibid., pp. 37–39.

6. Ibid., pp. 62, 65–69.

7. Ibid., pp. 71–76.

8. Ibid., pp. 92–93, 97–99.

9. Ibid., pp. 115–20, quote p. 119.

10. Ibid., p. 188. See Irwin Edman's comments in his foreword to *Creative Evolution*, trans. A. Mitchell (New York: Random House, 1944), p. ix: "The general public, and that relatively private clique known as the philosophical public, had long ago fallen into the habit of thinking of Bergson as dead. Only on the publication of the dramatic news of Bergson's decision to renounce all posts and honors rather than to accept exemption from the Anti-Semitic laws of the Vichy government was the world reminded that he was still alive."

This last point makes later Politzer's vicious celebration of Bergson's death all the more tasteless. In "Aprés la mort de M. Bergson," in the clandestine *Pensée Libre*, no. 1 (February 1941), Politzer claims that the German occupation press covered Bergson's death with "embarrassed amusement" since Bergson had provided language and concepts later appropriated by fascism. Contained in *Ecrits I: La Philosophie et les mythes* (Paris: Editions Sociales, 1969), pp. 274–81. Politzer forgot that fascists also appropriated Marxist and Leninist language and concepts, and that a bourgeois philosopher can be an antifascist bourgeois philosopher.

11. Politzer, *La Fin*, p. 155.

12. Georges Politzer, *Critique des fondements de psychologie* (Paris: Rieder, "Collection Esprit," 1928; reprint, Paris: Presses Universitaires de France, 1967), p. 20. All citations are from the 1967 edition. Listed in *Psychological Abstracts* #3353, 2, no. 12 (December 1928) pp. 754–55, resumé by Math. H. Piéron of the Sorbonne.

13. Politzer, *Critiques des Fondements de psychologie*, pp. 1–10, 27–29.

14. Ibid., condensed from discussion chaps. 1 and 2.

15. Ibid., discussion chap. 3, especially pp. 144–53.

16. Ibid., chap. 4.

17. Ibid., pp. 11–12.

18. Ibid., pp. 51–53.

19. Ibid., pp. 247–53.

20. Kenneth Burke, *Permanence and Change* (New York: New Republic, 1935); *The Philosophy of Literary Form* (Baton Rouge: Louisiana State University, 1941); *A Grammar of Motives* (New York: Prentice Hall, 1945); *A Rhetoric of Motives* (New York: Prentice Hall, 1950). There is a rapidly growing critical literature regarding Burke as well. Burke informed me that although he knew Guterman, he is not familiar with Politzer's writings (personal correspondence, 10 May 1986).

21. See Martin Jay's discussion of Fromm in *The Dialectical Imagination* (Boston: Little, Brown, 1973), especially pp. 88–89.

22. Georges Politzer, "Editorial," *Revue de la Psychologie Concrète*, no. 1 (February 1929) and no. 2 (July 1929); reprinted *Ecrits II: Les Fondements de la Psychologie* (Paris: Editions Sociales, 1969) pp. 55–56. There are several listings for *Revue de la Psychologie Concrète* in *Psychological Abstracts*, including one by Piéron (3, no. 7 [July 1929]), and one each from R. R. Willoughby (3, no. 6 [June 1929]) and N. L. Nunn (3, no. 8 [Aug. 1929]), both of Clark University in Massachusetts.

23. Georges Politzer, "La Crise de la Psychanalyse," *Revue de la Psychologie concrète*, no. 1 (February 1929): 135–38; in *Ecrits II*, pp. 189–94. All page references for quotes from Politzer's articles will be from *Ecrits II*.

24. Georges Politzer, "La Psychologie gènèrale et la psychotechnique," *Revue de la Psychologie concrète*, no. 1 (February 1929): 132–34; *Ecrits II*, pp. 248–51.

25. Fritz Giese, "Theorie et Pratique en matiere de psychologie," *Revue de la Psychologie concrète*, no. 1 (February 1929): 65–74.

26. Hans Prinzhorn, "La Crise de la Psychanalyse," *Revue de la Psychologie concrète*, no. 1 (February 1929): 140–54.

27. Otto Rank, "Remarques sur la Crise de la Psychanalyse," *Revue de la Psychologie concrète*, no. 2 (July 1929): 259–66.

28. André Hesnard, "A propos d'une pretendue crise de la psychanalyse," *Revue de la Psychologie concrète*, no. 2 (July 1929): 267–81; *Ecrits II*, pp. 201–18. See also Edith Hesnard-Fèlix, "Le Docteur Hesnard et les Débuts de la Psychanalyse en France," *Europe*, no. 539 (March 1974); and M. Francioni with M. A. Schepisi, *Storia della psicoanalisi francese* (Turin: P. Boringhieri, 1982), part 1, chap. 2. See also Richard Keller, "Forgetting Freud: Language, Psychoanalysis and the Body in France 1913–1932," master's thesis, University of Colorado, 1996, especially chap. 3 devoted to Hesnard's role in French psychoanalysis.

29. *Ecrits II*, p. 218; see Politzer's "Reponse au Professor Hesnard," *Revue de la Psychologie concrète*, no. 2 (July 1929): 282–93, and in *Ecrits II*, pp. 218–34; and Hans Prinzhorn's "Sur l'article de Hesnard," *Revue de la Psychologie concrète*, no. 2 (July 1929): 294–97. Also see Francioni with Schepisi, "Psicoanalisi e 'psicologia conc-

reta.' La polemica con Politzer," in *Psicsanalisi francese*, pp. 141–56, especially section 3, pp. 147–51.

30. Georges Politzer, "Psychologie mythologique et psychologie scientifique," *Revue de la Psychologie concrète*, no. 1 (February 1929): 8–64; *Ecrits II*, pp. 57–131; quote from p. 70 of *Ecrits II*.

31. Politzer, *Ecrits II*, pp. 80–81.

32. Ibid., pp. 101–102.

33. Georges Politzer, "Editorial," *Revue de la Psychologie concrète*, no. 2 (July 1929): 161–63; *Ecrits II*, pp. 132–35. Quote from *Ecrits II*, p. 134.

34. Georges Politzer, "Où va la psychologie concrète?" *Revue de la Psychologie concrète*, no. 2 (July 1929): 164–202; *Ecrits II*, pp. 136–88; quote from *Ecrits II*, p. 139.

35. Politzer, *Ecrits II*, p. 187.

36. Jean Prévost, "D'une nouvelle orientation de la psychologie," *Europe*, no. 66 (June 1928): 281–90.

37. Henri Gouhier, "Les Livres de la philosophie," *Nouvelles Littéraires* (9 February 1929): 8.

38. Metenie, "Bergson et Bergsonisme," *Monde*, no. 43 (30 March 1929).

39. Roldolphe Loewenstein, "Critique des fondements de la psychologie," *Revue Française de Psychanalyse* 2, no. 3 (1928): 578–87.

40. Henri Piéron, "Critique des fondements de la psychologie," *Année psychologique*, 29e année (1928): 249–50.

41. Bischler, "Critique des fondements de la psychologie," *Archives de Psychologie*, tome 22, no. 85 (September 1929): 115.

42. Etienne Pialat, "Critique des fondements de la psychologie," *Archives de Philosophie*, vol. 7, supplement bibliographique no. 3 (1930): 17–19.

43. Henri Piéron, reviews of *Revue de la Psychologie concrète* in *Année psychologique*, 30e année (1929): 211–15, 235–36.

44. J. C. Flügel, "Politzer: Critique des fondement de la psychologie," *International Journal of Psycho-Analysis*, vol. 11 (1930): 237–38; considering the authoritative position of the *IJPA* and of Flügel, his review is actually extremely supportive of Politzer as a younger colleague.

45. "Revue des Revues," *Nouvelles Littéraires* (2 March 1929).

46. Jean Wahl, "Revue de la Psychologie concrète," *Nouvelle Revue Française*, no. 188 (May 1929): 743–44. *Monde* only mentioned the new review and listed the contributors, no. 38 (23 February 1929).

47. Lucien Roure, "Politzer: Critique des fondements de la psychologie," *Etudes*, tome 198 (January–March 1929): 754–55.

48. Léon Pierre-Quint, "Les caracteres religieux du communisme," *Europe*, no. 79 (July 1929): 472–79.

49. Georges Politzer, "Note preliminaire sur l'Aperçu historique du mouvement psychanalytique français," *Revue de la Psychologie concrète*, no. 1 (February 1929): 102–105. *Ecrits II*, p. 197–200.

50. Andre Hesnard and Edouard Pichon, "Aperçu historique du mouvement psychanalytique français," *Revue de la Psychologie concrète*, no. 1 (February 1929): 105–20.

51. *International Journal of Psycho-Analysis* 9 (1928): 395–97.

52. *International Journal of Psycho-Analysis* 11 (1930): 357–58.

53. Ibid., p. 520.

54. There are an increasing number of works on the subject of psychology in France. The following are most useful: J. Benrubi, *Les Courants de la Philosophie Contemporaine en France* (Paris: Alcan, 1933); D. Essertier, *Philosophes et Savants Français du XXe siècle* (Paris: Alcan, 1929) tome 4; I. and R. Barande, *Histoire de la Psychanalyse en France* (Paris: Privat, 1975); H. Baruk, *La Psychiatrie française de Pinel à nos jours* (Paris: Presses Universitaires de France, 1967); M. Francioni with M. A. Schepisi, *Storia della psicoanalisi francese* (Turin: P. Boringhieri, 1982); E. Roudinesco, *La Bataille de cent ans: histoire de la psychologie en France* (Paris: Ramsay, 1982), tome 1 (1885–1939); Jean-Pierre Mordier, *Les Débuts de la psychanalyse en France 1895–1926* (Paris: Maspero, 1981); André LeBois, "Psychanalyse et Freudisme en Sorbonne," *Nouvelle Revue Critique*, no. 95 (October 1936); and A. de Mijolla "La Psychanalyse en France," in *Histoire de la Psychanalyse*, ed. R. Jaccard (Paris: Hachette, 1982). Note that in this last, there are two mentions of Politzer in the essay devoted to Soviet psychoanalytic thought, but none in the very interesting essay on the movement's history in Hungary. There is some chance that Politzer may have been influenced by current Soviet debates regarding psychoanalysis. On these debates, see Martin A. Miller, "Freudian Theory Under Bolshevik Rule: The Theoretical Controversy During the 1920s," *Slavic Review* 44, no. 4 (winter 1985), especially pp. 635–41.

55. "Félix Arnold" [Georges Politzer], "La Lutte pour le matérialisme," *Revue marxiste*, no. 1 (February 1929): 93–100. In August 1936, Jean Grenier provided the most accurate comment on Lenin's effective but very simplistic polemic: "On peut s'imaginer que Lénine est un philosophe tant qu'on n'a pas lu *Materialisme et Empirio-criticisme*. Après l'avoir lu le doute n'est plus possible," in "L'Orthodoxie contre l'intelligence," *Nouvelle Revue Française*, no. 275 (August 1936): 305. Unfortunately, Grenier appears to have never commented on Lenin's more sophisticated "Philosophic Notebooks."

56. "Félix Arnold" [Georges Politzer] "Au-delà du marxisme ou en deça de la réalité," *Revue marxiste*, no. 3 (April 1929): 349–62.

57. Ibid., pp. 356, 359, and other references to Freud and *freudistes* passim.

58. Georges Politzer, "Psychanalyse et Marxisme," *Commune*, no. 3 (1933); *Ecrits II*, pp. 252–81. See also Francioni with Schepisi, *Psicsanalisi francese*, pp. 151–54.

59. "Th. W. Morris" [Georges Politzer], "La Fin de la psychanalyse," *Pensée*, no. 3 (October–December 1939); *Ecrits II*, pp. 282–302.

60. Ibid., p. 295.

Chapter 4

The *Revue marxiste*

(1929)

F alling at the midpoint of the interwar era, the *Revue marxiste* affair
neatly divided the exuberant revolutionary excitement of the 1920s
from the more disciplined militancy of the 1930s. Contemporaries
and scholars alike point to the brief success and noisy failure of this journal
in 1929 as one of the pivotal events of the period between the wars. Some
participants would later charge that the entire affair was orchestrated from
Moscow and represented a Stalinist effort to destroy an independent
French school of Marxism, and with it any hope for an independent French
Communist Party. Scholars of the Party and of French Marxism have
repeated these claims, but without examining the case too deeply. The continuing interest in that increasingly distant scandal lies both in the fact that
the major participants figure among the leaders of twentieth-century
French intellectual achievement and because the affair in part structured
the relationships between the French Communist Party and its intellectual
allies. Yet there has been no effort to explain why the *Revue marxiste* was so
important or to unravel the mysterious scandal that destroyed it.

During an interview a half-century afterward, Lefebvre claimed that
he and his friends "entered into the Party and into Marxism as into a new
order, I was going to say a monastic order."[1] Perhaps the Philosophies in
1928 had not changed too dramatically from the days when Morhange
wrote of their dreams of monastic lives and warrior spirit as argumentative

students. That they retained a certain amount of naivete is very evident. Lefebvre, in all of his memoirs, indicated that in 1927–1928 the group semiseriously explored the possibility of buying an island in the Gulf of Morbihan and establishing a platonic or monastic "Ilse du Sagesse" as a refuge for exiled socialists, with Trotsky as the first resident. When not preoccupied with this scheme, Lefebvre was charged with the merger negotiations with the Communist Party. He met with a member of the Party's Central Committee—and handed him copies of *Esprit*! Any militant's reactions to the writings in that periodical can be imagined.[2] Meanwhile, Guterman shifted from translating Dostoyevsky's mysticism to pieces on Lenin. And during the 1928 elections, Friedmann supposedly approached a Party dignitary named Paul Boutonnier with an offer to place some of his personal resources at the Party's disposal. For his pains, he was chased out as a police provocateur![3]

In the autumn of 1928, the Philosophies turned to a new, more serious project, the founding of their own publishing house, Les Revues. The necessary capital came, once again, from Friedmann. A project as ambitious as Les Revues required the efforts of a large number of dedicated intellectuals, and Jean Bruhat, Jean Fréville, Claude Glaymann, and other young Party militants brought their talents and energies to the enterprise. The aging Guesdist Charles Rappoport left his post at *L'Humanité* to serve as the group's mentor.[4] While the full impact of his participation did not become clear until well into the 1930s, Paul-Yves Nizan, a close friend of Friedmann's from the École Normale Supèrieure, became the important addition to the Philosophies.

As a small publisher, Les Revues began rather well. As part of their *Librarie materialiste*, they released a series of pamphlets during 1929, including Politzer's critique of Bergson. Politzer's *Revue de la Psychologie concrète* appeared in February and July 1929, and received considerable international attention. In the planning stages they had another review with the Dickensian title *Mauvais Temps*, a pet project of Morhange's.[5]

Without doubt, the most important part of their program was their *Revue marxiste*, first released in February 1929.[6] The editorial board originally included Morhange (as director), Rappoport, "Albert Mesnil" (Guterman, who also served as secretary), and one Victor Melora (who vanished after the second issue). *Revue marxiste* was an altogether more

serious project than their previous journals as the long, self-indulgent ram-
blings of *Philosophies* and *Esprit* vanished. Significantly, the importance of
Revue marxiste did not lie in what the Philosophies and their colleagues
wrote themselves. Their reviews and commentaries pale beside the importance of what they read and published.

During the late fall of 1928, a bulky package from Moscow arrived at
the offices of Les Revues. Since the materials it contained were in Russian,
they were handed over to the Warsaw-born and multilingual Guterman for
his opinion. In this first of several intellectual grab bags, Guterman found
copies of recent Soviet journals, literary and philosophic publications, and
issues of *Arkhiv K. Marksa i F. Engel'sa*, the major house periodical of the
Marx-Engels Institute. The source was David Riazanov, the Institute's
director, who is generally recognized for his dedication to the dissemination of Marx's writings and for his penetrating wit. Presumably he had sent
the texts to Les Revues as a courtesy to Charles Rappoport, his friend on
the editorial board. Guterman and his colleagues found they had received
some of the most important and controversial pieces written by the major
theorists of Marxism. The Philosophies purposefully relegated their own
writings to a secondary role in order to publish translations of these sem-
inal pieces.[7]

The very first article in February's issue was a portion of Marx's
"Third Economic and Philosophic Manuscript of 1844," translated and
prefaced by Guterman. A second segment from the "Third Manuscript"
was carried in the June issue. Engels's "On the Dialectic" appeared in April.
The compilation known as "The Political Testament of Engels" was serialized in May and June, while Marx's "Letters to Lavrov" also appeared in
the May issue. Along with reviews of the French and Russian editions of
Lenin's collected works, *Revue marxiste* published his essay "On the Significance of Militant Materialism," one of Lenin's last writings in which he
urged cooperation between Communist and non-Communist intellectuals,
emphasized the study of Hegel, and called for the formation of a circle of
materialist friends of the Hegelian dialectic, exactly what the Philosophies
were attempting to forge. Beside these major translations, *Revue marxiste*
printed writings by leading Soviet intellectuals, including Abram Deborin,
the "Hegelian" Marxist and former Menshevik who was just triumphing
over the "Mechanists" in a major theoretical debate; the embattled histo-

rian E. Tarlé's long study of the workers' movement in Lyon; and Riazanov himself. A passing reference to Karl Wittfogel's writings on geopolitics marked the first faint contact between the Philosophies and the German Frankfurt School theorists.[8]

The introduction to these writings had a massive impact on the development of the Philosophies. From 1924 until the end of 1928, they had been embedded in a general French intellectual discourse concerning literature and philosophy, with some excursions into a broader European philosophical tradition. Suddenly they confronted the crucial texts that have been at the center of debate within Marxism ever since. The writings of Marx, Engels, and Lenin that they held in their hands all emphasized the overriding importance of Hegel for creative dialectical thought. The fortuitous arrival of the then totally unknown "Economic and Philosophic Manuscripts" came on the heels of their study of Hegel and Schelling, allowing the Philosophies to grasp immediately Marx's links to German Idealism. With one wrench, the Philosophies were torn out of the comparatively protected cultural greenhouse of Parisian intellectuals and placed, in 1929, a half-dozen years ahead of the most sophisticated French commentators on Marx and Hegel, exploring questions that did not become common intellectual fodder until after 1945.

The Parisian intellectual world watched the efforts of Les Revues closely, and commented extensively on both periodicals and the pamphlet series. In particular, there was a tremendous response to a *Revue marxiste enquête*: "What are your objections to Communism?" Twenty-four answers—from Jean Cocteau, Gabriel Marcel, René Lalou, and others—appeared in *Revue marxiste*, while others appeared in a variety of other periodicals, including Léon Pierre-Quint in *Europe* and Albert Thibaudet in *Nouvelle Revue Française*.[9] These responses, as respondent Emmanuel Berl perfectly put it, demonstrated "the stunning ignorance" of French intellectuals when it came to Marxism, socialism, and communism.

The oddest set of commentaries came from Pierre Naville and the "left oppositionists" clustered around *Lutte de Classes*, the newest incarnation of the old *Clarté*. They ignored the *enquête* completely, instead of using it as an opening for criticizing the Philosophies and the PCF. Since experienced militants and polemicists like Naville and Gérard Rosenthal (the "Francis Gérard" of *Philosophies*) surely recognized the opportunity offered by the *enquête*, the decision to employ a different tactic must have been deliberate. Their first critique of *Revue marxiste* ignored Morhange, Politzer, and Lefebvre, while singling out Rappoport as responsible for the *Revue* that "prides itself on its veritable Marxist independence and . . . scientific honesty."[10] The translation of Lenin's "Of the Significance of Militant Materialism" in the March *Revue marxiste* was displayed as the best example of Rappoport's honesty. *Lutte de Classes* recalled that the piece first appeared in French in Souvarine's *Bulletin Communiste* during September 1922. A comparison of the texts showed that the *Revue marxiste* version lacked Lenin's original opening sentence, beginning "Comrade Trotsky has already said everything necessary, and said it very well. . . . " And at the end of the article a rather childish substitution was unearthed, for where Lenin had written "a Marxist review will have to wage war . . . ," the editors had substituted "La *Revue marxiste*"! "A Marxist review," *Lutte de Classes* scolded, must be dedicated to not creating falsehoods. By playing pranks, those connected with the review had shown themselves to be "false scholars and 'materialist' frauds of the most miserable sort." And the notice taken of *Revue marxiste* in May was briefer—recommending the pieces by Marx, Tarlé, and Dachkowski—and pronounced the contributions of the French collaborators to be "feeble and reproduce the opinions of *Cahiers du Bolchevisme*."[11]

The final commentary dealt with the seventh issue of *Revue marxiste* and appeared in October. The *Lutte de Classes* reviewer struck a tone bordering on fraternal concern about the apparent ill health of a respected competitor with the opening sentences:

> This review is diminishing in volume in a disquieting fashion. It is even said that it will cease publication.[12]

Riazanov's discussion of marriage and communism was given prominent mention, and the importance of the Zimmerwald Conference documents underscored. Again, criticisms were directed solely at Rappoport. Three very straightforward and simple commentaries, but noticeably unlike the earlier denouncements Morhange and the Philosophies suffered and certainly expected again! With the past hostilities between Naville and the Philosophies and with current antagonisms over the direction of the Communist movement in France, *Lutte de Classes* should have been filled with some scathing sarcasms or belligerent verbal sniping. Yet there were no blood-and-gore aphorisms, no suggestions of cowardice or lack of militancy.

A particularly flattering compliment came from the newest enterprise of Henri Barbusse, the weekly *Monde*, which expressed the hope that *Revue marxiste* would fill "a grave lacuna" by operating as an independent Marxist journal.[13] And, when *Monde* launched its own *enquête* on socialist doctrine in July—seeking responses from Leon Blum, Jacques Doriot, Clara Zetkin, Karl Kautsky, Norman Thomas, Max Eastman, and even Stalin, Bukharin, and Trotsky—right at the top of the list were the names Rappoport and Morhange.[14]

Even more heady was the immediate notice of *Revue marxiste* by the leading theoretical journal in the Soviet Union, *Pod Znamenem Marksizma*. The brief, polite compliments of the reviewer, one M. Leonovich, so delighted the French newcomers that they joyfully expanded his simple wishes for success into fraternal greetings from the leading Soviet journal of Marxism to its counterpart in France.[15]

Although the Philosophies could not have known it, the Comintern received word of the success of *Revue marxiste* as well. The source was a Party report, highlighting the importance of the review by indicating its printing run of one thousand copies per issue.[16] And Rappoport was, of course, the Paris correspondent of *Izvestia*, with numerous established friends and colleagues within the international Socialist and Communist movements. Surely he discussed the journal in his correspondence and sent complimentary copies abroad. His young collaborators unknowingly addressed an international audience.

The success of Les Revues and *Revue marxiste* even allowed for some good-natured humor. When an innocent Parisian photographer specializing in portraits of famous writers inquired about the possibility of a sitting with the long-dead Russian author Alexander Pushkin, Morhange and his friends returned the letter with the notation "M. Pushkin has left without leaving a forwarding address."[17]

Then, within one month of the peak of success in July 1929, *Revue marxiste* vanished and Morhange fell into disgrace. In a few chaotic weeks, everything the Philosophies had built in the preceding year was threatened by a complex series of events and circumstances. Thirty years later,

Lefebvre wrote that it would take a volume to explain what occurred.[18] To grasp even approximately what occurred requires a reconstruction of the situation of the French Communist Party and French leftist intellectuals during 1928–1929, for it was this context which ultimately determined the viability of the *Revue marxiste* project.

After carrying with it the bulk of the old Socialist Party at Tours, the Parti Communiste (technically still the "Section française de l'Internationale Communiste") began its existence with a precipitous decline in membership.[19] From the more than one hundred thousand adherents the Party claimed in October 1921, the number slid to forty-five thousand in 1923 and then rose to about sixty thousand during 1924, a revival attributable to the Party's antimilitaristic program. A period of stabilization and slower decline followed, with membership hovering between fifty and fifty-five thousand militants.

During the period 1928 through 1933, a sharper decline occurred as membership plunged by roughly 3 percent each year, from forty-five thousand in 1929 to thirty-eight thousand in 1930, and finally to about thirty thousand in 1932 and 1933. Even these figures are deceptive, as Osip A. Piatnitsky, an old Bolshevik and Comintern functionary, frequently admitted. At the March 1931 plenum meeting of the Executive Committee of the Communist International, Piatnitsky prefaced his report on the membership of the French Party with the statement:

> I have no exact figures. We had to search for the figures.... However, the French Party is taking in new members all the time and in spite of that it is going downwards.[20]

Still, being able to provide rough estimates was a marked improvement over his 1930 report, when Piatnitsky could suggest no numbers whatsoever, or his 1934 report, when he had to revise the numbers downward. The fact that a functionary as thorough and as important as Piatnitsky could not discover the exact figures is indicative of the Party's internal chaos.

This deterioration of the French Communist Party was due to two linked developments. From mid-1928 on, the Party had been subjected to increased government efforts to destroy it. Leading Party militants were imprisoned and its deputies were stripped of their parliamentary immunity. Paul Vaillant-Couturier, editor of *L'Humanité*, was arrested in 1928, two months after his scheduled appearance at L'Atelier with Morhange, and remained in prison until the summer of 1929, only to be rearrested almost immediately. Living a clandestine existence since 1927, Maurice Thorez managed to remain at liberty until June 1929. Imprisoned until the spring of 1930, Thorez and Vaillant-Couturier, both acquainted with Morhange and company, were unable to intervene in the *Revue marxiste* affair. The strongest assaults against the Party came during the summer of 1929. Government efforts to prevent violent clashes between police and Communists increased after the pitched battles of Ivry in 1928. Prior to May Day 1929, in the Paris region alone, four thousand preventive arrests were made. Then, only one month after rather accidentally apprehending Thorez, the police managed to arrest ninety leading militants gathered for a national conference. The organizational coherence of the Communist Party was being shattered.

Simultaneously, the Party was torn by a series of factional disputes concerning control of the Party's remains. The shift to the "Class-versus-Class" program may have explained quite neatly the new wave of government suppression, but it tore the Party apart. Supporters of Trotsky who had managed to retain Party membership until 1928 were expelled or quit, only to engage in ceaseless and useless arguments with those who had left the Party in earlier schisms. Attempts to discipline the errant leaders of the Party's organization in Alsace-Lorraine led to a dramatic loss of militants as well. Then, in November 1929, a major dissident group was expelled. As a result, the much maligned Barbé-Célor group exercised control over the Party because, quite simply, there was no one else available.

This disruption of the Party also underscored important ideological differences within its various component substructures. The Jeunes Communistes, personified by Henri Barbé and André Célor, effectively controlled the Party by the late summer of 1929, and generally took an extreme workerist position. *L'Humanité*, the Party's popular daily newspaper, had been the personal preserve of Vaillant-Couturier and the Party's intellectuals. By education, by age, and by position, these militant intellectuals preferred to pursue broader front tactics designed to attract more diverse supporters. Ironically, the very militancy of the "Class-versus-Class" policies that attracted the Philosophies and other rebellious intellectuals automatically made them targets of suspicion because of their nonproletarian backgrounds.

This quarrel between intellectuals and *ouvriéristes* emerged as early as 1927 as a battle for control of *L'Humanité.* At that time, Vaillant-Couturier and his coworkers fended off efforts by the Political Bureau to more closely regulate the paper. Then a partial "purge" of the editorial staff was carried out during April 1928. To compound problems, after mid-August 1929, *L'Humanité* faced a sudden and nearly catastrophic financial crisis when the government closed the Banque ouvrière et paysanne, and demanded the immediate payment of a debt, totaling more than six million francs, that the newspaper had accumulated with the bank.[21] Finally supporters of Barbé and Célor seized the offices of *L'Humanité* and replaced most of the staff in September 1929, even deposing Vaillant-Couturier himself.

While *L'Humanité* reeled from these crises, the Party's theoretical organ, *Cahiers du Bolchévisme,* confronted its own troubles. Faced with chronic financial woes and a continuing turmoil among its editors, *Cahiers du Bolchévisme* shifted from a twice-monthly to a monthly schedule in 1928. During 1929, only eight separate issues appeared, although technically, half of these were double issues. Moreover, *Cahiers du Bolchévisme* reached perhaps 750 subscribers in 1929, three-quarters of the printing run of *Revue marxiste.* Thus, at the very moment when Communist militants most needed direction, the two major Party publications were hampered in reaching them. Efforts to remedy the situation during the first half of 1929 were frustrated. The June issue of *Cahiers* announced a new editorial committee. Of the five new editors, two were already in jail when the issue appeared! Of special interest were the readers' criticisms of the *Cahiers.* Given the harsh political climate, many readers complained of the luxurious printing of the *Cahiers,* its large size which made concealment difficult, and its paper of unnecessarily high quality. The editors noted that "in general these comrades criticize the lack of system in the choice of articles, the lack of regularity of the rubrics, the nonexistence of a 'Lenin corner' and of the publication of good unedited or little known pages of Marx, Engels, Plekhanov, etc." In sum, Party militants criticized *Cahiers du Bolchévisme* for not being *Revue marxiste!* And the editors of *Cahiers du Bolchévisme* admitted their critics were absolutely right![22]

In addition, *Revue marxiste* obstructed the ambitions of other militants.

The most striking example was a periodical—to be titled *Devenir social*—planned by Charles Hainchelin and André Thirion. A leading Party intellectual, Hainchelin was not only fluent in Russian, but he also had connections in the Comintern and at the Marx-Engels Institute in Moscow. Thirion, a Surrealist who had adhered to Communism earlier than most of Breton's associates and who was still within the Party, received a note from Hainchelin in early 1929 which read in part:

> Yesterday morning, another letter from Riazanov. He's sending me the *Marxist Annals*, the philosophical works of Plekhanov, the works of Deborin, and several periodicals (*The Academy Bulletin*, etc.). . . . This augurs well for the review we're thinking of starting.[23]

The works mentioned by Hainchelin—of Plekhanov and Deborin, the *Vestnik Kommunisticheskoi Akademii*, and the *Arkhiv Marksa-Engel'sa*—matched those received by Les Revues. And the program of *Devenir Social* exactly matched that of *Revue marxiste*.

Further complications came from the Surrealists. Breton's circle had adhered to the Communist Party as a bloc during 1927, but after a brief embattled membership, most either left willingly or were expelled. In part this rapid exodus was traceable to the hostilities of established Party intellectuals like Rappoport, Barbusse, and Vaillant-Couturier, who detested the Surrealists as intensely as they were detested. In part, the Surrealists were themselves to blame, for they entered the Party proclaiming their intention of establishing Surrealist hegemony over the production of Party literature. Their scheme to create an "association of revolutionary writers" paralleled similar efforts by leftist literary groups, such as Prole'kult, Smithy, and Oktobr, to gain the literary franchise in the Soviet Union itself, much to the annoyance of Lenin and Trotsky.

In the aftermath of their party experiences, the Surrealists underwent a multiple fissuring, as the fragments of the movement turned upon each other with the fury and violence previously reserved only for others. In mid-February 1929, Breton, Aragon, and their supporters gathered together for a series of exclusion hearings. The bulk of their anger was directed at Naville and *Lutte de Classes* and toward the independent Surrealists around *La Grand Jeu*, but the original Philosophies core of

Guterman, Lefebvre, Morhange, and Politzer also figured among those to be exorcized.[24] In early March, Breton and his colleagues reconvened their hearings. Mentions of Morhange, *Philosophies, Esprit,* and *Revue marxiste* appeared in several denunciations, but the major attack came from none other than André Thirion, who found in the past evolution of the Philosophies proof of their untrustworthiness, and thought that in *Revue marxiste* would be found "the collection of everything that a communist will be obliged to combat." From a simmering literary tempest, the proceedings became public knowledge when published as a special issue of the Belgian periodical *Variétés* in June.[25]

The final disruptive ingredient was the increasingly bad relationship between Politzer and Nizan on one side and Morhange and Guterman on the other. Politzer and Morhange argued violently about the finances of *Revue de la Psychologie concrète* and the possibility of increasing the printing run of *Revue marxiste.* While Politzer's links to his old gang deteriorated, he and Nizan developed a friendship Mme. Nizan later described as the closest in Nizan's life, "after Sartre."[26] Unfortunately, Nizan's relationship with Morhange and Guterman also disintegrated quickly. In his memoirs, Lefebvre insisted that Nizan provided daily reports to someone in the Party about the goings-on at Les Revues.[27] As proof, Lefebvre claimed correspondence disappeared from Guterman's desk, only to reappear after several days.[28] Guterman himself later claimed that he caught Nizan in the act itself, and confronted him on the matter.[29]

In their collaborative biography on Nizan, Annie Cohen-Solal and Henriette Nizan appended two letters addressed to Nizan by Politzer.[30] The first, of which only the undated final page was published, appears to have been drafted before the end of July 1929. The quarrels within Les Revues had become so disruptive that Politzer skeptically raised the pros and cons of arbitration to resolve the disputes:

> It is evident that I have not the right to take all alone the responsibility
> of provoking the scandal, but I no longer have the right, simply, of per-
> mitting that it will be again and always stifled.

The second note, dated 29 August 1929, is complete. Clearly, some new catastrophe had occurred, as Politzer's violent tone shows:

It has become evident that all work with Morhange and Guterman is impossible, not only because of their total lack of seriousness, not even because of their maneuver, but because their position vis-à-vis the Party is, independent of what may be their ambitions, frankly oppositional. Without any quality, without experience, Morhange and Gut[erman] set themselves up as judges; they will not hear talk of any control. This fact suffices.... One of these days the Party itself may take the initiative of a verification, and then if we are not frankly and publicly separated from them, it's exclusion for all and WITH REASON.

Moreover, Politzer reminded Nizan that they were not the only ones conspiring against "the two dictators":

You certainly know the new comrade on whom Morhange has based all his hopes. M[orhange]. and G[uterman]. have taken him for an idiot and wish to use him against Rapp[oport]. But he proved that he is anything but an idiot and that he already began to doubt several things at the moment when—about ten days ago—I met him at the store where he replaced Lefebvre. I profited from this encounter by putting him on guard.... Beyond him, there is Lefebvre who the two "dictators" seek to get rid of as well. He, who for some years permitted Morhange to publicly entitle himself chief of the philosophic school at his expense, and on whom Morhange has played some particularly disgusting dirty tricks, has decided now to have M[orhange]'s hide.[31]

Politzer believed that at the next editorial meeting scheduled for mid-September, Morhange and Guterman would be presented with an ultimatum: Either turn power over to an editorial collective or face a Party inquiry. Politzer anticipated the support of everyone except Claude Glaymann, but, since Rappoport was on vacation, cautioned patience so that the conspirators' motives and actions would be beyond reproach.

Yet there is evidence of other plans in each of the letters. In the undated letter, Politzer told Nizan

that our project corresponds more and more to a necessity. I am very pleased to see that we are succeeding little by little in constituting a good group of collaborators, and who are not improvised specialists. If we continue in this way, *les Annales* will be a reality at the date planned.[32]

And in his postscript Politzer added "Bruhat has received [the?] third. All the better for *les Annales*." Only slightly more information can be found in the 29 August note: "Concerning *les Annales*, no one knows anything and may know nothing until your return." Along with cautious hopes of seizing control over *Revue marxiste*, Politzer and Nizan were planning to launch a new periodical of their own. They left no description of the program of their *Annales* but, with their newfound militancy and the cooperation of Jean Bruhat and "*une bonne équipe*" of specialists, the journal certainly would have been of high intellectual quality and, presumably, theoretically inclined.

In a wild flurry there were two theoretical journals in existence (*Cahiers du Bolchévisme* and *Revue marxiste*) and at least two more planned (*Devenir social* and *Annales*). This sudden surge of editorial fervor indicates that Party intellectuals were dissatisfied with the existing range of official publications and yearned for a theoretically inclined, "serious" forum under their control. In their own ways, the animators of all four journals were setting themselves up as the possessors of Truth and Orthodoxy, and condemning their competitors as heretics leading the masses astray.

The real scandal of Les Revues must have occurred after the appearance of the July issues of *Revue marxiste* and *Revue de la Psychologie concrète*, as well as after the first of Politzer's letters, but prior to Politzer's letter of 29 August. The "new comrade" Politzer referred to may have been the same mysterious figure Lefebvre would later describe as the "Eye of Moscow," a handsome, picturesque, and rather playboyish Slav, accompanied by an "attractive" wife and a "beautiful" dog. The most likely candidate for this mysterious character was one Stefan Minev, a Bulgarian Comintern agent who replaced the urbane Swiss Communist Jules Humbert-Droz as supervisor of the Latin Secretariat of the International in late 1928. With his access to the topmost ranks of the Party hierarchy, Rappoport certainly knew him, more so since a number of Party publications and even pieces in periodicals directed by Rappoport were written by Minev.[33]

This Minev met with Morhange in the late spring or early summer of 1929, and suggested that if Les Revues was to succeed, far larger sums of money were needed than Friedmann could provide. In the hope of silencing Politzer's demands and increasing the scope of their activities, Morhange and the others naively agreed to several schemes. Apparently, the first plot was to play the stock market at the Bourse. Some profits were made, but at a tediously slow rate. The next attempt was a foolproof system of winning at roulette in Monte Carlo. Again, a small sum was advanced with some success. Finally, a huge sum of two hundred thousand francs was risked. In one night, almost everything was lost.[34]

Les Revues did not fold immediately. A small sum remained, since initially Friedmann was willing to donate more funds, and operations would continue until late 1931. But the internal problems at *Revue marxiste* paralyzed the periodical. With the return of Rappoport from vacation, Guterman, Morhange, and the others vied for his attention and advice. On one occasion, Guterman was followed by two Party strong-arms to Rappoport's home, where he was accosted in the foyer and told to admit to the theft of Party funds. In the ensuing shoving, Guterman (a rather small man) threw the only punch, knocking out one harasser's tooth. The concierge's call for *les flics* sent everyone scurrying.[35] The supposedly disgruntled Lefebvre stood with Guterman and would later claim that one September night, again outside Rappoport's home, he told Politzer exactly what he thought of his concrete psychology.[36] The meeting Politzer had so looked forward to must have been a wild free-for-all. And, unsurprisingly, the commotion caused the Party to hold an inquiry.

The Party's Control Committee published the results of its inquiry in *L'Humanité* on 24 October.[37] Morhange, "Mesnil" (Guterman), and "Yankel" (Glaymann) were expelled from the Party. Morhange was ousted for "dissipating funds destined for revolutionary propaganda" but more importantly for "removing the *Revue marxiste* from the political and financial control" of the Party and "for having formally refused to submit that enterprise to Party control." Morhange and Guterman were also guilty of "trapping [!] a comrade [Nizan? Politzer?] who signaled to the Party the scandalous management of *Revue marxiste*." Guterman was further condemned for having a fistfight without regard for the possible scandal or police intervention in a Party matter. As Politzer had predicted, all militants were ordered to break contact with the trio immediately, and the review closed down.

André Breton crowed triumphantly. In his *Second Manifeste du Surréalisme* of December 1929, Breton declared the Party had received ample forewarning of Morhange's "bad faith" and feigned amazement at the ability of the "Morhanges, Politzers and Lefebvres" not just to "capture the confidence of the Party directors" but also to drop "in one day at Monte Carlo a sum of two hundred thousand francs which had been confided to them for purposes of revolutionary propaganda." Breton knew perfectly well the origins of the money lost at roulette, since he indicated that Friedmann had provided five million francs for Les Revues. Still, his mistaken belief that Lefebvre and Politzer had been involved at the tables indicates that his information was far from perfect.[38]

When the issue was mentioned in the *Nouvelle Revue Française* review of the *Second Manifeste du Surréalisme* in February 1930, Morhange wrote back to deny Breton's claims and to announce he would explain everything in *Mauvais Temps*.[39] *Mauvais Temps* never appeared. Morhange never made public his version of the affair. The only clue Morhange offered was a poem published in *Cahiers du Sud*, "Georges Politzer":

> Le traitre rigole, mais rigole.
> Il n'a pas même été éclaboussé.
> Derriere le monde
> Dans sa chambre
> Il raconte à sa complice,
> Avec sa bouche prise à un mort,
> Avec ses yeux égaux à deux bougies,
> Qu'il a aujourd'hui rudement défendu la justice,
> Que c'est bien, qu'il a soif,
> Que c'est bon d'être rentré chez soi,
> «Qu'il les a écrasés loin d'ici».
> Puis il éteint ses yeux
> Et entre dans un terrier de la Nuit:
> Elle cache sa tête de traitre
> Dans son drapeau ignoble.[40]

These were the events of the notorious affair. Morhange, Guterman, and their supporters clearly displayed exceedingly bad judgment in trusting anyone—even "an Eye of Moscow"—claiming to have an infallible system of raising money. Yet at any other time, their error would have been no more than a passing amusement for the back pages of literary journals. Only in the specific context of 1928–1930, when the PCF struggled to survive while cliques of intellectuals quarreled in and around it, could the losses at roulette become *L'Affaire de la Revue marxiste*.

There is no basis for blaming the *Revue marxiste* affair of 1929 on some premeditated attempt to squash any independence of theory or practice in France. In the realm of theory, the *Revue marxiste* circle was simply publishing either the unobjectionable writings of Marx, Engels, and Lenin or pieces by the leaders of official Soviet thought, a project that the readers of *Cahiers du Bolchévisme* were pleading for. There could have been no objections to publishing the writings of Deborin, who, while usually aligned with Bukharin on theoretical matters, was the recognized expert in matters of philosophy and method. Indeed, Deborin and his adherents had just prevailed in the Mechanist controversy and were at the pinnacle of their influence. Riazanov's prestige was also at its peak, and contact with the Marx-Engels Institute would not have led, in 1929, to an assault on a Parisian periodical. The debates over Marx's early writings and the possible uses of Hegel lie ahead, and were not yet the divisive issue they would become. The French Marxists, with Lefebvre in the lead, retained considerable theoretical independence until the 1939 appearance of the official *History of the Communist Party (bolshevik)*, with its dogmatic exposition of the crudest form of "dia-mat."

Nor has any evidence been unearthed to support some theory of "the long arm of Stalin" or similar diabolic intervention. The brief life and noisy demise of *Revue marxiste* occurred at the precise moment when the Soviet leadership was locked in a battle over the future of their revolution. Stalin was preoccupied with his struggle against Bukharin between April and November 1929, and throughout Communist organizations in the Soviet Union and internationally there was an uneven, drastic, and chaotic turnover in top- and middle-level leadership. Uncertainties surrounded the meanings and the durability of the new "Class-versus-Class" policies, and insufficient administrative controls were in place to monitor the activities of distant functionaries. In such a situation it is improbable, if not paranoid, that the *Revue marxiste* affair can be attributed to an omnipotent and omniscient Stalin (or Stalinist henchmen) who both knew of and cared in the least about a small group of young intellectuals in far-off Paris. The Comintern representative Minev, if he was in fact the "eye of Moscow" involved in the affair, was operating independently for the first time and with minimum oversight. Rather than a simple tool implementing a conspiracy hatched in the Kremlin, Minev should be viewed as a loose cannon who took advantage of an opportunity to enjoy himself royally at the expense of some naive intellectuals. Or, to word the issue more simply, surely if Stalin or any major figure in the Comintern or French Party hierarchy wanted to sabotage *Revue marxiste*, far more direct methods would have been used then a charade involving the Bourse and trips to Monte Carlo!

The rejection of a conspiracy theory to explain the *Revue marxiste* scandal also raises a broader question regarding theories of the *bolchévisation* of the French Communists. There is no denying that the Soviet leadership repeatedly intervened in serious quarrels within the French Party, most notably at Tours, in the case of Souvarine and later against Doriot. However, the continuing changes in leadership and policies within the Soviet Party and the Comintern meant that this process was usually limited to crisis interventions regarding major issues of leadership and tactics, whereas the *Revue marxiste* could only have been viewed as of minor interest. Hence, instead of trying to fit the *Revue marxiste* incident into a theory of bolshevization implying a program totally imposed onto the French by the Soviets, it seems more useful to view it as part of a long-standing debate within French socialism about control of the movement.

The causes of the *Revue marxiste* affair lay primarily in the immediate situation and the history of the French Party. The crisis facing the French Communist Party in the late summer of 1929 was clearly acute. The arrests of the Party's leaders put serious strains on those remaining to run Party affairs. Those who had worked with the Philosophies before and who might have intervened on their behalf, such as Thorez and Vaillant-Couturier, were imprisoned, and the latter was out of favor himself. Rappoport's influence had waned after Tours, and he exercised little leverage among the younger militants directing the Party. *L'Humanité* faced extinction, and the editors of the beleaguered *Cahiers du Bolchévisme* must have looked uneasily at this successful sister review. Militants of longer standing than the Philosophies found their own projects blocked by the upstart *Revue marxiste*. The denunciations of the Surrealists—especially of Thirion, who was still within the Party ranks—coupled to those of Nizan and Politzer, brought about the initial investigation by the Party. Faced with external pressure and internal fragmentation, the last thing the Party's remaining leaders wanted to deal with was a small bunch of troublesome scribblers.

Newcomers to the Party, the animators of *Revue marxiste* may have seen themselves (or may have been perceived by others) as attempting to fulfill Lenin's criteria for a party leadership drawn from *declassé* intellectuals. Such a simplistic attempt or perception would have surely provoked the resistance and hostility of established militants and especially of the *ouvrièristes* then running the Party. This very real tension between workerists and intellectuals evident in 1928–1930 has its roots in specific French precedents and can be traced back to the prewar era. Generational misunderstandings between older, established movement leaders and younger "bolshevizing" militants were fueled by the Comintern's 1924 organizational blueprint designed to emphasize and enhance the proletarian nature of its member parties. And while this tension between intellectuals and workers never totally disappeared, it is arguable that the success of the Party in attracting and retaining intellectuals from the early 1930s on can in part be attributed to the adoption of a "Gramscian" solution, in short, with the selection as Party General-Secretary of a working class militant respected for his ability to work with intellectuals. Ample evidence exists that this need is exactly one of those Maurice Thorez filled, at least until 1939.[41]

What was at stake was the definition of the relationship between the Party and its militants. *Revue marxiste* technically was not a Party publication, although its contributors were tied to the Party. Everyone, within the Communist Party and without, knew the lost money was Friedmann's and not the Party's. The real issue ultimately was the age-old dilemma of how much compliance and self-effacement a voluntary, ideologically founded organization can demand of its members. The question was not the misuse of "funds designated for revolutionary propaganda" but the inability of Morhange and Guterman to work inside the Party with a proper display of *partijnost*, of party spirit. In brief, they did not know when to stop arguing and shut up. And at some long-forgotten meeting of the remaining, harried Party leaders, the decision was made to simply be rid of them.[42]

If *bolshévisation* is redefined as the French process of building the institutions and the internal discipline of the Communist Party in the two decades between the wars, then clearly the incidents surrounding *Revue marxiste* furnished unmistakable signals to potential militants. The achievements and failures of *Revue marxiste* were of considerable interest to other French intellectuals, many of whom would soon be deciding just how active to become in Popular Front activities or even whether to adhere to the Party outright. The experiences of Morhange, Lefebvre, Nizan, Politzer, and their colleagues served as a warning by defining the boundaries of intraparty debate and public disagreement. The unfortunate and accidental affair of 1929 was an incident that fixed the limits of intellectual debate and independence for the next decade and indeed well beyond.

The blunder of the roulette table led to some harsh judgements by the Party. By publishing the actual names of Guterman and Glaymann along with their pseudonyms, the Party effectively handed them over to the police since, as nonnationals, they legally were not permitted to engage in political activities on pain of deportation. Rather than face the prospect of returning to a Poland controlled by an anti-Communist military, Guterman sailed for the United States, where he joined the staff of the *New Republic* and later worked with the exiled Frankfurt School.

A rather ironic question must be posed. Was Nizan, the author of *Les Chiens du Garde* (1932), parachuted into *Revue marxiste* to keep an eye on Morhange and company? Fifty years later, both Lefebvre and Guterman still believed so. It is an acknowledged fact that, only a year later, Nizan took over as editor of *Bifur* with explicit directions to turn that journal into a Party periodical. And in the spring of 1931, Nizan was charged with the task of bringing Henri Barbusse himself and his *Monde* under tighter Party control and orthodoxy. Given his earlier brief adhesion to the Communists and his almost simultaneous association with Faisceau, Nizan was under more pressure than most to clearly demonstrate his commitment to the Party. If Nizan was willing to play the role of Party watchdog in 1930 and 1931, then it is not terribly far-fetched to imagine him similarly cast in 1929 as well. Many commentators believe that Nizan later used his knowledge of the Philosophies and *Revue marxiste* as the raw material for his award-winning novel *La Conspiration*. Yet his tale is essentially an account of the hopes and failures shared by all the little *équipes* of the twenties, an indictment of all the vanities common to the entire *nouvelle génération*, and not simply a fictionalized history of Les Revues.

How influential could *Revue marxiste* have been, if it lasted only seven brief months and ended so ignobly? Several distinct pieces of evidence are available. Leaving aside the historiographic interest in the journal, the memoirs of anyone even remotely connected to *Revue marxiste*—Lefebvre, Friedmann, Thirion, Bruhat, and Guterman most obviously—all mention the review as an important stage of their intellectual and political lives. More importantly, leading figures among the French intellectual and cultural elite recognized *Revue marxiste* as an important innovator in French intellectual and political life. In his 1931 collection of essays, the noted critic Benjamin Crémieux wrote:

> The single authentically Marxist effort which has been made [in France] has been by the group of the review *Philosophies*, which later became *l'Esprit*, and later still *La Revue marxiste*. Unfortunately this effort has been solitary and unable to sufficiently develop itself so one might build on it.[43]

In late 1939, *Archives de Philosophie* published as a volume a collection of essays devoted to "La Philosophie du Communisme." Alexandre Marc and the other writers belonged to a new wave of disquieted youth, *les nonconformistes des années trente*, clustered around a new variety of periodicals and movements. On the very first page of their introduction, the editors cited "Albert Mesnil"—that is, Guterman—and the editorial opening *Revue marxiste*. On the following page there were two references to a 1936 work by Friedmann, and one to an anthology edited by Guterman and Lefebvre. In this display of critical scholarship published a decade after the disappearance of *Revue marxiste*, the different writers referred to it a half-dozen times as the definitive example of "what the Marxists are really all about."[44]

Perhaps the most poignant example of the enduring symbolic importance of *Revue marxiste* occurred in 1961, when a group of post-Stalinist *gauchistes*, including those old antagonists Henri Lefebvre and Pierre Naville, launched a new theoretical periodical. This ephemeral journal, successor to the short-lived *Tribune marxiste* and a symbol of the break with the crude diamat of the Stalinist era, was given the title *La Nouvelle Revue marxiste*.

A final question imposed itself on the apparently disintegrating Philosophies. Long after the affair, Lefebvre suggested that:

> The unhappiness of those who came to Marxism between 1925 and 1930 lie in the fact that they never surmounted their spontaneous romanticism in

a natural and reflective manner, in retaking the road of Marx, in elevating the *dépassé* to a higher level, in passing from the aspiration to knowledge and of the authenticity of concepts. They arrived at Marxism over the ruins of their youth.... Over the ruins of their absurd and unlimited hopes.[45]

Faced with the apparent ruins of their faith in the Bolshevik mystique, the question was where would the Philosophies turn next.

NOTES

1. Henri Lefebvre, *Les Temps des mèprises* (Paris: Stock, 1975), p. 66.

2. Henri Lefebvre, *L'Existentialisme* (Paris: Editions du Sagittaire, 1946), p. 45: "Mais ceci est encore une autre histoire" is all Lefebvre tells of that meeting!

3. Lefebvre, *Temps des mèprises*, pp. 68–69. Danielle Tartakowsky denies the incident occurred, based on the evidence of Victor Fay, "Le Marxisme et les intellectuels," *Pensée*, no. 205 (May/June 1979): 36, n. 14.

4. Rappoport was a Guesdist Socialist who broke from the Section française de l'Internationale ouvrière (SFIO) at Tours. Within the French Communist Party, his influence appears to have waned from about 1923 on, although he retained membership until 1938. He was also involved in the publication of the small periodicals Revue Communiste (March 1920–February 1922), *Militant Rouge* (November 1925–January/February 1927), and *Brochure Populaire* (1934–1935), as well as *L'Humanité*. Hence, his participation in *Revue marxiste* was not an unusual activity.

5. The 1929 publications of Les Revues included Georges Politzer's *Fin d'une parade philosophique*; Aline, *Lenine à Paris*; Pushkin, *Poèmes révolutionnaires*; Matveev, *Les Hommes du 1905 russe*; Blok, *Chants d'amour et de révolte*; Chpilevski, *Les Matelots rouges*; and the announced but apparently unreleased *Anthologie des poètes Yiddisch* translated by Norbert Guterman and Pierre Morhange. *Mauvais Temps* was originally announced in *Monde*, no. 44 (6 April 1929): 3, and continued to be in the planning stages for the next year before being given up. Les Revues advertized extensively, especially in *Monde, Europe*, and *Nouvelles Littéraires*, and its publications and journals were widely and usually very positively reviewed throughout the French press. The press continued until August 1931, and would be bought out by the *Lutte de Classes* circle, yet another evolution of the *Clarté* group that the Philosophies worked with in 1925.

6. *Revue marxiste*, no. 1 (February 1929) through no. 7 (August/September 1929); issues 1–5 contained 126 pages each, while numbers 6 and 7 had 96 pages each, a huge shrinkage of 30 pages or 25 percent, an indication of possible financial problems.

7. Norbert Guterman, personal communications of 18 April 1981, 8 and 16 May 1982, 1 August 1982, 4 September 1982, 24 August 1983, and our final meetings of April 1984. D. B. Riazanov was a long-exiled member of the Russian Social Democratic Party who worked primarily with the group around Trotsky. Dedicated to the reunion of the feuding factions of Russian socialism, he joined the Bolsheviks in 1917 with Trotsky and his close friend Anatole Lunacharsky, the future commissar of education. An advocate of the Workers Opposition and staunch critic of the Party's bureaucratic tendencies, Riazanov punctuated Party meetings with sarcasm and unanswerable wit. Riazanov's major contribution was his dedication to the location and dissemination of Marx and Engels's writings, an activity given greater substance when he founded and headed the Marx-Engels Institute in Moscow, later one of the key components of the Institute of Marxism-Leninism. The Institute itself received the 1844 manuscripts from a group of German intellectuals later known as the Frankfurt School, giving the first tenuous triangular contact between Paris-Frankfurt-Moscow for the Philosophies. Riazanov was removed from his positions in 1931 on trumped-up charges. There is no full-length biography of Riazanov or history of the Marx-Engels Institute. See my "D. B. Riazanov and the Marx-Engels Institute: Notes Toward Further Research," *Studies in Soviet Thought* 30 (1985), the separate bibliographic annex covering the Institute's periodicals through 1932 located in the same issue, and the bibliography of the post-1932 *Arkhiv Marksa I Engel'sa* 37, no. 1 (1989) and of the *Leninskij Sbornik*, part 1, 32, no. 3 (1986), and part 2, 39, no. 1 (1990).

For an examination of the origins of the texts received and translated by the *Revue marxiste* collective, see the appendix to my "The *Revue marxiste* Affair: French Marxism and Communism in Transition between the Wars," *Historical Reflections/Réflexions historiques* 20, no. 1 (winter 1994): 162–64.

8. On Soviet intellectual life during this period see David Joravsky, *Soviet Marxism and Natural Science 1917–1932* (London: Routledge and Kegan Paul, 1961); Loren R. Graham, *Science and Philosophy in the Soviet Union* (New York: Knopf, 1972); Edward J. Brown, *The Proletarian Episode in Russian Literature 1928–1932* (New York: Columbia University, 1953). The writings of Shelia Fitzpatrick are particularly useful, including "Culture and Politics Under Stalin," *Slavic Review* 35, no. 2 (June 1976); "Cultural Revolution in Russia 1928–1932," *Journal of Contemporary History* 9, no. 1 (January 1974); and "The 'Soft' Line on Culture and Its Ene-

mies: Soviet Cultural Policy 1922–1927," *Slavic Review* 33, no. 2 (June 1974). Overall, the implications of the positions of John Barber, "The Establishment of Intellectual Orthodoxy in the USSR 1928–1934," *Past and Present*, no. 83 (May 1979), are most likely to prove fruitful for a synthetic overview. On Deborin, see R. Ahlberg, "Abram Deborin: The Forgotten Philosopher," in *Revisionism*, ed. L. Labedz (New York: Praeger, 1962).

9. For an analysis of this *enquête*, see my "Revealing Thoughts: French Post-War Cultural Disarray and the *Revue marxiste enquête* of 1929," *Contemporary European History* 2, no. 3 (June 1993): 225–41.

10. "Un faux," *Lutte de Classes*, no. 9 (March–April 1929): 264.

11. "Revue marxiste," *Lutte de Classes*, no. 10 (May 1929): 280.

12. "Revue marxiste," *Lutte de Classes*, no. 13/14 (October 1929): 354.

13. *Monde*, no. 37 (16 February 1929): 3. Since *Bibliographie de France* refused to mention *Revue marxiste*, the editors of *Monde* urged their readers to ask their local book dealers to carry the magazine.

14. "Nouvelle enquête du 'Monde,'" *Monde*, no. 59 (20 July 1929), and replies in issues from no. 76 (16 November 1929) through no. 122 (4 October 1930). On *Monde*, see in particular Nicole Racine's writings listed above, as well as her "L'Association des écrivains et artistes révolutionnaires," *Mouvement Sociale*, no. 54 (January–March 1966); "Le Comité de Vigilance des Intellectuels Antifascistes (1934–1939). Antifascisme et pacificisme," *Mouvement Sociale*, no. 101 (October–December 1971); "Le Parti Communiste Français devant les Problèmes ideologiques et culturels," *Cahiers de la Fondation Nationale des Sciences Politiques*, no. 175 (1969); *Le Communisme en France et Italie* (Paris: Armand Colin, 1969); and, with Louis Bodin, ed., *Le Parti Communiste Français pendant l'entre-deux-guerres* (Paris: Armand Colin, 1972). See also Guessler Normand, "Henri Barbusse and his «Monde» (1928–1935): Progeny of the Clarté movement and the review «Clarté»," *Journal of Contemporary History* 11, no. 2–3 (April–July 1976).

15. M. Leonovich, "La Revue marxiste," *Pod Znamenem Marksizma*, no. 2/3 (February/March 1929): 255–56; "Les Revues Soviétiques," *Revue marxiste*, no. 4 (May 1929): 499–502.

16. Annie Cohen-Solal and Henritte Nizan, *Paul Nizan, Communiste impossible* (Paris: Grasset, 1980), pp. 81 and 134, n. 7, citing Danielle Tartakowsky's, "Editions et Ecoles communistes 1921–1933," (Université of Paris VIII, 1977, thèse du 3e cycle); in its published version as Tartakowsky's *Les Premiers Communists français: formation des cadres et bolchévisation* (Paris: Presses de la Fondation Nationale des Sciences Politiques, 1980), there is a single reference to *Revue marxiste*, p. 201, n. 34 to

chap. 5. The relevant document is given as in côte 452, Institut Maurice Thorez. See also Tartakowsky with Claude Prévost, "Les Intellectuels et le P.C.F. 1920–1940," *Cahiers de l'Institut Maurice Thorez*, no. 43, ns# 15 (January–March 1976); and her "Le Marxisme et les intellectuels de 1920 à 1935," *Pensée*, no. 205 (May–June 1979).

17. *Nouvelles Littéraires*, no. 337 (30 March 1929): 2.

18. Henri Lefebvre, *La Somme et le Reste* (Paris: Bélibaste, 1973), tome 2, p. 397.

19. Precise membership figures for this period are still not available today, but the accepted figures are those provided by Annie Kriegel, in her "Le Parti Communiste Français sous la Troisième République (1920–1939), Evolution de ses effectifs," *Revue Française de Science Politique* 16, no. 1 (February 1966). Kriegel's figures appear to be compatible with those later used by Party historians, as the contributions in *Le Parti Communiste Français: étapes et problèmes 1920–1972* (Paris: Editions Sociales, 1981) indicate.

20. O. A. Piatnitsky, *Urgent Questions of the Day* (New York: Workers Library, 1931), p. 38.

21. "Vie du Parti: Rapport sur l'Humanité," *Cahiers du Bolchévisme*, no. 66 (February 1927): 228–35; Pierre Milza, "Les Problèmes financiers du journal «L'Humanité» de 1920 à 1939," *Revue d'Histoire Moderne et Contemporaine* 20, no. 4 (October–December 1973); O. A. Piatnitsky, *World Communists in Action* (New York: Workers Library, [1930?]), pp. 51–52; and *The Communist Parties and the Fight for the Masses* (New York: Workers Library, 1934): 42.

22. "Vie des Cahiers," *Cahiers du Bolchévisme* 8, no. 2 (15 January 1933): 133; "A nos lecteurs," *Cahiers du Bolchévisme* 4, no. 16 (June 1929); "Avis du Comité de rédaction des Cahiers du Bolchévisme," *Cahiers du Bolchévisme* 4, no. 19/20 (September/October 1929): 649–50; in the December 1929 issue ("Note de la rédaction," pp. 918–19), the editors admitted their critics were right! See also "Vie du Parti: Pour une transformation des Cahiers du Bolchévisme," *Cahiers du Bolchévisme* 5, no. 1 (January 1930): 103–108. There was a stunning lack of any mention of *Revue marxiste* in the pages of *Cahiers du Bolchevisme*, a major divergence from normal Party etiquette.

23. André Thirion, *Revolutionaries without Revolution*, trans. J. Neugroschel (London: Cassell, 1976), pp. 207–208, and also pp. 100–101.

24. David Caute neatly summed up the Surrealist situation when he noted that "intellectuals abandoned the Party before 1927 as Trotskyists. Surrealists joined the Party in 1927 as semi-Trotskyists, while the Trotskyists denounced them as irresponsible idealists," *Communism and the French Intellectuals 1914–1960* (New York: MacMillan, 1973), p. 98.

25. André Thirion in André Breton et. al., "A suivre: Petite Contribution au dossier de certains intellectuels à tendances révolutionnaires," *Variétés*, special issue (June 1929); collected in Jose Pierre, ed., *Tracts Surréalistes et Déclarations Collectives* (Paris: Terrain Vague, n.d.), tome 1, p. 102. Thirion, *Revolutionaries*, p. 166–68, stated the Philosophies and others were purposely uninformed of the "hearings," although Breton implies in the transcript of the 6 March purge that they were told in advance. Guterman claimed he never received any warning, but was aware of Breton's *Second Manifeste*.

26. Cohen-Solal and Nizan, *Paul Nizan*, p. 80.

27. Lefebvre, *Temps des méprises*, p. 71.

28. Ibid., p. 77.

29. Norbert Guterman, personal communications, 4 September 1982, 1 August 1982, and April 1984.

30. Cohen-Solal and Nizan, "Annexes," in *Paul Nizan*, pp. 271–74. All emphasis as in originals. Incidentally, the reference to "our Weitling" in Politzer's correspondence did not mean the "mysterious Spector" of the Roulette affair. Wilhelm Weitling was a conspiratorial Communist involved with Blanqui. A tailor, autodidact, and author of socialist tracts, Weitling was in 1846 (in Edmund Wilson's phrase) the victim of "the first Marxist party purge" for his Utopianism. Weitling is remembered for his attempt to infuse a Christian socialism into the workers' movement. Hence, Politzer's sarcasm was about Morhange.

31. Ibid., pp. 271–72. In fact, Lefebvre was quarreling with Morhange and Friedmann, as described in *L'Existentialisme*, p. 55–56; on the next page he praises Guterman for saving him from his struggle to support his family as a factory worker and as a cabdriver. See also *La Somme et le Reste*, tome 1., p. 296–98.

32. Cohen-Solal and Nizan, *Paul Nizan*, p. 274. A slightly differing version of the origins of *Revue marxiste* can be found in Jean Bruhat with Michel Trebitsch, *Il N'est Jamais Trop Tard* (Paris: Albin Michel, 1983), p. 56, and in Cohen-Solal and Nizan, *Paul Nizan*, p. 76, but in light of the Politzer correspondence these events appear to concern the *Annales* project. Bruhat and Trebitsch, *Il N'est Jamais Trop Tard*, p. 56, n. 24, indicated the allusion to *Annales* meant nothing to him. Also Politzer's letters offer precise dating regarding the fate of *Revue de la Psychologie concrète*, for in the first note, he reminded Nizan not to forget to send an article, presumably not a reference to Nizan's review that appeared in the July issue. In the note of 29 August, Politzer informed Nizan about efforts by Morhange to convince the *Revue marxiste* circle that the only common interest with Politzer was

publication by Les Revues, and therefore, Politzer decided, *Revue de la Psychologie concrète* should be abandoned, as secondary to "le scandale des Revues."

33. Stefan Minev was born in Bulgaria in 1893, and studied medicine in Switzerland during 1914–1918, where he worked with Willi Münzenburg and the Zimmerwald left. From 1919–1939 he was attached to the Comintern's Latin Secretariat, first as an aide to Humbert-Droz, but apparently independently in 1928–1930. Later, he and his wife (who answered to the name Lebedeva) were in Moscow as part of the prosecution case against the Barbé-Célor leadership group. Minev apparently left France for good in 1934, but then appears in Spain during the civil war. The last mention of this elusive internationalist was that he was ill during the retreats of 1941 and retired from active political life. All published evidence is fragmentary. See M. M. Drachovitch, ed., *The Revolutionary Internationals* (Stanford: Stanford University, 1966), pp. 197–98; Pierre Broué, ed., *Du Premier au deuxieme Congres de l'Internationale Communiste* (Paris: Etudes et documentations internationales, 1979), p. 28; Roland Gaucher, *Histoire Secrete du Parti Communiste Français* (Paris: Albin Michel, 1974), p. 212; Philippe Robrieux, *Histoire intérieure de Parti Communiste* (Paris: Fayard, 1980), tome 1, pp. 288, 315, 317–18, 362–77; Jules Humbert-Droz, *De Lenine à Staline: Memoirs de* (Neuchatel: de la Baconniere, 1971), tome 2; Branko Lazitch, "Two Instruments of Control by the Comintern: The Emissaries of the ECCI and the Party Representatives in Moscow," in *The Comintern*, ed. Lazitch and Drachkovitch (New York: Praeger, 1966), pp. 45–65.

34. There are various versions of the "affair" in the following: Lefebvre, *L'Existentialisme*, pp. 47–49; *La Somme et le Reste*, tome 2, part 4, chap. 6, pp. 425–35; *Temps des méprises*, p. 66–77; Georges-Philippe Friedmann, *La Sagesse et la Puissance* (Paris: Gallimard, 1970), pp. 379–80; Norbert Guterman, personal conversations and correspondence from April 1981 through 1984; see also the versions in Pascal Ory, *Nizan, Destin d'un revolte* (Paris: Ramsay, 1980), pp. 87–95; and especially Cohen-Solal with Nizan, *Paul Nizan*, p. 75–85. Any study of Nizan will contain some version of the "eye of Moscow" tale, usually derived from Lefebvre's *La Somme et le Reste*. I have followed the version provided by Guterman, which included as the first step an investment in stocks, followed by two trips to the gaming tables. Madame Nizan only briefly mentions the *Revue marxiste* episode in her *Libres Mémoires* written with Marie-José Joubert (Paris: Robert Laffont, 1989), pp. 138–39.

35. Guterman told essentially the same tale to Cohen-Solal (*Paul Nizan*, p. 83), but mentioned only one assailant named Frauenglass. The version Guterman shared with me differs in several details: He had been pressured repeatedly to either admit his own complicity in the loss of funds or to denounce Morhange.

One night, two Party strong-arms (the first tall, heavy, and speaking French with a Polish accent; the second slighter and less forceful) followed him to Rappoport's home. The taller man grabbed Guterman by the lapel, leading to some pushing and shoving, and one punch was thrown. Guterman, a small man himself, knocked out the taller fellow's tooth. The concierge threatened to call the police and the two fled (personal communication, 8 May 1982).

Guterman also provided a third version in a written statement provided to the U.S. Federal Bureau of Investigation and dated 20 April 1955. This statement appears on page 10 of a report on Guterman prepared by the FBI New York City Office and dated 18 May 1955 (Bureau file 100-384556, NYC file 105-4005). This version differs from the others: "In August or September 1929 a man who represented himself as a Communist emissary came to see me and requested me to testify in behalf of the Party. When I refused, he threatened that I would be publicly denounced and discredited; thereupon I violently ejected him from my premises."

Guterman remained rather ambiguous about Rappoport. On the one hand, if he did not trust Rappoport, he (and the others) would not have continued to frequent his home and seek his advice. On the other hand, Guterman recalled arguing over the decision to publish Marx's 1844 manuscript, and even claimed that Rappoport, in an effort to find out just what Guterman and Morhange were doing, asked his redheaded secretary to wheedle information from them (personal communication, 16 May 1982).

36. Lefebvre, *L'Existentialisme,* p. 50.

37. "Vie du Parti: L'Affaire de la «Revue marxiste»," *L'Humanité* (24 October 1929); cited in full in Cohen-Solal and Nizan, *Paul Nizan,* pp. 83–84. Guterman repeatedly denied having been an official Party member and invariably added: "I was excluded even though I was never included. How can you exclude someone who doesn't belong?"

38. André Breton, "Second Manifeste Surréalisme," *Révolution Surréaliste,* no. 12 (December 1929).

39. *Nouvelle Revue Française,* no. 197 (February 1930): 291–93 and Morhange's note in *Nouvelle Revue Française,* no. 198 (March 1930): 440.

40. *Cahiers du Sud,* no. 116 (November 1929): 655.

41. This understanding of the bolshevization of the French Party is, perhaps, closest to Ronald Tiersky's views in the second chapter of his *French Communism, 1920–1972* (New York: Columbia University, 1974), although in the particular example of the *Revue marxiste* it is possible to argue that the process was much more chaotic and the intervention of Moscow much less direct than Tiersky's

broad framework allows. Irwin M. Wall captures the essence of this problem when he notes "Stalinist bureaucratic techniques proved to be adaptable in France for specifically internal reasons," in his *French Communism in the Era of Stalin* (Westport, Conn.: Greenwood, 1983), p. 11.

42. Two further possible contributing factors for the problems of *Revue marxiste* merit discussion. First, the Philosophies circle may have been mistaken for Trotsky-ists. They, like many enthusiasts in the Soviet Union and abroad, glorified the revolutionary leadership and especially Trotsky. Morhange and his friends had contact with the "Trotskyist" *Clarté* movement during the alliance against the Rif War, but those ties had dissolved in well-publicized mutual abuse. Also, Lefebvre's efforts to create the "Ilse du Sagesse" with Trotsky as guest may have been publicized, and certainly would have raised the eyebrows of Parti Communiste functionaries. And finally, in 1931, Les Revues would be sold to Pierre Naville and the *Lutte de Classes* group. However, in 1929, the Philosophies were known to be extremely and openly hostile to the recognized leaders of French Trotskyism, and there are no indications of support for Trotsky in *Revue marxiste*. Thus it seems unlikely that such a miscomprehension could have led to the problems of *Revue marxiste*.

The second possible factor may have been anti-Semitism. Morhange, Guterman, Friedmann, Glaymann, and others were of Jewish heritage, although none were religious or active in the Jewish community. Still, when joining the Party in 1928, Morhange organized a series of conferences including topics such as "L'Appel au Proletariate juif de Paris" and "La Traite des ouvriers en Palestine," as advertized in *Europe* in March and June 1928. While these topics suggest a link to the creation of a "Jewish Section" of the Party in June 1927, direct evidence is nonexistent, nor do Morhange and the other Philosophies ever act as "Jewish Communists." See on this point Maurice Rajsfus, *L'An prochain, La Révolution: Les Communistes Juifs immigrés dans la Tourmente Stalinienne 1930–1935* (Paris: Mazarine, 1985). However they perceived themselves, it is possible that the animators of *Revue marxiste* were the target of a combination of anti-Semitism and anti-intellectualism by the Party's *ouvrièristes*, a feasibility given the fact that Morhange, Guterman, and Glaymann were singled out for punishment and public denunciation by the Party.

43. Benjamin Crémieux, *Inquiétude et Reconstruction* (Paris: Correa, 1931), p. 224.

44. "La Philosophie du Communisme," essays by A. Marc, A. Etcheverry, B. Romeyer and G. Jarlot, *Archives de Philosophie* 15, no. 2 (November 1939): 1.

45. Lefebvre, *La Somme et le Reste*, tome 2, p. 404.

Chapter 5

And So Ends
the Avant-Garde (?)

(1930–1940)

Despite Politzer's gleefully vicious prediction that Morhange and the others would disappear, the amazing fact was that the Philosophies did not really "go" anywhere: Having found the resolution to their cultural crisis, they remained within or close to the Party and the broader Communist movements, and continued to explore Marxist theory. As individuals and as a collective, the Philosophies continued to exist and cooperate in their project, and equally important, were still viewed as a collective by their peers. This collaboration was made more difficult by the geographic dispersion of the group members, as most assumed teaching posts at provincial lycées, and with Guterman planning to settle in the United States.[1]

But despite distances and disrupted friendships, Les Revues continued operations into 1931, issuing works by Engels, Plekhanov, Ilya Ehrenburg, Bertrand Russell, and Riazanov. Morhange and Guterman jointly translated an anthology of poetry by American workers, and Guterman was one of the translators of Mayakovsky's *Nuage dans le pantaloons*, with an introduction excerpted from one of Trotsky's essays, providing Nizan with the ammunition to label him a "Trotskyist."[2]

If anything, it did appear that Morhange—and possibly Lefebvre and Guterman—would break to the extreme Left. While the solicitousness of Naville and *Lutte de Classes* during 1929 was inexplicable, the improved relationship of 1930–1931 was due to the mutually cautious flirtation between the Philosophies and *Lutte de Classes*. With Trotsky's exile and the continued bleeding of militants from the PCF, a number of the small oppositional groups banded together as the Ligue communiste in April 1930. *Lutte de Classes* became its theoretical journal, while *Vérité* (also founded and animated by Naville and Rosenthal) served as its weekly paper.[3] In the summer of 1931, *Lutte de Classes* announced that it was now being sold at the Librarie Materialiste, the bookstore connected with Morhange and Les Revues.[4] But by late 1931, the relationship between Naville and the Philosophies returned to normal, as he and Lefebvre started a running quarrel regarding the direction of the *professeurs union* and the radical caucus (*Minorité oppositionelle révolutionnaire*) within it.[5] Thus, the Philosophies remained as an identifiable grouping on the Left—more scattered and less cohesive than before but still retaining a collective identity.

Simultaneous with this courtship by Naville and the Left opposition, Morhange and Les Revues enjoyed a degree of partial protection by Henri Barbusse and *Monde*. In the midst of the *Revue marxiste* scandal, *Monde* carried one of Morhange's poems—a piece innocent in itself, but its publication at that moment suggesting quiet patronage.[6] These connections, which originated with Friedmann's activities with the original *Clarté* and later the new *Monde*, benefited Guterman as well: When Barbusse visited New York City during his 1933 world speaking tour, he introduced the exile to Kenneth Burke and Malcolm Cowley of the *New Republic*, who brought Guterman into their magazine as a literary critic and translator.[7]

The difficult context confronting French leftist intellectuals in the early 1930s is best illustrated by the particularly tangled situation surrounding Henri Barbusse. Since its founding in 1928, his *Monde* quite openly pursued a course of broad-based unity in opposition to Party and Comintern directives. Indeed, the Party set up its own *Cercle de La Russie Neuve* to compete with his *Amis de l'U.R.S.S.*, and Nizan and others tried to gain control over *Monde* for the Party in 1931. On top of these antagonisms, Barbusse had been "directed" by the International Union of Revolutionary Writers to set up a similar organization in France, a task he failed to undertake to satisfaction. Sharply criticized at the 1930 Kharkov Second Congress of the International Union, literally besieged in his own office by Party militants, and with *Monde* suffering from chronic financial problems, Barbusse and his newspaper alike appeared ready to disappear.

Then the entire net entangling Barbusse's premature Popular Front movement came apart. RAPP—the Union of Proletarian Writers in the Soviet Union and the quarrelsome sectarian driving force behind the International Union—was dissolved and replaced by the Association of Soviet Writers and Artists. The PCF under Thorez slowly opened to a broader spectrum of tactics and began to woo French intellectuals. Working with Paul Vaillant-Couturier, Barbusse ignored his own Groupe des Ecrivains Proletariens launched in January 1932 to organize the Association des Ecrivains et des Artistes Révolutionnaires (AEAR), the long-awaited French section of Revolutionary Writers, in March 1932. With the success of the Barbusse-inspired Amsterdam Conference against war and fascism in August 1932—a success due in no small part to the French Communists—the quarrels that plagued Barbusse faded away. By his tenacious dedication to the principles of a broad unity of the Left despite the denunciations of his own Party, Barbusse paved the way for the organizations within and around which the Popular Front took shape. When Barbusse died in August 1935, the unity he worked so relentlessly for was not as impossible as it had once appeared.[8]

The reasons for this change in climate lay in political changes across Europe—most obviously the years of Stalinism in the USSR and the rise of National Socialism in Germany—combined with a series of convulsions that the Communist Party and the broader leftist movements in France underwent between 1930 and 1932 before settling down into new patterns. As militants continued to slip from the Party, Barbé and Célor were removed from their positions, and Maurice Thorez was named General Secretary. While membership continued to decline until 1933, Thorez infused greater efficiency into the Party apparatus and allowed for a greater degree of individual deviance on minor matters. Yet since the official Comintern line remained the "Class-versus-Class" program, in his official and written commentaries Thorez upheld the policy and therefore continued to refer to "social-democratic vomit" and other crude expressions of the program. If Jacques Doriot, his last remaining challenger for power within the PCF, was willing to openly advocate a French "Popular Front" strategy despite the disapproval of the Comintern, Thorez was not about to ignore the program binding the international Communist Parties together. And it is possible that Thorez's experience during the 1925 Rif crisis enabled him to recognize that incidents like "l'Affaire *Revue marxiste*" simply stemmed from overzealous attempts to control intellectuals. Thus, Thorez's less-dogmatic pragmatism allowed for a greater degree of discussion, if not deviance on major issues, for the Party's intellectuals.

Suddenly, French intellectuals were able to participate in a growing number of Party organizations. As one concrete example, instead of the handful of struggling periodicals available to leftist intellectuals during the 1920s, there was a rapid expansion in the number, diversity, and quality of Party-connected publications. The total number of publications may have reached as high as forty by 1934, peaked at about a hundred during 1937, and remained high until the French government closed all Party-linked periodicals in 1939. A corresponding increase in Party organizations was also evident, with, for example, the *Cercle d'Etudes marxistes* in 1930, charged with developing a cadre of intellectuals to guide the Party. To these were added an *Academie matérialiste* (or *Groupe d'Etudes matérialistes*) in 1933, and the *Comité de Vigilance des Intellectuels antifascistes* a year later.[9]

Like the pre-1914 German Socialists, the PCF after 1931 began expanding into every area of culture and daily life. A policy more congenial for intellectuals also implied diversity of class origins and increased debate within the PCF, or in other words a more "Popular Frontist" atmosphere, at least in unofficial practice. Far from being a foreign graft, these quiet innovations were independent, perhaps accidental, probably intentionally pragmatic, and very well suited to their French context.

*   *   *

Of the Philosophies, Friedmann quickly moved into prominence. Throughout these years, Friedmann continued to explore the classics of philosophy. He wrote extensively on Spinoza and Liebniz, the two philosophers who influenced his early development, as part of a project reaching fruition with his 1946 *thèse Liebniz et Spinoza*.[10] Friedmann devoted other essays to Descartes and Bergson, and consistently wove a discussion of classical philosophy into both his theoretical and sociological works. Rather surprisingly, Friedmann's first success came as a novelist and poet. His verses inspired by the city of Marseilles were published as *Ville qui n'as pas de fin* by Gallimard in 1931, to the acclaim of critics.[11] Friedmann's novels, also published by Gallimard, did equally well. The quasi-autobiographical tale of the son of a Parisian banker, Friedmann's first volume of "Jacques Aron," *Votre Tour Viendra,* traced the youth's life from childhood through a distant appreciation of the horrors of the Great War to his father's death at its end. In the second volume, *L'Adieu,* Aron (the name was obviously borrowed from Raymond Aron) participated in a quarrelsome leftist circle, publishing the review *Demain,* modeled as much on Friedmann's *Clarté* experiences as on *Revue marxiste.* Friedmann gave the series the definitive title of *Lutte pour la Vie* to emphasis Aron's struggle to overcome his class and educational background.[12] But Friedmann left his tale hanging and his hero stuck in the mid-twenties when he turned more strictly to theory and sociology, as will be examined in chapter 6.

The eminent sociologist Celestine Bouglé brought Friedmann and his friend Raymond Aron back to Paris as assistants at the Centre de documentation sociale of the École Normale Supérieure during 1931–1934.[13] In his post, Friedmann found himself straddling several innovative movements in the development of French and international sociological theory. Within the French sociological tradition, Bouglé, one of Emile Durkheim's staunchest supporters, had strong links to Henri Berr's *Revue de Synthèse,* that innovative attempt to bridge the hardening lines between different scholarly disciplines. This connection expanded to include the new professional periodical launched by Marc Bloch and Lucien Febvre in 1929. Their *Annales d'Histoire économique et sociale* underwent several changes of title and format before emerging as *Annales: Economies, sociétés, civilisations,* the center of one of the century's most influential scholarly movements. Friedmann quickly became a frequent contributor of reviews and articles, and was named a member of the *Annales* editorial board in January 1939, at the same time as Jacques Soustelle and Ferdinand Braudel. His *Annales* colleagues frequntly joined Friedmann in his Popular Front activities, appearing as speakers or contributing articles to journals he edited.[14]

These blurred overlaps between academic and political discourses were equally evident in Friedmann's contacts with another circle of theorists. Bouglé was not only a collaborator with *Revue de Synthèse,* a first connection with *Annales,* and a powerful figure in French education; he was also a contributor to the *Archiv für die Geschichte des Sozialismus und der Arbeiterbewegung,* a journal usually referred to as the *Grünberg Archiv* after its founder and animator Carl Grünberg. The first openly Marxist theorist to hold a university chair in Germany, Grünberg gathered around his Institute for Sozialwissenschaft in Frankfurt a number of younger scholars including Max Horkheimer, Theodore Adorno, Herbert Marcuse, Leo Lowenthal, and Frederick Pollock—the famous Critical Theorists of the Frankfurt School. With these colleagues, Grünberg arranged for the copying of manuscripts by Marx and Engels, and their delivery to his old friend and coworker, David Riazanov, at the Marx-Engels Institute in Moscow! Thus, the package of Institute publications which the Philosophies received at Les Revues in 1929 had its origins in the labors of German scholars of the Frankfurt School. With Grünberg's death, the *Archiv* was renamed *Zeitschrift für Sozialforschung*, and the leadership of the Institute passed to Max Horkheimer. When forced out of Germany by the Nazi rise to power, Bouglé and his younger associates arranged for the opening of a Paris office of the Institute and for the publication of the *Zeitschrift* by Editions Felix Alcan.

Partly through chance, partly due to the restricted size of the international academic community, the Philosophies became part of an unorthodox intellectual cosmos, with Friedmann serving as the linchpin in a series of institutional convergences tying their project to those of the Frankfurt School theorists and the innovative Annales movement in the 1930s, and to the Durkheimian movement of the fin-de-siècle represented by Bouglé. Even Guterman's links to the *New Republic* and his later collaboration with Leo Lowenthal and the Frankfurt School during its New York exile were ultimately due to Friedmann. For one brief moment, the major movements of theoretical innovation were bound together, with Frankfurt, New York, and Moscow joined through Paris.

*   *   *

Throughout the early thirties, Lefebvre continued to be frustrated with his projects.[15] A long critique of contemporary academic philosophy was turned down by Editions Rieder, since the pamphlets of Nizan, Politzer, and Emmanuel Berl already saturated the market. His plays and film scripts were left unfinished, and when he completed reports on the French cement and silk-weaving industries and turned them over to a Party official for prepublication approval, the manuscripts disappeared, only to surface in *Pravda* some time later.[16] The typical frustration came when Léon Brunschvicg turned down yet another thesis topic, this time on Hegel:

> You know [Lefebvre recalled Brunschvicg saying] Hegel had the mental age of a seven-year-old. He thinks of a concept like a cow thinks of green: because she browses indiscriminately among grasses, leaves, hay, she has a concept of green.[17]

It was with relief that Lefebvre planned to escape on a long vacation in Germany during 1932.

This "vacation" jerked Lefebvre out of his intellectual lethargy. Shocked by the ardor of the Hitler youth and the bureaucratic rigidity of the German Communist Party, he was even more disappointed that "the German workers allowed themselves to be seduced and won over by national-socialism, because the latter presented itself as socialist and revolutionary, more revolutionary in the national setting than the German Communists."[18] Lefebvre returned to France with a set of problems urgently requiring analysis, and poured his energies into the struggle against fascism.

Soon after his return, Lefebvre figured among those up-and-coming intellectuals asked to contribute to the famous "Cahiers de Revendications," a collection of statements by representatives of the "new youth" that *Nouvelle Revue Française* carried in December 1932. The bulk of the contributors represented a new wave of dissenting movements emerging after 1927, clustered around new periodicals such as *Plans, Action française, Combat, Jeune Europe, Ordre nouveau,* and especially Emmanuel Mounier's *Esprit.* In his concluding summation, "A prendre ou à tuer," Denis de Rougemont (who worked with both *Esprit* and *Ordre nouveau*) argued that the new, widely divergent movements of young nonconformists agreed at least about what they were breaking away from, and to some degree on what goals they sought.[19]

Following the success of his polemic *Chiens du Garde,* Nizan was an obvious choice as representative of the younger Communist intellectuals. In "Conséquences du refus" Nizan denied that the confrontation was between capitalism and *l'Esprit,* but rather was between capitalism and proletariat. The cure Nizan advocated lay in the adherence of disillusioned intellectuals to the cause of the workers, but he prophesied that those who refused to accept the consequences of their anticapitalist rejection would ultimately go over to fascism. The discussion continued in Nizan's "Sur un certain front unique" in *Europe* of January 1933, in which he rejected de Rougemont's contention of a "possible common cause" uniting the squabbling groups of young intellectuals, and led to an exchange of letters in the February issue between Nizan and de Rougemont.[20]

The unexpected contribution came from Lefebvre, whose new intellectual focus was evident in his "Du culte de «l'esprit» au matérialisme dialectique." Lefebvre tied individual rejection of existing society to the search for an absolute, pure life of *"esprit,"* in the sense defined by Valéry and Arland a decade earlier. Such a search, Lefebvre now argued, led to absolute silence and retreat. Unless one was prepared to watch as young intellectuals became "a lumpenproletariat of thought," Lefebvre argued, only one solution was possible. There was plenty of work remained to be done within the PCF and workers' organizations, such as the new AEAR:

> The proletarian revolution and communism are total solutions, but not inevitable. The revolution cannot make itself. It must be organized. It may be aborted. We might be defeated and the land covered by the blood of wars and of aborted revolutions. This is even—this barbarism—the sole "chance" for our adversaries! Truly revolutionary youth musters, prepares and organizes, with a sense of its human and in some way cosmic responsibility, the Revolution.[21]

His German experiences fed Lefebvre's antifascist enthusiasm throughout the thirties, as manifest itself in his 1935 *Le Nationalisme contre les Nations* and the 1938 *Hitler au Pouvoir*, both published by the Party. But the immediate expression of his determination appeared in the new review, *Avant-Poste*, launched in the summer of 1933.

Avant-Poste was the final periodical animated by a sizable number of the original Philosophies. Lefebvre (as *gérant*) and Guterman were the major animators, with Morhange as a regular contributor. Henriette Valet, Lefebvre's wife, served as secretary. *Avant-Poste*, a revue of literature and criticism, set three tasks for itself. In philosophy, contributors were to analyze the movement of ideas and their social roles by using the methods of dialectical materialism. The announced literary goal was to transform readers' sensibilities by unveiling the oppression of distress and the unhappiness of living in capitalist society, while expressing the desire for a new world. Finally, a polemical role was envisioned as part of a struggle against a culture disguising the problems of everyday life.[22]

"Honest, too honest, this number of *Avant-Poste*," Lefebvre commented in the second issue of August, "not an element of bluff, not the least little bit of fraud."[23] Honest was actually an understatement, for *Avant-Poste* reviewers violently demolished the writings of Gide, Martin du Gard, and other major figures. Lefebvre himself piled invective on Breton, on Miguel de Unamuno—the old hero of *Philosophies*—on Victor Serge, and on others. The *Avant-Poste* editors greeted the creation of *Commune*, the official periodical of the AEAR, with an odd little welcome, expressing their pleasure to be followed so quickly by another revolutionary periodical, and condescendingly dismissing the faults of its "comrade review" as only the usual errors made in a new journal![24]

Lefebvre's critique of Louis-Ferdinand Céline's *Voyage to the End of Night* led to a sharp exchange of letters. The success of the novel could not, for Lefebvre, disguise the ultimate unreadability of Céline's massive volume, with its tone of a victimized "*pauv' mec*" that Lefebvre found nauseating.[25] Céline shot back a note, leading to a farcical exchange as Céline snarled:

> I see you have set off on the right foot for reforming humanity. Tomorrow is the fourteenth of July. The city is ours! Don't hesitate! But which flag are you going to plant above the others? The swastika? The sickle? The hammer! The rake! . . . One goes astray, colleague, when trying to take you seriously. . . .

And Lefebvre sneered back:

> You can speak of the fourteenth of July, you fortune-teller of lies for crowds of dawdlers in rags and old shoes, for gapers who cry "oh, that is beautiful!" . . . During this brawl, do you think to get out of it by sleeping with the wife of a cop? Or will you remain somewhere comfortably scrawling on the tops of café tables, chasing the ashes of your cigarette butt across the paper. . . . You and your type, you say "It's a dog's life" and

later are content with having said it with a pretty tone. We, we say "It's a
dog's life" and we really grumble, and we are going even further. There's
the difference.[26]

The rhetorical violence of *Avant-Poste* was a symptom of its efforts to
set itself apart from the mainstream of both literary and political criticism.
The importance of the three issues of *Avant-Poste* lies in four specific areas.
The first, and not the least, of these was the publication in the first two
issues of the closing segment of Marx's "Third Economic and Philosophic
Manuscript of 1844," entitled "The Critique of Hegel's Dialectic and
General Philosophy." The translation of this fragment thus linked *Avant-
Poste* to the efforts begun in *Revue marxiste*, and marked a partial fulfillment
of the earlier project.[27]

The second important contribution of *Avant-Poste* was the joint
attempt by Lefebvre and Guterman to work out a rigorous analytical
Marxism in their articles "Individu et Classe" in the first issue and "La
Mystification" in the second. "In bourgeois society," Lefebvre and
Guterman declared in the former piece,

> the individual has above all a comfortable feeling. He is familiar with
> himself. He says: "Me" like he says "my feelings and my opinions," like
> he says "my" house, "my" wife, "my" belly, "my" butt, "my" bed.[28]

But efforts to move beyond self-definition by possession led to a double
abyss, where psychology and biology served as diversions from the real
definition by class. Lefebvre and Guterman argued that race and nation as
ideological concepts subsumed the individual, while sociology devoted
itself to the study of ill-defined groups. For Lefebvre and Guterman, only
definitions derived from class relations provided a definition of individual:

> Class is not an abstraction. It corresponds to the practical and daily life
> common to many others. It defines the conditions of this daily life. A pro-
> letarian has the daily life of a man belonging to a class deprived of the
> means of production. Individuals are not real each by himself, they are
> real in the ensemble of their reciprocal relations, by and in class. Con-
> versely, class is the reality of the ensemble of individuals that it envelops.[29]

From this rather orthodox definition Lefebvre and Guterman turned immediately to the question of class-consciousness, and in particular why individuals of any class may not be aware of their true social position. Unfortunately,
in 1933 they were only prepared to offer a schematic—and simplistic—
analysis: The bourgeoisie denies class as a defining concept and substitutes
ideological constructs, like the cult of individualism, to disguise the real conflict. The workers, lacking economic, political, and cultural power, absorb this
ideology and, viewing themselves as free and equal citizens of a nation,
remain subservient. Ultimately, Lefebvre and Guterman argued, if only the
individual matters, humanity became a meaningless and passive herd.

Yet Lefebvre and Guterman managed to work in a curious critique of
Lefebvre's earlier positions, condemning the cult of action they called
"adventure." Desiring to define oneself in opposition to the masses, individuals engaged in socially contentless acts, driven by interior impulses
easily diverted into harmless pastimes. The only hope, the two wrote, was
to realize that the individual may only become real through class.[30] This
first effort of Lefebvre and Guterman was, therefore, primarily a statement
of orthodoxy, but did contain the rather original if brief self-criticism of
Lefebvre's earlier espousal of a philosophy of action.

With the second article, "La Mystification: Notes pour une critique de
la vie quotidienne," Guterman and Lefebvre began to explore a higher
analytic level. They argued that modern philosophy divorced existence
and essence, and that only modern materialism, Marxism, reunited the two
in its concept of totality. Lefebvre and Guterman then sketched out a preliminary materialist theory of knowledge, working from the present
totality of the unity of bourgeois culture in an attempt to arrive at the general laws of "mystification."[31]

For Lefebvre and Guterman, the most striking aspect of bourgeois culture was the apparent diversity of its manifestations. Yet behind the seemingly different abstractions of Bergson, Valéry, Proust, and others was the fact
that all appealed in the end to an abstract "*esprit*" as the all-encompassing
source of ultimate reality. From the vantage point of this hypothetical *esprit*,
the diversity of cultural products was reduced to unity in fragmentation, to
monotony before "the grand symphony of *esprit.*" Moreover, supposedly elite
culture was embedded in so-called popular culture, that mass-produced
world of films and cheap novels geared toward entertainment. Bourgeois cul-

ture, they concluded, offered unreachable Absolutes and a diversity of enter-
taining evasions in place of reality, and thereby maintained order.

Yet, Lefebvre and Guterman argued, while disguising reality, this same
culture in fact revealed the forms of bourgeois culture in alienated and
mystified ways. Values like sincerity, the uniqueness of the individual, and
the primacy of spiritual life served as rallying points away from the issues
of collective interests and definitions. Everything appeared topsy-turvy,
masquerading as its opposite: Fascism paraded as revolution, and nationalism hid imperialism.

Curiously, only at the end of the article did Lefebvre and Guterman
provide summary definitions for their key concepts. First they added
fetishism, borrowing directly from Marx to describe those confrontations
of men with the products of labor in which the social labor process was not
recognized and the product acquired an independent "life" of its own.
From this arose alienation, the estrangement of man from man and from
his own individuality. During those historical stages when societies become
immobile, when changes could not be made without rupturing the entire
system, human consciousness becomes mystified. The true roots of the
"unhappy consciousness," Lefebvre and Guterman wrote, lay in the projection of human desires and consciousness into an impossible search for
comfort in an unrealizable Absolute.[32]

With their projected "critique of everyday life," Lefebvre and Guterman
moved on to totally new terrain, at least in terms of French Marxism. But
from these rough beginnings they would continue their collaboration
through the end of the thirties. These works, along with Lefebvre's lifelong
continuation of this project, will be explored in chapter 7.

The third major project of *Avant-Poste* was to demystify fascist ideology. In the second issue, Lefebvre evaluated the present state and possible future of fascism in France itself. In 1933 Lefebvre acknowledged
there were obviously small reactionary groups, but added "one may not yet
properly speak of a fascism in France." In part, Lefebvre thought this
absence was due to the peculiarities of French history, for nationalism had
been classified as "on the political right" for a longer period than in the
newer nations of Germany and Italy, and the civilizing mission and supra-
national stance France adapted toward the colonies undercut racism, since
cultural identity provided the basis for integration and unity.

Perhaps, Lefebvre suggested, racist and nationalist elements were not essential for the development of a fascist ideology. He noted a tremendous enthusiasm for the abstract idea of Revolution, tied to a violent critique of capitalism, in the periodicals of the different groups of disenchanted youth. A similar rejection of capitalism in the name of "spiritual values" had occurred elsewhere, Lefebvre added, particularly in Germany where young *inquiéts* had worked out themes like depersonalization and generational conflict, themes later assimilated and employed by the Nazis. French nonconformists around *Esprit, Pamphlets, Revue Française,* and other journals were providing the materials for a French fascist movement, according to Lefebvre. A revolution that denied Marxism led to the Right, he claimed, and a denial of class conflict in the name of a spiritual renaissance ignored the real problems of economic and political domination. With the promise "to be continued," Lefebvre truncated his effective but crude assault on the nonconformists as protofascists.[33]

The fourth contribution of *Avant-Poste* was an *enquête* on the possible spread of fascism in France, launched in June 1933, just prior to the fusion of the Amsterdam-Pleyel movements. A limited number of writers were asked to respond on questions such as whether a fascist government could appear in France, what form it would take, the best means of fighting fascism, and in particular what roles writers could play. Unfortunately, the list of those polled was not published, and the demise of *Avant-Poste* prevented the publication of all responses. To an extent, the replies were predictable. Léon Pierre-Quint began with his invariable disclaimer: The questions posed require a long and detailed study, *but*, in his view, democracy was being wrecked by the economic crisis of the Depression, and the proper role of intellectuals was to avoid adherence to any party while studying the causes and proposing solutions to those economic problems.[34] But most respondents thought a French fascism unlikely. If one did develop, the suggestions as to its form were all derived from French historical experiences, as Alain thought of Boulangerism, and Bernard Lecache pointed to the "Liberal Empire" and Bonapartism. Others—Jean-Richard Bloch most notably—followed a comparatively orthodox Marxist position: Fascism was a symptom of the decomposition of capitalism, and drew upon the disaffections of those groups most seriously affected by that decay—workers, the petite bourgeoisie, and the intellectuals.[35] Writers, the contributors (all writers themselves, of course) generally agreed, could assist in the fight against fascism by creating a new literature and cultural hegemony to replace the decayed remnants of bourgeois culture.

The most interesting responses came from Henri Barbusse, Louis-Fernand Céline, and André Malraux. Barbusse was in the midst of organizing antifascist committees and meetings, and had no doubts about the counterrevolutionary, antiproletarian nature of fascism. Yet he was almost alone among the respondents in claiming that a form of fascism was being developed in France. But what this French fascism was he did not specify, adding only that while it would not appear similar to its German and Italian relatives, the consequences would be identical.[36]

Céline was outrageously insulting to Valet, who had signed the letters of inquiry as secretary of the review:

> I read nothing in the heavens but it is easy to predict that if the franc falls by half, it's going to get tough!
>
> Dictatorship? Why not? It would be good to see that we are not capable of it as well! But with intelligence, of the press, not of those gross excesses which revolt our admirable sense of French moderation! In two weeks it may be entirely old gossip. After one sees.
>
> Defense against fascism? You must be joking, you have not been to war, Mademoiselle, that leads, you see, to some parallel questions. When the military takes command, Mademoiselle, there are no more resistances, one doesn't resist the dinosaur. It bursts by itself—and us with it—in its guts, Mademoiselle, in its guts.[37]

Malraux on the other hand took a more thoughtful position, suggesting his future political trajectory. In France, Malraux thought, there was

> a confusion between fascism, on the one hand, and strong government on the other. I call fascism a movement which arms and organizes the petite bourgeoisie, pretends to govern in its name against the proletariat and capitalism. . . .The present relative feebleness of the French proletariat seems to me therefore to block the appeal of fascism, and leaves possible a "strong" government of the Clemenceau type, jacobin and radical. In the present, a workers' movement does not have, to my mind, any chance of taking power in France. Its chances are linked, in the future, to revolutionary circumstances: profound crises, famine or war. For reasons that

it would take too long to develop here, an important part of the French petite bourgeoisie remains tied to democracy, and hostile to fascism.[38]

Malraux directly tied the struggle against fascism to the union of the proletariat with elements of the petite bourgeoisie, in an as yet nonexistent organization.

This focus on fascism and mystified bourgeois culture, interwoven as it was with violently worded diatribes against prominent intellectuals, predictably led to a continuation of the polemics that began with the *Nouvelle Revue Française* "Cahiers de Revendications" of 1932. The nonconformists around *Esprit* were particularly outraged by the verbal assaults they received. In the September 1933 *Esprit*, Edmond Humeau decried the entire *Avant-Poste* project as a giant mystification of Marxist functionaries:

> the Marxists of *Avant-Poste* are rendering to "Marxism" services analo-
> gous to those the surrealists rendered to "Freudism": They are suc-
> ceeding in showing the philosophic mediocrity, the intellectual petrifica-
> tion, the shabby literature and the polemical address of the Stalinists.

Humeau jeered at the mixture of Hegel and Marx as mere "scientific sur-realism" and was incensed by Guterman and Lefebvre's description of the new *Esprit*'s search for absolutes as "onanistic mysticism." Infantile provo-cations and theoretical illusions like those of *Avant-Poste*, Humeau mocked, explained why "if there has not been a strong movement of theoretical Marxism in France, as the editors of *Avant-Poste* say, that may be due to the childishness of the arguments that they utilize for their propaganda."[40]

Lefebvre shot back a brief comment in the closing pages of *Avant-Poste* no. 3, asking that someone inform "that spiritualist eunuch" that *Commune*, and not *Avant-Poste*, was the organ of AEAR.[41] Beyond Humeau's ignorance about who was who on the Left, Lefebvre sensed "more than a trace of a passion, make that hate. He grimaces and gnashes."

Support came from Paul Nizan, in one of his most often quoted pieces, "Les enfants de la lumière" in *Commune*. Nizan ignored Humeau and went after Emmanuel Mounier, Thierry Maulnier, and other more prominent nonconformist writers. Their chase after the individual and the Absolute left social reality and the alienation of individuals untouched, Nizan empha-sized. The unique common front of youth, of which de Rougemont wrote, was already fragmenting, as those who retained some interest in Christianity and its ethics began to balk at the aristocratic and essentially fascist solutions—the so-called revolution—others sought. Still, the bonds between the two groups were strong enough that Nizan could foresee "the defenders of the Person, in fascist uniforms, will be then truly and publicly in the eyes of all the bourgeois, will be then, more than ever, the 'Children of the Light.' "[42]

Humeau continued his assault with a second article in November's *Esprit*. Lefebvre and Guterman's "Mystification" became a philosophy of "fetishism" embracing all of daily reality, and Humeau found the *enquête* on fascism mediocre and pretentious. Humeau gleefully spotted the obvious disharmony between *Avant-Poste* and *Commune*, and noticeably between Guterman and Nizan, in the second issue. He rejected Nizan's attempt to lump all the nonconformists together as fascists, and claimed Nizan and Lefebvre missed the point since, Humeau persisted, the goal of the new youth was to purify spiritualism and not just to grapple with the simple, temporal causes of alienation.[43] However, the public identification of *Esprit* with the young Right at this time was so strong that Emmanuel Mounier personally added a postscript to Humeau's article, restating for the benefit of Left and Right alike the independence of that fragment of nonconformist youth gathered around the journal.[44]

Lefebvre and Nizan moved to the sidelines of this particular debate, but the quarrel itself continued. In *Commune*, during December 1933, Jacques Bartoli used the example of the original 1926–1927 *Esprit*—that of the Philosophies—to underscore the correct resolution of intellectual alienation. Bartoli noted that in the mid-twenties, revolution and pursuit of the eternal was confused by Lefebvre, Friedmann, Politzer, and company in much the same manner as by Mounier, Izard, and their friends in 1933. Unless the new *Esprit* intended to remain dupes and refused to learn from others, Bartoli urged they follow the example of their predecessors and explore Marxism.[45]

Jean Grenier followed a similar line of thought from the opposite direction in *Nouvelle Revue Française*, a full year after Bartoli. Tracing their history from Philosophies to *Avant-Poste*, Grenier suggested:

> The young writers of the first review *Esprit* are swiftly reappearing within the second (to tell the truth, they may have kept their religion for themselves, because messianism goes very well paired with revolution).[46]

Moreover, Grenier continued, the new *Esprit* faces the same quandary:

> They want a social revolution which will be at the same time spiritual.
> They are simultaneously revolutionaries and believers. But this is a diffi-
> cult position to take in our times and in our country. If you are [a] revo-
> lutionary, you are practically obliged to be Marxist. If you are [a] spiri-
> tualist, you cannot be Marxist.[47]

Grenier recognized that intermediate positions existed, but brushed them
aside as ultimately untenable. When the members of the new *Esprit* found
themselves confronted by the choice between religion or revolution, Grenier
wrote he would not be surprised if many followed the path of the first *Esprit.*

This quarrel, lasting from 1932 through 1936, marked the stages of
Catholic and Communist relations during those years. By the time of the
Popular Front, the new movements of the thirties and especially *Esprit* had
meandered to the Right and then to the Left in search of the answer to
their form of the *mal du siècle*. As Grenier had predicted, many nonconformists did choose revolution over religion, although many remained with
Mounier and the independent *Esprit*. The comparison of the "old" *Esprit*
with the "new" highlighted several key points. Obviously, the comparison
only made sense if everyone sharing in French intellectual debate knew
who was being discussed, demonstrating that the trajectory of the Philosophies was well known. Second was the not unrealistic possibility of
Lefebvre and friends serving as role models for others, a point made by
Bartoli and Grenier. Finally, perhaps most glaring was the continuity of
the problems facing French intellectuals between the wars. Although many
of the early sufferers of *inquiétude* and the *mal du siècle* had, to a large
extent, faded from prominence into the silence Lefebvre had spoken of, the
new nonconformist youth emerging at the end of the 1920s confronted and
debated the same problems as their immediate forerunners. These new
nonconformists might have had a stronger recognition of social causes and
may have grounded themselves more firmly in philosophy than in poetry,
but the dilemma they sought to escape remained the same.

*   *   *

By 1932 there were signs that the tensions that divided Nizan, Lefebvre, Friedmann, Guterman, and Morhange were being forgotten. As early as 1930, Nizan had written a short, generous review of the *Poèmes des ouvriers americains* prepared by Morhange and Guterman, a gesture followed by a continuous stream of public support.[48] When Guterman and Lefebvre prepared their Marx anthology, Nizan compiled the first half, entitled "Marx philosophe." And the preface to Lefebvre's *Nationalisme contre les Nations* came from Nizan as well. Perhaps most indicative of this change came at the end of the decade, when Nizan published what amounted to defenses of Friedmann's *De la Sainte Russe à l'U.R.S.S.* and Lefebvre's *Nietzsche*—against Politzer.

The others reciprocated in these expressions of goodwill. Friedmann praised Nizan's *Aden Arabie* in *Cahiers du Sud*, and arranged that an excerpt from Guterman and Lefebvre's introduction to Lenin's philosophic notebooks would be included in a special issue of *Europe* devoted to Descartes.[49] As editor of the prestigious series "Socialisme et Culture," Friedmann ensured the publication of Nizan's *Materialistes de l'Antiquité* in 1936 and Lefebvre's *Nietzsche* in 1939.[50] Lefebvre responded in kind, reviewing Nizan, Friedmann, and Morhange's writings whenever possible.[51] While Politzer remained silent about his old colleagues until 1938, the only bitter note came from Norbert Guterman, who heaped abuse on Nizan's *Chiens du Garde* in the second issue of *Avant-Poste*:

> For reviving Marxism in France, at least among the intellectuals, some original works would have more effect than a repetition of elements and of formulas already vulgarized and refuted. . . . One cannot go through the school on rue d'Ulm and through the besotting university examination without leaving something there and without placing oneself a little on their terrain. . . . Style does not save the work. . . this demagogy recalls a little those rich young men who put on a [worker's] sweater and cap to go into meetings. . . .[52]

Parallel to this calming of angry relations among themselves was the demergence of Friedmann, Nizan, Politzer, and then Lefebvre as major figures among those most active in the Popular Front movement. Friedmann served as secretary of the *Cercle de Russie Neuve*, before which Politzer spoke on Bergson, and Lefebvre on fascist ideology.[53] Friedmann and Politzer were important members of the *Academie materialiste*, along with Charles Hainchelin.[54] All frequented the Maison de la Culture in Paris and were among the original adherents to the Association des Ecrivains et Artistes Révolutionnaires. At the AEAR-sponsored Congress for the Defense of Culture during June 1935, Friedmann addressed the association on "Machinisme et Humanisme" while Nizan followed with "Sur l'Humanisme."[55] Nizan was in a prominent position within the AEAR, as his signature on a directive from the International Union of Revolutionary Writers indicates, and Friedmann appeared as a frequent speaker on Soviet labor policies.[56] Along with these activities, Politzer, Friedmann, and Nizan managed to teach a "Cours de Marxisme" at the Mutualité during 1935–1936.[57] At the Université ouvrière, Politzer team-taught the course on philosophy the following year, while Friedmann lectured on the scientific organization of labor.[58]

At the same time, Nizan, Friedmann, and Politzer also assumed important positions within the Popular Front press. Friedmann joined the editorial board of *Europe* when it swung closer to the PCF in April 1936, while Nizan edited the PCF evening paper *Ce Soir* and served as an editorial secretary for the AEAR journal, *Commune*. Friedmann, Nizan, and Politzer were listed as among the collaborators of a new, Popular Front incarnation of *Clarté* from 1936 through 1939. More importantly, in 1937 all three served as members of the *L'Humanité* collective: Nizan as a member of the editorial board and a literary contributor, Friedmann as a literary and scientific collaborator, and Politzer as scientific collaborator.[59]

By the mid-thirties, then, several of the Philosophies had carved out niches of prominence within French intellectual life. Nizan in particular was doing well. As a writer, his novels enjoyed considerable popular and critical success. As a Party journalist Nizan occupied positions on the editorial boards of several of the most important Party periodicals. And as an advisor to the Central Committee, he could exert a degree of influence over policy formulation.

Friedmann's success embraced literature, philosophy, and sociology, along with a considerable outpouring of reviews and essays for periodicals. By assuming a position next to but not in the PCF, Friedmann exercised a tremendous influence over nonaligned intellectuals. While Nizan demonstrated that Party militants could combine extreme political positions with insightful cultural commentary and literary creativity, Friedmann exemplified the aligned but independent intellectual working as a partner of the PCF.

*   *   *

In Georges Politzer a different model of militant intellectual was evident.
Having dropped psychology, Politzer devoted himself for most of the 1930s to
political economics, on which he wrote extensively for *L'Humanité* and *Cahiers
du Bolchevisme* from as early as 1932. Moreover, he frequently attended the
meetings of the Party's Central Committee as an advisor, and he appeared
with great regularity at a wide range of meetings as the official Party spokesman.[60] His lectures at l'Université Ouvriére were reconstructed after the war
from student notes, and published as *Elementary Principles of Philosophy*.[61]

Politzer's dedication to the Party could at times border on the overzealous. Note has already been taken of his nonautocritique in *Commune*,
and his outright rejection of any reconciliation between Marxist and
Freudian thought. Again in *Commune*, Politzer wrote the concluding
overview for the *enquête* "Pour qui ecrivez vous"—the slogan of "for who
do you write" which mobilized American intellectuals of the 1930s. Rather
than provide an optimistic evaluation of the tremendous support among
intellectuals that the responses demonstrated, Politzer focused on the hostile remarks, like that of Drieu la Rochelle, and criticized liberals for lack
of sufficient militancy.[62] In *Cahiers du Bolchevisme* throughout 1936, Politzer
drew sharp lines to distinguish what was and what was not possible under
the Popular Front.[63] Perhaps these latter pieces were necessary and official
statements of the PCF's position, but his division of sheep from goats in
the avowedly popular frontist review *Commune* contrasts strikingly with the
purposes of the journal and the AEAR.

Only during the last prewar years did Politzer seriously return to
writing about philosophy, and more correctly about the history of philosophy. In all his essays of this period, Politzer offered a selective defense of
French philosophy, claiming that real French philosophy

> has been characterized in the course of the most essential moments of its
> history by an impulse toward truth, toward the solution of problems, the
> possibility of which the greatest French thinkers have always believed in,
> because they have always thought that it would be possible to resolve
> problems by the means of science.[64]

Politzer's defense of this national intellectual tradition ran from the mechanistic elements of Descartes's writings, through the Encyclopedists of the Enlightenment, and to the early French utopian socialists, especially Saint-Simon. Politzer heavily larded his writings with references to the canons of Marxism. Thus, following Engels, Politzer pronounced the Enlightenment "a preeminently French century," and asserted that "French materialist philosophy of the eighteenth century became the creed of the French Revolution."[65] This orthodox history led to the obvious conclusion that Marxism

> is the sole legitimate heir and continuer of the philosophy of Enlightenment. And it alone may be the heir and continuer: Materialism can only keep up with modern science by being dialectical, and there does not exist any other scientific conception of history than historical materialism.[66]

In part, Politzer's writings of this period can be considered a popularization of a basic Marxist historiography, and indicative of PCF efforts to portray itself as the "sole heir" of everything progressive extractable from three hundred years of French history—a position to which the Party had as much rightful title as any other claimant. Perhaps the unoriginality of these repetitive essays can be attributed to Politzer's antifascist efforts, since the theme linking his writings during the late 1930s was the defense of this French rationalist heritage against the foreign and irrational threat of Nazi racism, against

> the suppression of the rights of science and of the consciousness, the interdiction of free scientific research, science and philosophy reduced to the level of the most vulgar apologetic.[67]

Perhaps the best known and most lasting of Politzer's activities during the thirties was his participation in the new review *Pensée, Revue du Rationalisme moderne*, founded in 1939. A quarterly, the first two issues were densely packed with a wide range of articles covering physics and atomic theory, genetics, music, and philosophy contributed by Paul Langevin, Georges Cogniot, Celestin Bouglé, Henri Wallon, Jacques Solomon, Pierre George, and other prominent intellectuals with Party ties.[68] Although Politzer was not listed among the editors, he is generally accorded a major role in the planning and daily operations of *Pensée*, and he was the single largest contributor to the journal. His "Philosophie et les Mythes" appeared in the first issue, the second contained "Qu'est-ce que le rationalisme?" and "Dans la cave de l'aveugle," and the third included his "Fin de la psychanalyse" signed "Th. W. Morris."

In "La Philosophie et les mythes," Politzer quoted the Nazi ideologue Alfred Rosenberg's own claim that the concept of racism was only a myth around which to rally Germans. To achieve the acceptance of this myth, Rosenberg asserted the need for faith against the "problem of consciousness." Politzer denounced this cynical manipulation as a tool for the preservation of capitalism. "Le mythe est mensonge et la mystique mystification," Politzer snapped:

> The myth is a lie and the mysticism a hoax. To work for this mystification, such is the task that Nazi obscurantism assigns to philosophy. Philosophy must become the servant of mythology.[69]

This obscuring mythology was seen by Politzer as slowly infiltrating into France, where it took the form of a championing of Being (Descartes's *sum*) over Consciousness (*cogito*). Politzer argued this philosophy, "called existential," in its efforts to simultaneously avoid idealism and abstract rationalism, was reduced to creating a mystique, a mystical theology obscuring reality. Politzer focused on two propagators of this new "philosophy of gloom," Jean Wahl and Gabriel Marcel. Despite their differences, Politzer lumped together Wahl the Kierkegaardian and Marcel the Heideggerian as theorists paving the way for a fascist mysticism.[70]

Politzer's assault on these old associates grew even more vicious in "Dans la cave de l'aveugle." Politzer denounced Marcel's professions of "radical experience" and a "poetic essence of life" as a faith in mysticism. After noting that Marcel had described "La Philosophie et les mythes" as "fairly naive" and that *Esprit* had dismissed *Pensée* as "a 175-page brick," Politzer struck back by linking the Existentialists as well as Bergson directly to Nazi ideology, a point he drove home by bracketing a quote from Marcel with one from Rosenberg.[71] "The antagonism of materialism and idealism, science and mysticism, rationalism and obscurantism," Politzer wrote in clear imitation of Lenin's writing style in *Materialism and*

Empirio-Criticism, could not be circumvented and posed a pressing problem requiring a solution.[72]

Ironically, it was one of the "irrationalists" Politzer denounced who had the final say on *Pensée*. Jean Wahl, in his *Nouvelle Revue Française* critique of the final issue, noted that the contributors to *Pensée* tended to carry some weighty credentials, like Henri Wallon (professeur au College du France) and Charles Parain (agrégé de l'Université). Titles did not spare them his critical eye, for Wahl noted in Wallon's "Scientific Psychology and the Study of Character" a slippage from a critique of Bergson into one against Heidegger, leaving Wahl to ask if such a conflation of philosophy and politics was really necessary. Still, Wahl enjoyed the "Fin de la psychanalyse" by Th. W. Morris (*sans titres*, he noted), a "study made by a very intelligent man, despite his dogmatism." In particular, Wahl took interest in the claim by Morris that the proper study of sexuality lie in the examination of the social conditions that determined it. Wahl wondered "which will absorb the other, Marxism or psychoanalysis? Or maybe one can unite them (does the author deny that?)."[73] But of course Politzer denied precisely such an attempt could work.

*   *   *

Quietly reintegrated into the Party after the *Revue marxiste* affair, Morhange adjusted to life away from Paris, and scored some small success with his poetry, notably in 1931, when *Europe* carried a number of pieces under the title "Gallia."[74] But his hopes for fame rode on his collection of verse *La Vie est Unique*, published by Gallimard in 1933, which brought together new poems like those dedicated to Jean Wahl and Norbert Guterman, as well as collecting previously published works.[75] Morhange's major themes throughout the collection were antimilitarism and the struggle to create oneself in the modern world.

Reviewing the work for *Nouvelle Revue Française*, Raymond Schwab rather surprisingly criticized a house publication sharply.[76] Schwab recalled the title had been announced as a work in progress by Norbert Guterman back in 1927, and decided this coincidence signified collective authorship (he also attributed to this collective Morhange the translation of Schelling!). While finding the verses theoretically interesting and

Morhange's expression ingenious, Schwab concluded *La Vie est Unique* left only a vague imprint and was a massacre of words.

Morhange's reply was carried in full in *Nouvelle Revue Française* in November.[77] Morhange rather politely corrected some of Schwab's misunderstandings about the authorship, and suggested that if Schwab needed to label his works the most appropriate title would be *poésie matérialiste*. These explanations in *Nouvelle Revue Français* were mild compared to the rebuttal Morhange published in *Avant-Poste*, where Morhange savaged Schwab as a pedantic, closed-minded, spiritual reactionary.[76] But after this sputter of indignation, Morhange devoted himself to teaching, family, and writing. Yet, both at the time and in retrospect, Schwab's criticisms ran counter to *Nouvelle Revue Français*'s own appreciation of Morhange's verse, since three selections from *La Vie est Unique* were contained in the prestigious 1936 *Anthologie des poètes de la Nouvelle Revue Française* as well as its 1956 edition.

Throughout the thirties, Morhange quietly continued to write and to teach. *Europe*, with Friedmann and other friends as editors, carried his wistful "Air de flute improvisé pour l'anniversaire de Henri Heine," as well as love poems dedicated to his wife.[79] Particularly biting were Morhange's antimilitaristic poems, such as the 1940 "Le Lieutenant Bicot."[80] Most indicative of Morhange's personal and emotional growth were his poems concerning anti-Semitism, about being Jewish, and his horrified incomprehension of the Nazi prison camps. The number of these pieces increased through late thirties and provide graphic proof of Morhange's efforts to grapple with his own heritage. "Bible," inauspiciously dated September 1939 and published in the Catholic *Esprit* in April 1940, captured Morhange's uneasiness:

> La pluie et toute la crépitude
> M'avaient jeté sur un versant
> Je chantais un chant nu
> Et seul, comme un mouton
> Je paissais l'effroi et la solitude
> Chacun est un Job ou un Jérémie
> De profundis ad te clamavi
> Inutilement, du triste génie de ma vie
> Un humble arbre vert, une feuille
> Que rien n'appelle et que rien n'accueille

Un soupir, un nom pronouncé
Mystère de la détresse nue et total
Le grain de la douleur, une larme étonnée
Que nul ne sait et ne saura jamais.[81]

The prophet within Morhange had been slowly fading throughout the 1930s: The zealot Jeremiah was being replaced by the long-suffering and doubting Job.

*   *   *

After the "Affaire *Revue marxiste*" the Philosophies denied neither Marxism nor the Communist Party. To reject Marxism would have meant rejecting the theoretical explanation and solution of the problem of inquietude. To turn their back on the PCF would have entailed foreswearing the possibility of a concrete resolution of their quandary.

Despite geographic dispersal and continuing tensions left by the arguments of 1929, the Philosophies retained a group identity throughout the 1930s. There was a tremendous overlap not only in their activities, particularly during the years 1932–1938, but in their individual projects as well. The Philosophies shared each other's quarrels, furthered each other's careers, and jointly produced publications. In general, Politzer remained aloof from his former colleagues, although his last articles of 1939 were strikingly but superficially similar in tone to the writings of Lefebvre and Guterman in *Avant-Poste* during 1933 as well as their 1936 *La Conscience mystifiée*. Yet the appearance of agreement masked hostilities extending beyond a defense of political orthodoxy.

NOTES

1. Henri Lefebvre, *Le Somme et la Reste* (1959; reprint, Paris: Bélibaste. 1973), tome 1, p. 298. Nizan became one of the few capable of living by the pen, see Paul Gerbod, "L'Université et la Littérature en France de 1919 à 1939," *Revue d'Histoire moderne et contemporaine*, tome 25 (January–March 1978). See also Georges-Philippe Friedmann, *La Puissance et la Sagesse* (Paris: Gallimard, 1970), p. 380.

2. The publications of Les Revues during these last years of its existence were, for 1930: Riazanov, *Communisme et mariage*; Plekhanov, *Materialisme militant* (preface Deborin); M. Beer, *Histoire gènèrale du socialisme* (trans. Marcel Olliver); Friedrich Engels, *Ludvig Feuerbach and la fin de la philosophie suivi par les theses de Marx sur Feuerbach* (trans. Olliver); *Poèmes des ouvriers americains* (trans. Pierre Morhange and Norbert Guterman); Bertrand Russell, *Le mariage et la morale*; Calverton, *La faillite du mariage*; Mayakovsky, *Le nuage dans le pantaloons* (intro. L. Trotsky, partial trans. N. Guterman); Ilya Ehrenburg, *La ruelle de Moscou* and *10 c.v.*; and for 1931: Georges Altman, *Ça c'est la drame!*; Hermynia zur Mühlen, *Le Rosier* (preface Barbusse); E. E. Kisch, *Paradis americain*; Chpilevskii, *Copains!*; A. Maraï, *Les Revoltés*. Note the number of pieces about marriage, an indication of the immediate personal preoccupations of the entire group. That eternal emigre Ilya Ehrenburg was a close friend of Nizan's and the fact that Les Revues published his works at this time suggests that the thawing relations between Nizan and the others may date from this period.

On Guterman's continuing quarrel with Nizan: Guterman, personal communication, 8 May 1982; the introduction to Mayakovsky matches that portion of Trotsky's essay "Futurism," beginning "Mayakovsky is a big, or as Blok defines him, an enormous talent. . . " in *Literature and Revolution* (Ann Arbor: University of Michigan, 1968), p. 147. Guterman also translated Mayakovsky's "Comme on fait une poème" for *Europe*, no. 127 (July 1933). While denying he was ever a Trotskyist, Guterman took great glee in baiting agents of the FBI, during a 10 January 1955 interview, with expressions of his admiration for Trotsky's literary writings and called him "a wonderful writer" and "brilliant man" (New York Office of FBI, file 105-4005, report of 26 January 1955).

3. There are a growing number of works, of vastly varying quality, devoted to the Trotskyist mouvement in France. Most useful for my purposes has been Jean-François Kesler, "Le Communisme de Gauche en France (1927–1947)," *Revue Française des Sciences Politiques* 28, no. 4 (August 1978). See A. Ariat, "G. Plekhanov: Materialisme militant," *Lutte de Classes*, no. 20 (April 1930): 316–17; and "Engels: Feuerbach et la fin. . . ; M. Beer: Histoire. . . ," *Lutte de Classes*, no. 21–22 (May–June 1930): 440–43.

4. *Lutte de Classes*, no. 34–35 (August–September 1931).

5. Pierre Naville, "Après le Congrès de l'Enseignement: La position de la MOR," *Vérité* (1 September 1931); collected in Naville's *L'Entre-Deux-Guerres* (Paris: Etudes et Documentations Internationales, 1975), pp. 320–22. Lefebvre wrote the supplement to *L'Ecole Emancipée* (26 April 1931), and worked with the Communist educators around *Cahiers de Contre-Enseignement*.

6. Pierre Morhange, "Poème inedit," *Monde*, no. 68 (21 September 1929): 3. Two prominent members of the French Trotskyist movement—Magdeline (Marx) Paz and Angelo Tasca —wrote extravagant reviews of Friedmann's novels and of Les Revues publications respectively for *Monde*. See, for example, Paz, "La Guerre et l'Homme—L'Adieu," *Monde*, no. 231 (5 November 1932).

7. Norbert Guterman, personal communication, 18 April 1981. See also Guterman's written statement to the Federal Bureau of Investigation (20 April 1955, NY Field Office, file 105-4005). According to Martin Peretz (personal communication, 30 January 1986), the records of the *New Republic* during the 1930s are scanty, and specific employment information regarding Guterman could not be provided.

8. On Barbusse's problems and the AEAR, see Nicole Racine, "L'Association des Ecrivains et Artistes Révolutionnaires," *Mouvement Sociale*, no. 54 (January–March 1966); Normand, "Henri Barbusse and his 'Monde,'" and the interesting work of C. G. Geoghegan, "Surrealism and Communism: The Hesitations of Aragon from Kharkov to the 'Affaire Front Rouge,'" *Journal of European Studies* 8, no. 1 (1978). See also Friedmann's brief message of adhesion in *Ceux qui ont choisi* (Paris: Editions de l'AEAR, 1933). For the international dimensions of the movement and the problems of Soviet writers see Edward J. Brown, *The Proletarian Episode in Russian Literature 1828–1932* (New York: Columbia University Press, 1953); or one of the many other thorough studies of pre-1941 Soviet literature.

9. On the Cercle de la Russie Neuve see Paul Laberenne, "Le Cercle de la Russie Neuve (1928–1936) and l'Association pour l'Etude de la Culture Sovietique," *Pensée*, no. 205 (May/June 1979). The Cercle was renamed the Association pour l'Etude de la Culture sovietique in 1936, and published *Documents de la Cercle* from 1930. Politzer's presentation to the Cercle were to be published in the unachieved vol. 2, part 2, of *À la lumiere du marxisme*. Laberenne also mentions the "Academie materialiste"/"Groupe d'Etudes materialistes" active 1933–1939. Parallel groups included Les Amis de l'URSS, founded by Barbusse and Francis Jourdain; the proceedings of the Congrès des Amis was published by the Party's Bureau d'Editions in 1928. In November 1930, *Cahiers du Bolchevisme* contained Servet's "Un Cercle d'Etudes marxistes est crée," (5, no. 11, pp. 1074–78); reprinted in *Cahiers de l'Institut Maurice Thorez* no. 43, ns# 15 (January–March 1976). Politzer apparently headed the economic section. On CVIA, see Nicole Racine, "Le Comité de Vigilance des Intellectuels antifascistes (1934–1939): Antifascisme et pacificisme," *Mouvement Sociale*, no. 101 (October–December 1971). Its journal was *Vigilance, Bulletin du CVIA*, 1934–1939.

10. See Georges Friedmann, "Lettres de Spinoza," *Cahiers du Sud,* no. 126 (November 1930), and "Errata" in the following issue; "Paul Vulliaud: Spinoza aprés les livres de ses bibliotheques," *Commune,* no. 19 (March 1935); "Leibniz et le Discours de Métaphysique," *Cahiers du Sud,* no. 128 (February 1931); "A propos d'inedits de Leibniz," *Commune,* no. 23 (July 1935); "A propos d'un livre sur Bergson," *Europe,* no. 106 (October 1931); "La prudence de M. Bergson," *Commune,* no. 30 (February 1936), provoking a response from Julien Benda, "Parlons d'eux, non avec eux," *Nouvelle Revue Française,* no. 274 (July 1936); "Descartes, Un Prince du Temps modernes," *Europe,* no. 175 (July 1937); also published in the anthology, Maxime LeRoy et. al., *Descartes* (Paris: Rieder, 1937); and *Leibniz et Spinoza* (Paris: Gallimard, 1946).

11. Georges Friedmann, *Ville qui n'a pas de fin!* (Paris: Gallimard, 1931). Quotes from excerpts published in *Cahiers du Sud,* the Marseilles-based literary review, no. 120 (April 1930): 163. The only extant copy in North America is located in the Rare Book Collection of Yale University: I have been informed its condition precludes photocopying. See reviews by Leon-Gabriel Gros in *Cahiers du Sud,* no. 136 (December 1931): 703–704; "Trois recueils de poèmes," *Monde,* no. 174 (3 October 1931): 4.

12. On *Votre Tour Viendra,* see Paul Nizan, *Europe,* no. 99 (March 1931): 430; Benjamin Cremieux, *Nouvelle Revue Française,* no. 210 (March 1931): 446–48, as well as Cremieux's passing comments in *Inquiétude et Reconstruction.* Also see Friedmann's interview with A. Habaru, "Classe 22," *Monde,* no. 130 (29 November 1930): 4. On *L'Adieu,* Magdeleine Paz, *Monde,* no. 231 (5 November 1932): 15; Eugene Dabit, *Europe,* no. 121 (January 1933): 136; Denis Saurat, *Nouvelle Revue Française,* no. 233 (February 1933): 348; Nizan, *Humanité* (2 December 1932): 4. Fernand Baldensperger, in his *La Littérature française entre les deux guerres* (Los Angeles: Lymon House, 1941), compared "J." [!] Friedmann's *Aron* to Galworthy's *Forsyth Saga,* Mann's *Buddenbrooks,* and Martin du Gard's *Thibault* cycle (p. 112).

13. Friedmann, *La Puissance et la Sagesse,* p. 113. Raymond Aron describes being brought back to ENS by Bouglé as secretaire du Centre, in his *Mémoires* (Paris: Julliard, 1983), p. 84; Aron also mentions contact with the exiled Frankfort School in ibid., pp. 85–88, and in *The Committed Observer, interviews with J.-L. Missika and D. Wolton,* trans. J. and M. McIntosh (Chicago: Regnery Gateway, 1983), p. 34. On the Frankfurt School's Parisian Branch, see the passing comment in Martin Jay, *The Dialectical Imagination* (Boston: Little, Brown, 1973), p. 37.

14. Should one characterize the early *Annales* as Marxist, on the Left, and so on? In reaction to the more conservative tendencies of the Braudellian *Annales,*

some younger scholars have emphasized the links discussed in this study. See, for example, Hervé Coutau-Begarie, *Le Phenomene 'Nouvelle Histoiré, Stratégie et idéologique des nouveaux historiens* (Paris: Economica, 1983), which has two second-hand references to Friedmann's work during the 1930s on p. 225. Supporters of the more conservative tendencies within *Annales* ignore or deny the movement's early ties to the Left and Marxism, and generally ignore Friedmann as well. J. R. Suratteau, "Les Historiens, le Marxisme et la Naissance des Annales," in *Au Berceau des Annales*, ed. C.-O. Carbonell and G. Livet (Toulouse: Presses de l'Institut d'Etudes politiques de Toulouse, 1983), offers perhaps the most sensible overview of the relationship between early *Annales* and Marxism. In sum, the scholarly preoccupations of the *Annales* scholars made a confrontation and utilization of Marxist theory inevitable, just as their individual political interests and historical context made it inevitable that some would gravitate toward the Popular Front. To claim more would be as deceitful as to claim less.

15. *La Somme et le Reste*, tome 1, pp. 48–49.

16. Ibid., tome 2, pp. 441–42; on his literary attempts, pp. 340–41, 437–39; and on the *Pravda* incidents, pp. 305, 442–44, and *Les Temps des mèprises* (Paris: Stock, 1975), p. 81.

17. Lefebvre, *Temps des mèprises*, p. 198.

18. Lefebvre, *La Somme et le Reste*, tome 2, p. 453; in *Temps des mèprises*, pp. 83 and 196, Lefebvre spoke of several trips to Germany.

19. The "Cahiers de Revendications" are well known and thoroughly discussed in the works of Loubet del Bayle and Winock listed below. There is a fascinating and growing historiography of French Catholic thinkers and their relations with both the political Left and Right. Among the major studies available see Jean-Louis Loubet del Bayle, *Les Non-Conformistes des Années Trente* (Paris: Editions du Seuil, 1969); René Remond, *Les Catholiques, le Communisme et les crises 1929–1939* (Paris: Armand Colin, 1960); Michel Winock, *Histoire politique de la Revue Esprit 1930–1950* (Paris: Editions du Seuil, 1975); Jean Touchard, "L'Esprit des Années 1930," in *Tendances politiques dans la vie français depuis 1789* (Paris: Hachette, 1960) and his *La Gauche en France depuis 1900* (Paris: Editions du Seuil, 1977). In this last, note Touchard's call for a study of the Philosophies on p. 38. See also Edward Rice-Maximin, "The Main Tendue," *Contemporary French Civilization* 4, no. 2 (winter 1980).

20. Paul Nizan, "Les Consequences du refus," *Nouvelle Revue Française*, no. 231 (December 1932); "Sur un certain Front unique," *Europe*, no. 109 (January 1933); "Lettres sur un certain front unique," *Europe*, no. 110 (February 1933).

21. Henri Lefebvre, "Du culte de «*l'Esprit*» au «Matérialisme dialectique», *Nouvelle Revue Française*, no. 231 (December 1932): 804–805.

22. *Avant-Poste, Revue de Littérature et Critique*, no. 1 (June 1933); no. 2 (August 1933); and no. 3 (October–November 1933). The planned publishing schedule was an unusual eight times annually. A fourth issue had been announced, a special double number devoted to "La Question juive," due out in January 1934. An *Avant-Poste did* appear then, dated January–February, but it contained articles by Catholic nonconformists: Robert Aron, "Le Vrai probleme du travail"; C. Chevalley and A. Marc, "Patrie, Nation, Revolution"; and H. Daniel-Rops, "Vers un ordre nouveau." The standard microfilm copy of *Avant-Poste* contains only the first three issues, and I cannot locate the "other" periodical utilized by Loubet del Bayle for his *Non-conformistes des années trente*. Very few mentions of *Avant-Poste* can be uncovered. Beyond those discussed in the text, see the short barb in the usually genial *Monde*, "Memento des Revues," no. 264 (24 June 1933): 11. Unlike his accounts of *Revue marxiste*, Lefebvre has provided only the briefest of passing references to *Avant-Poste* in *Temps des mèprises*, p. 73.

23. Henri Lefebvre, "Autocritique," *Avant-Poste*, no. 2 (August 1933): 142.

24. Signed "AP," "Une nouvelle revue révolutionnaire: Commune," *Avant-Poste*, no. 2 (August 1933): 139.

25. Henri Lefebvre, "A propos du livre de L. F. Céline," *Avant-Poste* 1 (June 1933): 78. The violence of Avant-Poste is clear from Lefebvre's closing line: "Le désespoir et la colère sont des choses vivantes, tandis que l'avachissement et les vieux râleurs impuissants, c'est encore une variété de la merde, mon vieux Céline."

26. L. F. Céline and Henri Lefebvre, "Lettres," *Avant-Poste*, no. 2 (August 1933): 143–44.

27. This text is the closing section of the "Third Economic and Philosophic Manuscript of 1844" and appeared in *Avant-Poste*, no. 1 (June 1933): 33–39, and in no. 2 (August 1933): 110–16.

28. Henri Lefebvre and Norbert Guterman, "Individu et Classe," *Avant-Poste*, no. 1 (June 1933): 2.

29. Ibid., p. 4.

30. Ibid., p. 9.

31. Henri Lefebvre and Norbert Guterman, "La Mystification, Notes pour une critique de la vie quotidienne," *Avant-Poste*, no. 2 (August 1933): 91–92.

32. Ibid., p. 106.

33. Henri Lefebvre, "Le Fascisme en France," *Avant-Poste*, no. 2 (August 1933): 68–71.

34. Léon Pierre-Quint, "Reponse," *Avant-Poste*, no. 3 (October–November 1933): 148–49. Other respondents included, in no. 2 (August 1933): Victor Margueritte, Jean-Richard Bloch, René Trintzius, Jean Cassou; and in no. 3 (October–November): Bernard Lecache, Alain, and Tristan Rémy. A long and surely provocative response from Emannuel Berl had been announced as well, but Berl yanked his contribution after being the target of some of Lefebvre's verbal bludgeoning, in no. 2, pp. 136–37, followed by further jeering in "Lettre d'un jeune à la jeunesse" in no. 3, p. 184. Lefebvre's intransigence was in marked contrast to Nizan's writings on Berl, Céline, and Drieu la Rochelle. Well into the thirties, Nizan mixed sharp criticism with encouragement, in an apparent effort to swing leading intellectuals of the Right over to the Left.

35. Jean-Richard Bloch, "Reponse," *Avant-Poste*, no. 2 (August 1933): 84.

36. Henri Barbusse, "Reponse," *Avant-Poste*, no. 2 (August 1933): 82–84.

37. L. F. Céline, "Reponse," *Avant-Poste*, no. 2 (August 1933): 87.

38. Andre Malraux, "Reponse," *Avant-Poste*, no. 3 (October–November 1933): 147–48.

39. Edmond Humeau, "Destin du spirituel: factionnaires endormis," *Esprit* 1, no. 11/12 (September 1933): 777. Humeau had already taken a passing shot at Nizan in "Le Jeu des dupes," *Esprit*, no. 8 (March 1933).

40. Ibid., p. 779.

41. Henri Lefebvre, "La revue «*Esprit*»," *Avant-Poste*, no. 3 (October–November 1933): 202–203.

42. Paul Nizan, "Les Enfants de la lumiere," *Commune*, no. 3 (November 1933). Also in Jean-Jacques Brochier, ed., *Paul Nizan, Intellectuel Communiste* (Paris: Maspero, 1967), tome 2, p. 31.

43. Humeau, "Destin du spirituel: catégories révolutionnaires," *Esprit* 2, no. 2 (November 1933): 276.

44. Ibid., p. 280–81.

45. Jacques Bartoli, "Crise de croissance et révolution de l'esprit," *Commune*, no. 4 (December 1933) especially pp. 458–60.

46. Jean Grenier, "*Esprit*," *Nouvelle Revue Française*, no. 255 (December 1934): 934.

47. Ibid., p. 935. Grenier continued his analyses two years later in *Nouvelle Revue Française* with "L'Age des Orthodoxies" in no. 271 (April 1936), and in "L'Orthodoxie contre l'intelligence," no. 275 (August 1936); fragments of Grenier's pamphlet *Essai sur l'Esprit d'orthodoxie* published by Gallimard in 1938. Georges Friedmann provided a response in "Autour d'une manifeste," *Europe*, no. 162 (June 1936).

48. Paul Nizan, "Poèmes des ouvriers americains," *Europe*, no. 94 (October 1930); "Votre tour viendra," *Europe*, no. 99 (March 1931); "Notes de Lecture (L'Adieu)," *L'Humanité* (2 December 1932); "Littérature feminine," *L'Humanité* (20 March 1937); "J. dos Passos: 1919," *Ce Soir* (20 January 1938). In 1932, Nizan also did an odd review of a novel by one "Baruch," *Aron, Friedmann et Cie* (Paris: Flammarion) for *L'Humanité* (20 January 1932): 4, which may have been written by either Morhange or Guterman.

49. Georges Friedmann, "Nizan: Aden Arabie," *Cahiers du Sud*, no. 132 (July 1931); Norbert Guterman and Henri Lefebvre, "Probleme du conscience," *Europe*, no. 175 (July 1937); this issue was also published as a volume entitled *Descartes* by Rieder in 1937.

50. See Jean Luc, "Socialisme et Culture," *Europe*, no. 170 (February 1937).

51. Henri Lefebvre, "Nizan: Materialistes de l'Antiquité; Friedmann: Crise du Progrès; Luppol: Descartes," *Zeitschrift für Sozialforschung*, vol. 6, 1937; "Friedmann: Crise du Progrès," *Nouvelle Revue Française*, no. 275 (August 1936); "Morhange et Matveev: Lettres de Lenine à sa famille," *Europe*, no. 177 (September 1937); Lefebvre also reviewed Henriette Valet's *Madame 60 bis* in *Nouvelle Revue Française*, no. 225 (December 1934).

52. Norbert Guterman, "Nizan: Chiens du Garde," *Avant-Poste*, no. 2 (August 1933): 140–41.

53. Paul Labrenne, "La Cercle de la Russie Neuve (1928–1936) et l'Association pour l'Etude de la Culture Sovietique (1936–1939)," *Pensee*, no. 205 (May–June 1979): 15, 18, 19.

54. Ibid., p. 23.

55. See Georges Friedmann's "Machinisme et Humanisme" and Nizan's "Sur l'Humanisme" published with other presentations from the International Writers' Congress in *Europe*, no. 151 (July 1935); Nizan's essay is also in Brochier's anthology, tome 2.

56. Nizan was one of the signatories of the famous "Lettre à l'AEAR," *Littérature Internationale*, 1934, pp. 119–22, instructing AEAR to simultaneously struggle against fascism, the Left opposition, and social democracy! Friedmann spoke on "«Esclavage» ou liberation" (comparison of labor conditions in the United States and the USSR) according to *Commune*, no. 23 (July 1935): 1338; on "Stakhanovisme" on 19 December 1935 according to *Commune* no. 29 (January 1936): 654; chaired with Lucien Febvre the sessions on Marxism and Science of 5 and 21 March 1936, according to Friedmann's own report in *L'Humanité* (15 March 1936): 8, and the *Commune* report in no. 32 (April 1936): 1040.

57. T. Ferlé, *Le Communisme en France* (Paris: Documentation Catholique, 1937), p. 104; bears the *nihil obstat* and imprimatur indicating official Church approval of the publication. This work (like the author's work on the Ligue des Droits de l'Homme) is often ignored, or shunned, due to Ferlé's links to the Church. Yet *Le Communisme* is a concise source of accurate and verifiable information, since Ferlé's purpose was encyclopedic not polemic.

58. Ibid., p. 99.

59. Ibid., p. 226–27.

60. Regarding Politzer's role as Party spokesman, see C. Cardon and G. Willard, "Intellectuels dans l'Action antifasciste: L'Exemple du CIVA," *Cahiers de l'Institut Maurice Thorez*, no. 33, ns # 5 (October-November 1973): 40–41; *Commune*, no. 16 (December 1934): 412; Ferlé, *Le Communisme*, pp. 93–95; Jacques Varin, *Jeunes comme J. C* (Paris: Editions Sociales, 1975), tome 1 (1920–1939) pp. 239, 249; *Commune*, no. 69 (May 1939): 671. In the words of Danielle Tartakowsky, "[Politzer] va jouer un rôle extrêmement important au niveau de l'élaboration politique: il suffit de rappeler son rôle dans l'élaboration des textes économiques du parti, la place qu'il joue dans le débat mené avec la SFIO sur les questions de l'unité organique, etc.; en dépit de toute l'estime que lui porte Maurice Thorez, il n'aura jamais officiellement un rôle dirigeant, memé s'il assiste comme invité aux sessions du Comité central." Tartakowsky with C. Prevost, "Les intellectuels et le PCF 1920–1940," *Cahiers d' Histoire de l'Institute Maurice Thorez* 9, no. 15, ns# 15 (January–March 1976): 62. Note the frequent and approving references to Nizan in Tartakowsky's writings of the 1970s.

61 Perhaps the most popularly known of all of Politzer's writings, *Elementary Principles of Philosophy*, has been repeatedly reprinted and translated. The second edition was entitled *Cours de Philosophies* (Editions sociales, 1948), tome 1, *Principes élémentaires*, with revised editions appearing in 1966 and 1975. There are several English translations including that made by B. L. Morris from the 1975 French edition (New York: International, 1976). A second volume, *Principes fondamentaux de philosophie*, was released in 1954, but instead of being a compilation of his other writings this was an expanded version of *Principes élémentaires*, listing Politzer with Guy Besse and Maurice Caveing as coauthors. This volume incorporated Politzer's lectures in a heavily revised form, for example his "L'Etat" from *Cours de Marxisme, Première année 1935–1936* (Paris: Bureau d'Editions, 1937), pp. 69–81.

62. Georges Politzer, "Pour qui ecrivez vous," *Commune*, no. 10 (June 1934); in *Ecrits I: La Philosophie et les Mythes* (Paris: Editions Sociales, 1969).

63. Georges Politzer, "L'unité ideologique du Parti," *Cahiers du Bolchevisme* 12,

no. 10/11 (15 May/1 June 1935); "Les Discussions sur le probléme du Parti Unique," *Cahiers du Bolchevisme* 13, no. 1/2 (15 January 1936); "A propos du programme du Rassemblement populaire," *Cahiers du Bolchevisme* 13, no. 3/4 (15 February 1936), reprinted *Nouvelle Critique*, no. 241, ns# 60 (1973); "L'Execution du Programme du Rassemblement populaire," *Cahiers du Bolchevisme* 13, no. 10/11 (15 June 1936).

64. Georges Politzer, *La Pensée française et le Marxisme*, part 1 of Politzer's "Cours de l'Université ouvrière," *Grands problèmes de la philosophie contemporaine* (Paris: Bureau d'Editions, 1938), p. 11.

65. Georges Politzer, "Philosophie des lumières et la pensée moderne," *Cahiers du Bolchevisme*, no. 8 (July 1939); reprinted in *Cahiers du Communisme*, no. 7 (1949); trans. W. Zak, in *Essays on the French Revolution*, ed. T. A. Jackson (London: Lawrence and Wishart, 1945); quotation as in *Ecrits I*, pp. 91–92.

66. Ibid., p. 116.

67. Georges Politzer, "Race, Nation, Peuple," *Commune*, no. 70 (June 1939); *Ecrits I*, p. 75.

68. *Pensée*, no. 1 (April–June 1939): 1–176; no. 2 (July–September 1939): 1–160; no. 3 (October–December 1939): 1–64. The publisher was Editions Sociales Internationales, with offices at 51, rue-le-Prince, two doors down from the old *Revue marxiste* office at no. 47! Politzer finally had his *Annales*. See A. Adler, "Georges Cogniot et la Naissance de «La Pensée»," and G. Milhau, "Georges Politzer et la Raison militante," both in *Pensée*, no. 205 (May–June 1979). Remarkably, *Pensée* released a third issue, despite the closure of all Party-affiliated publications after the Hitler-Stalin pact. While shrinking to a mere 64 pages, *Pensée* still listed ESI as publisher.

69. Georges Politzer, "Philosophie et les mythes," *Pensée*, no. 1 (April–June 1939); *Ecrits I*, pp. 131–32.

70. Ibid., p. 137–42.

71. Georges Politzer, "Dans la Cave de l'aveugle," *Pensée*, no. 2 (July–September 1939); *Ecrits I*, pp. 264–65. Actually, the *Nouvelle Revue Française* review by Jean Guérin appeared in no. 309 (June 1939): 1082; see also Guérin's comment on *Pensée* no. 3 in *Nouvelle Revue Française*, no. 317 (February 1940): 288. The *Esprit* review appeared in no. 81 (June 1939): 450.

72. Politzer, "Dans la Cave de l'aveugle," p. 265.

73. Jean Wahl, *Nouvelle Revue Française*, no. 318 (March 1940): 421–22. See Nizan's review in *Ce Soir* (15 June 1939): 2, and also the review "Philosophie et les mythes" in *Commune*, no. 71 (July 1939) by Georges Sadoul.

74. "Gallia," *Europe*, no. 102 (June 1931): 203–204.

75. Pierre Morhange, *La Vie est Unique* (Paris: Gallimard, 1933); Mme. Mathilde Morhange, in the introductory note to Pierre Morhange's posthumous poems, indicated that Gallimard would be issuing a reimpression (*Europe*, no. 528 [April 1973]: p. 149); I have found no confirmation that a new edition was released. Individual poems were published prior to *La Vie est Unique*, and others were anthologized in *Action poètique*, no. 18 (October 1962). Note Morhange's two poems to "Guter," p. 122–25.

76. *Nouvelle Revue Française*, no. 241 (October 1933): 638–39.

77. *Nouvelle Revue Française*, no. 242 (November 1933): 799–800.

78. *Avant-Poste*, no. 3 (October–November 1933): 204.

79. Pierre Morhange, "Air de flute improvisé pour l'anniversaire de Henri Heine," *Europe*, no. 170 (February 1937): 264–66; and "Poémes d'amour," *Europe*, no. 181 (January 1938): 34–40.

80. Pierre Morhange, "Séparations," *Esprit*, no. 91 (April 1940): 53.

81. Pierre Morhange, "Bible," *Esprit*, no. 91 (April 1940): 54; in *Le Sentiment lui-même* (Honfleur: Editions Pierre Jean Oswald, 1966), p. 46.

Chapter 6

Friedmann:
That Man Might
Become Man

F riedmann's literary career and his activities as an independent scholar of the Left were but a fraction of a hectic professional life embracing teaching, sociological research, philosophic debate, and literary criticism. Throughout the 1930s, Friedmann combined a close scrutiny of the industrial organization of labor with an impassioned but critical support for socialism and the Soviet experiment. In his efforts to comprehend and transform social realities, Friedmann drew from Marxist theory the elements he needed to develop his own methodology, a process culminating in his major works, *La Crise du Progrès* in 1936 and *De la Sainte Russie à l'U.R.S.S.* in 1938. Yet Friedmann's achievements within French political and theoretical debates would be threatened by the changing political contexts and vicious sectarianism on the eve of the Second World War.

Central to Friedmann's intellectual growth were Marx's, Engels's, and Lenin's philosophical writings. Along with his friends of the Philosophies, Friedmann thrilled in his discovery of the *Economic and Philosophic Manuscripts of 1844*, *The German Ideology*, and Lenin's *Philosophic Notebooks* during 1929. The impact of these texts on Friedmann was evident in a shift in what he wrote about. From 1923 through 1930, the writings of Georges Friedmann can be described as broadly philosophic, political, or literary. In early 1931, the first of his writings on the organization of labor and mechanization appeared, themes occupying an increasing and finally a dominant position in his oeuvre. To better understand the labor process of his times, Friedmann engaged in the usual scholarly activities of collecting statistics, carrying out surveys, and critically absorbing the relevant academic literature. Most unusual, however, was his decision to work as an apprentice machinist during the year 1932–1933 at École professionelle Diderot in Paris, the sort of training avoided by most academics like the plague. His firsthand experience with machines, combined with his continuing theoretical studies, enabled Friedmann to focus on the qualitative aspects of the labor process in a way that few others could.

Despite Friedmann's tremendous productivity during the 1930s, he never provided a single coherent statement of theory, no detailed exposition specifically outlining his method. While several procedures offer insight into recreating Friedmann's theoretical position in the 1930s, the most useful is to focus on Friedmann's writings containing repeated references to specific Marxist texts. Most frequently, one can find *Ludvig Feuerbach and the end of classic philosophy* (the Les Revues pamphlet of 1929), *From One Holy Family to Another*, *The German Ideology*, *Capital*, *The Manifesto*, *The Poverty of Philosophy*, and the *Philosophic Notebooks* of Lenin. Anthologies of Marx's, writings like *Oeuvres philosophiques*, *Etudes philosophiques*, and *Morceaux choisis de Marx* were frequently cited, along with letters written by Engels. Each of the specific references by Friedmann was to a text or passage in which Marx, Engels, or Lenin wrote on methodology. For example, in *L'Humanité*, 22 October 1935, Friedmann reviewed a French anthology of Lenin's writings, and, after the obligatory homage to *State and Revolution* and *Materialism and Empirio-Criticism*, devoted the bulk of his review to "On the Importance of militant materialism," the essay contained in *Revue marxiste* six years earlier.[1]

How Friedmann employed these texts to construct his own analytical methods can be reconstructed from a number of short essays and published lectures on Marxism he presented during the 1930s. The earliest and best known of these was his "Matérialisme dialectique et action réciproque," contained in the first volume of *À la Lumiere du Marxisme*, a 1934 anthology representing an important introduction of Marxist theory into French academic discourse. Friedmann's essay was given added weight when also printed in *Commune*. Friedmann denied the prevailing view that Marxism was simply an economic fatalism where all details of noneconomic life were determined by production. To reconstruct Marxism, he turned back to the history of philosophy and found that "the historians of Marxism are recognizing more and more completely the considerable influence of Spinoza on the philosophic formation of Marx and Engels."[2] For Friedmann, Spinoza remained a revolutionary thinker, affirming the existence of an infinite Nature which caused itself without divine intervention. Hegel's idealist transcendence of Spinoza established the relations between phenomena, and especially the reciprocity between *esprit*, as mind and spirit, and its material reality. When Marx and Engels stood the Hegelian dialectic on its feet, therefore, they had absorbed and transformed the heritage of Spinoza. Nor was it surprising that, along with this emphasis on the heritage of his favorite philosopher, Friedmann also recommended *Les Cahiers philosophiques* of Lenin as the "crucial document for the study of the philosophic foundations of Marxism."[3]

Friedmann dated the emergence of Marxist dialectics to the *German Ideology*:

> The dialectic had become materialist. Causality, which, for Hegel, goes, in the last analysis, always from idea to idea (the material world was only itself considered as a dispersion of the Absolute Idea), goes here [in the *German Ideology*] essentially to the material—and more precisely to the relations of production where men are active,—toward the social, the political, the spiritual.[4]

This reversal clarified the role of human free will in history, but Friedmann thought it was itself clouded by the interpretation of some of Marx's own texts. This dilemma within Marxism was, for Friedmann, was summed up in that troublesome phrase of the *Eighteenth Brumaire*, "Men make their own history, but not as just they please; not under conditions they themselves have chosen but under the conditions directly given and inherited from the past." The confusion of many, Friedmann claimed, lie in the mental substitution of cause for condition. Instead of the rigid determinism displayed by detractors and even some supporters of Marxism, Friedmann envisioned Marxism as a method of analyzing the conditions restricting the range of possible options for human activity. And, at the heart of Marxist analysis, Friedmann located labor as the key to comprehending human social existence:

> This constant exchange of action between nature and man had its origin in labor. It is by the production of the means of existence that Man commenced his history properly human, and that a simply biologic, animal evolution—where Man is himself absorbed into Nature and its evolution—gave way to the development of interaction between Man the producer and milieu. . . .[5]

In his understanding of Marxism, then, Friedmann embedded the labor process as transformative and establishing the material conditions of life. Equally important was his insistence that these conditions limited but did not absolutely determine or cause human activities or consciousness.

Friedmann explored this intersection in "Machine et Humanisme," presented to the Congrès International des Ecrivains la pour Défense de la Culture, held in Paris during June 1935 and published in *Europe* in July. If the interactions between men and between Man and Nature, as well as human history itself, all originate in labor, then, Friedmann argued, these relationships are mediated through machines. In a series of brief reflections Friedmann underscored the liberating potential embedded within the mediating machine. Having defined the potential goal of human history as a reintegration of human thought and action through labor with machines, Friedmann then measured the world around him against this ideal. The scientific organization of capitalist societies "has increasingly separated from each other the idea and the process of working," and hence accelerated human alienation, *l'inquiétude*.[6] But, in 1935, another option appeared possible, "the Machine controlled by the finally fraternal collaboration of scholars and of engineers with the workers."[7] In other words it appeared as if the resolution could be achieved, was being achieved, in the Soviet Union. And, in *De la Sainte Russie à l'U.R.S.S.* and other writings, Friedmann would measure Soviet success and failure by the same criteria he applied to capitalist societies: Was human alienation being overcome?

The last of Friedmann's articles on Marxism, "Les rapports de la conscience des hommes et des conditions économiques," was published in *Cours du Marxisme 2e année*. Friedmann again scolded those adversaries and supposed defenders of Marxism who omitted or deemphasized the importance of self-conscious human action: "How could there be a revolutionary doctrine which denies its efficacy to [human] energy, to action?"[8] And again, he turned to the dilemma of the *Eighteenth Brumaire*:

On the one hand, the will of men: Men make their own history. But they make it within conditions that they have not chosen:—in sum the influence of historical conditions and on the other hand the will of men who are inserted into those conditions.[9]

Friedmann posed the obvious question himself:

One can see that, in this manner, Marxism reinserts the living and active man into a totality, and there with him places his consciousness and his beliefs. But then, if there is reciprocal action of the economic conditions and of consciousness, where is the decisive action?[10]

His answer was a very brief, apparently orthodox statement:

The decisive action, Marx and Engels have clearly affirmed, is that of the economic, because labor, the production of the means of subsistence, had for them a fundamental importance.[11]

But note well how Friedmann chose his words: The economic is defined as the same thing as labor. For Friedmann, it was the concrete, specific, and synthetic processes of laboring, and not the statistical or structural abstractions of the economy, that really mattered. And, as Friedmann noted, when one says labor one speaks of machines as mediations.

In his choice of Spinoza and Leibniz as guides, Georges Friedmann revealed himself as representative of the new generation of inquiet youth and defined the problem he would devote his life to. In his autobiographical *La Puissance et la Sagesse*, Friedmann suggested the link between his earlier *inquiétude* and his interest in Marxism:

I was driven to reconcile the texts of the great theorists, Lenin included, with my fervent quest for a humanism founded on free will, my tension toward a socialist society where all the essential problems of existence would be resolved (and even many disorders, sufferings of mental and emotional life that I placed much too easily to the account of organic faults of capitalist society).[12]

In turning to Marxism for a remedy for the "sufferings of mental and emotional life," Friedmann consciously sought to comprehend and to banish *la mal du siècle*, the *inquiétude* of his generation. Thus, the fortuitous arrival of the "1844 Manuscripts" and other works of Marxist theory at the offices of Les Revues in 1929 provided the bridge for Friedmann to overcome, in the classic sense of *aufheben* and *depasser*, his *inquiétude*. Marx's "Manuscripts" led Friedmann back to the Lord-Bondsman relationship in the *Phenomenology of Spirit*, to the mediating "thing" interposed in social relations and between Man and Nature, to the machine. With these insights, the abyss dividing the individual and the universal, human alienation (*inquiétude*) and the absence of any unifying vision of the world (*la mal du siècle*) became resolvable problems. In an unorthodox Marxism offering the liberation of both Spirit and Matter, Friedmann found what he and his suffering generation desired above all things: a method leading to salvation.

Yet in his 1936 *Crise du Progrès*, Friedmann warned that the road he and so many others sought was in danger of being blocked. Incorporating several published essays, Friedmann had worked on *La Crise* for the previous two years. The result of his efforts was a remarkably lucid, even lyrical, presentation of the entwined relations between the political, economic, strictly philosophic, and broad cultural developments of the West in the previous half-century. Unlike the crude generalizations of most panoramic works, Friedmann fashioned minute details from industrial economics and from the most abstract contemporary philosophers into a convincing portrait of modern human existence as a totality. A perceptive and incisive exposé of the anxieties of the time of its composition, *Crise du Progrès* retains a continuing relevance, an insistent pertinence, for the last decades of a century that shares many of the preoccupations and anxieties of its earlier years.

To understand Man and to envision history in its fullness, Friedmann focused his inquiry on those fears and desires represented by the idea of progress:

> The idea of progress is one aspect of the reflection of Man on his destiny. It is one of the principle value judgments that Man places on his condition, in the past, in the present and in the future.[13]

Better still, Friedmann added, to speak of multiple ideas of progress, each composed of extremely complex and variable elements, and reflecting widely variable levels of human maturity as well. Moreover, in the variety of these images where Man regards and judges his condition and his future, Friedmann located the search for the eternals and absolutes of life, the basic questions posed by all individuals.

Friedmann provided a broad survey of the tremendous transformations of the past two centuries, when confident perceptions of science and philosophy marched hand in hand with the industrial and political revolutions. Yet Friedmann also found these same years witnessed a resurgence of ideologies hostile to science and the values of progress, exemplified by Bergson as the key antagonist in the struggle against the mechanistic and materialist excesses of early psychology and biology. However, Friedmann continued, Bergsonism also

> constituted a pole of attraction for all the irrationalist movements in France and abroad. One knows that this intuitionism, with its persevering critique of intelligence and of science, with its scale of values where the highest degrees are always reserved, beyond the conceptualizing and superficial intelligence, to the "profound" realities, life, *durée*, instinct, with its marked sympathy for religious life,—one knows that this doctrine in fact supplied all the adversaries of progressive ideas in the struggle that they engaged in at the beginning of the century.[14]

The fin-de-siècle schisms developing within bourgeois consciousness also were, Friedmann observed, reflected within the working class movements, where the apocalyptic visions of Sorel jostled the mechanistic orthodoxy of Kautsky. With the cataclysm of the Great War, both paths of led to disaster. Only a few pockets of activists around the world—in France, in the Industrial Workers of the World of North America, and in the Bolsheviks—retained the confidence and the vision of earlier days.

This failure within the socialist movements permitted a resurgence of capitalist domination. Along with political liberalism, as exemplified by the global vision of Wilsonian democracy, Friedmann saw the early postwar years as dominated by the figures of Frederick Taylor and Henry Ford, offering, despite apparent differences, new justifications for capitalist domination. Taylor advocated collaboration between employer, engineer, and employees in the "scientific" organization of industrial labor, a swindle in Friedmann's eyes that merely intensified the fragmentation of human activities and increased individual alienation. Ford, by advocating the rational utilization of machines, promised a harmonious collaboration between industry and general public, an endless flow of products, ever-increasing wages with which to buy, and ever-increasing employment. An admirable loop on paper, Friedmann sneered, if one ignored the increasing speed of contrived social and economic changes, the artificiality of consumer needs, the lag time between parity in prices and wages, and basic questions of the proportional redistribution of buying power between classes. Liberty for Ford, Friedmann scoffed, lay in the ability to consume products, the need for which was artificially created—by Ford! Where, Friedmann asked, was the liberty of Man in that?

Twentieth-century thought, Friedmann remarked, reacted in its own fashion to the war, to the economic and political crises, and to the simple mechanistic materialism underlying capitalism. Friedmann argued that contemporary phenomenology, as typified by Heidegger and Husserl, abstractly reflected material realities by granting primacy to extratemporal essences accessible only through intuition and thus relegating the existence of immediate forms, of science, and of contingency to inferior theoretical positions. What became of reality, of Nature and of Man in phenomenology, Friedmann asked, if:

> Phenomenology demands even of itself a fundamental sacrifice, a sort of abandonment of all questions concerning the reality of objects which correspond to essences. All the material of the sciences, of Nature, and of the sciences of Man is, so to speak, placed between parentheses—and reserved.[15]

For Friedmann, this refusal to judge, to compare, to affirm or deny was common within phenomenological thought, but particularly, distastefully present in Heidegger, who left the isolated individual confronting unknowable and overpowering daily forces, to be finally overwhelmed in an anguished confrontation with nothingness.

Friedmann presented these worries, debates, and irrationalisms as parts of the totality of his times and reflective of postwar realities. According to Friedmann, the postwar era constituted a crucial stage within the development of the idea of progress, requiring a clear-cut solution. Friedmann argued that the only solution was a revival of the idea of progress, and moreover asserted:

> The idea of progress is at the heart of Marxism, renewed by the dialectic. It is at this point today that, in the West, spiritualist intellectuals strain themselves in the battle recalling and deforming this characteristic.
>
> Everything is tension within Marxism. Tension of the will of a class to transcend [*depasser*] its condition, heavy with its revolutionary energy, in good position and at the right moment, above social contradictions. Hopes for a true democracy where liberty ceases to be irremediably abstracted by the alienations of Man, where equality authentically becomes equality at the start of unequal courses. . . . It demands that each individual may in all justice take his chance, his progress.[16]

Marxism, for Friedmann, required an alliance of humanist reason with science, a bond necessary so that Marxism "may look reality in the face."[17] The insights of science could be used to open new doors on the future, to correct mistakes, and to define the possible. But ultimately human beings make their own history, and thus require an ever-evolving ethical vision of human perfectibility and progress. As such, Friedmann's Marxism was scientifically grounded protest against the alienation of humanity's potential within class societies, and Marxism became, in its vision of human liberation, "a technique of human progress."[18]

La Crise du Progrès was received with tremendous excitement and acclaim, and remains as a monument to Friedmann's vision of the world as it existed—and could exist. The hope in the future of human progress Friedmann proclaimed was widely shared, and even as the book rolled off the presses of Gallimard, was taking concrete form in the French Popular Front.

Ironically, those hopes were being undermined at the same moment. André Gide, that prestigious if unreliable acquisition of the Popular Front, published his *Return from the U.S.S.R.* in late 1936. His experiences during a summer's tour led Gide noisily away from the Popular Front at precisely the moment when it was enjoying its greatest support. Gide claimed he had been driven to visit the USSR by the unfairness and stupidity of its critics. Gide's *Return* conveyed his impressions Maksim Gorky's funeral, and of his contacts with Soviet intellectual and political figures. But outside the major Soviet cities, Gide found himself receiving preferential treatment, isolated from the everyday people around him, and increasingly dismayed by what he saw. Gide noticed that to obtain the most basic goods, endless queues formed, although he was struck by the orderliness of crowds and the lack of coercive controls. But discussions with Soviet intellectuals and Party members led him to bemoan a general loss of individualism, of conformity to the Party line, and a parallel decline in artistic creativity. The growing cult of Stalin was disconcerting but understandable, Gide thought, who did credit Stalin with the implementation and overall success of the five-year plans. Overall, Gide presented the Soviet Union with, at best, an extreme caution tinged by a slight optimism, and at worst as a failing experiment to be avoided:

> Good and bad alike are to be found there; I should say rather: the best and the worst. The best was often achieved only by an immense effort. That effort has not always and everywhere achieved what it set out to achieve. Sometimes one is able to think: not yet. Sometimes the worst accompanies and overshadows the best; it almost seems as if it were a consequence of the best. And one passes from the brightest light to the darkest shade with a disconcerting abruptness.[19]

Gide's *Return* quickly became a best-seller, frequently quoted by critics of the Soviets and the Popular Front. Unsurprisingly, Gide and his memoir were sharply attacked by Popular Front supporters as a threat to their hard-won and newfound political position.

Among all the responses to Gide, *Nouvelle Revue Française* commented in May 1937, the best was that of Georges Friedmann.[20] In fact, of all French observers of Soviet life, Friedmann was perhaps the most qualified to write about the Soviet Union. Friedmann had been publishing articles on the economic and social organization of the USSR, drawing upon the firsthand experiences of three trips to the Soviet Union during 1932, 1933, and 1936. Nor were his writings mere hymns of praise for the five-year plans, for Friedmann constantly measured stated goals against actual progress. His series of articles in *Monde,* begun during 1931, were collected as *Problèmes du machinisme en U.R.S.S. et dans les pays capitalistes,* released by Editions Sociales Internationales in 1934.[21] The journal *Europe* frequently served as a prepublication sounding board for Friedmann.[22] The scholarly significance of Friedmann's research was highlighted by the fact that some of his pieces on the Soviet experiment were carried in *Annales d'Histoire économique et sociale,* which tolerated neither shoddy craftsmanship nor polemical partisanship. For many French intellectuals, Friedmann was the expert on Soviet social, economic, and cultural life.

In his response to Gide, carried as the lead article of *Europe* for January 1936, Friedmann avoided the polemics of other reviewers and drew on his personal knowledge of the Soviet Union. "The testimony of André Gide on the Soviet Union poses a series of problems important to look in the face," Friedmann admitted, and suggested that "to comment on it, it would take another book consecrated to the USSR."[23] Friedmann allowed Gide some leeway, since the novelist at least admitted being disinterested in and even baffled by social and economic questions. But, as Friedmann pointed out, it was precisely those aspects of Soviet life that mattered most. Thus, Friedmann the specialist patiently corrected Gide's misconceptions.

On conformism, Friedmann noted that Gide only had direct contacts with intellectuals. But he admitted that the brilliance of Lenin and the early Bolsheviks was being replaced by prolonged polemics where unpleasant epithets and rote repetition of formulas and citations were hindering scientific and philosophic research. Friedmann himself thought such a low level of debate insufferable and alien to the founders of Marxism. Still, he was willing to try to comprehend the situation as a necessary manifestation of Soviet domestic problems as the Party and citizens struggled to transform their country. This same explanation served to answer Gide's complaints about the decline of the creative arts, since if art was subservient to political and social needs, there could be no cult of pure art of the type Gide espoused. What Gide ignored, Friedmann claimed, was the basic fact that the cultural level of the people had been raised at a tremendously fast pace. Illiteracy was disappearing, and the libraries were crowded with the previously ignorant seeking to absorb all of the great works of literature, reflecting popular efforts to forge a new humanity through education.

Still, there remained elements of Gide's *Return from the U.S.S.R.* that Friedmann could not attribute to lack of direct contact or insufficient understanding. In particular, Friedmann was surprised that "this series of psychological, moral impressions, is also, on the most diverse questions, the most broad and protruding, a series of verdicts."[24] Friedmann thought Gide overlooked the political impact of his book, and failed to take the measure of the specific historical situation in which it would appear. For Friedmann, Gide failed to assume responsibility for this impact, and for his tendency to slide from the psychological to the political.[25] "Dear André Gide," Friedmann concluded,

> I do not approve of all that I have seen in the Soviet Union. I have told you that. I've said it, on my return, to some friends of the USSR more senior and more constant. We retain, we also, our critical spirit before the enormous soviet reality.[26]

When Gide attempted to respond to his critics by publishing *Retouches à mon Retour de l'U.R.S.S.*, Friedmann responded a second time, in part by quoting his own denunciation of "irresponsibles"—that critique of intellectuals who shirked the political and social battles of their day—originally published in *Esprit* back in 1926.

And, in 1938, Friedmann published the book he thought was necessary to answer Gide and other vacillating critics of the Soviet Union. All of Friedmann's explorations and anxieties of the twenties, all of his purposeful self-immersement into the theory and practice of labor, his search for philosophical guides leading to human liberation, and his scrutiny and adoption of Marxism—in brief, Friedmann's intellectual and political trajectory for a decade and a half—was poured into his most important work of the interwar years, *De la Sainte Russie à l'U.R.S.S.*

Friedmann, mindful of his own criticisms of Gide, clarified the limits and purposes of his work in order to minimalize misunderstandings while enhancing its effectiveness:

> I know the limits of this book which has no pretense of being a "Summa" on the USSR. I have deliberately restricted myself to domains which I have personally investigated in the course of three stays between Sep-

tember 1932 and October 1936: education, industry, the material and intellectual conditions of the workers, the discussions in the realm of practical morality, of art, of science, of philosophy have held my interest the longest. . . .

This adherence to limitation presents some inconveniences that I weighed from the first and an advantage which appears to me decisive: The USSR is a complex world where more than elsewhere, as a consequence of the planned structure of the social economy, everything happening is closely tied together. Would it not be better to know several links of the chain than to allow it, in the end, to slide totally through one's hands and be left holding nothing?[28]

De la Sainte Russie opens with an overview of the social and economic structure of Imperial Russia on the eve of the Great War. Friedmann contrasted the disparity between the gigantic natural resources of Russia and its actual level of development, and its dependence upon the more industrialized producers of Europe. Friedmann, like many others, noted that the recent introduction of industrial techniques into Russian society created islands of highly advanced industrial centers surrounded with extremely backward countrysides. Yet while the industrial workforce in 1914 might have totaled perhaps 7 percent of the Russian population, the bulk of these workers were concentrated in factories employing more than a thousand, dwarfing, as Friedmann pointed out, most French industries. The intellectual stranglehold of the state-controlled Orthodox Church, the corrupt and inefficient imperial bureaucracy, and the extreme misery of the peasantry all made czarist Russia, in Friedmann's eyes, a land out of the Middle Ages and not of the twentieth century.

From the Russia of 1914, Friedmann turned immediately to the situation of the USSR in the 1930s, focusing primarily on education and industry. Friedmann emphasized that, from the onset of the October Revolution, the planning, development, and success of the Soviet educational system had been a continuous priority, and, as Friedmann himself worded it, "the life and the efforts of the school, mirror of all the struggles, of the difficulties and the problems which have risen in the other domains" were at the very heart of the Soviet experiment.[29] To cope with an illiteracy rate approaching 63 percent, the commissariat of instruction linked manual and intellectual instruction as essential parts of all education, and devoted its energies to constructing the Soviet system of education. Polytechism, as Friedmann reminded his reader, was a dream central to all socialist theorists,

> precisely one that should allow the child, as future citizen, to take from the multiplicity of modern techniques the common elements which will permit him to be a skilled worker—but also, beyond depressing specialization—of being a man.[30]

Yet the initial attempts to create "Soviet Man" and develop a comprehensive program of socialist humanism suffered before the realities of developing Soviet institutions and programs, and before the continual redefinition of problems as attempted solutions succeeded or failed. Despite all difficulties, Friedmann emphasized the dramatic annual expansion of Soviet education, in terms of numbers of students enrolled, of the number of schools built, and of the increasingly comprehensive programs. Friedmann even compared the rapid decline of illiteracy in the USSR to the persistence of low literacy rates among military recruits from the French departments abutting the Pyrénées!

Friedmann placed Soviet industrial achievements into the contexts of the end of the civil war, when the country lay in ruins, and the practical and necessary respite of the New Economic Policy (NEP) years. The unevenness of the Soviet preparations for the leap into massive industrial development of the five-year plans was evident to Friedmann on all levels, from regional disparities to the intangibles of individual lives. For example, in even the most progressive plants he visited, Friedmann witnessed both the confidence of some workers in their confrontation with technology and the indifference of their coworkers who remained staring spectators instead of working. While the use of Fordist methods led some alarmed observers to decry an idolatry of the machine, Friedmann argued that this emphasis on the machine indicated

> the combat of the Machine against the Russian Middle Ages, simultaneously in the material world (the Machine permitting the exploitation of this very rich portion of the Earth) and within the mind (transition from the mystical and ignorant masses toward a rational attitude).[31]

Even more astounding, Friedmann emphasized, was that the process was only just begun:

> Soviet industry is not therefore a finished fact. Any truly modern industry in the world is never finished, in the USSR even less than elsewhere where all is being made ... schools, theaters, museums, scientific institutes—dockyards and workshops—are constantly, according to the expression that I have heard a hundred times, in "grand renovation." Minds as well. Nonetheless the achievement is considerable.[32]

Friedmann saw the 1930s as a heroic time in which the pioneer and the machine were joined on the frontiers of human history. For Friedmann, in creating this new economic basis, the constraints of the past were being broken and the minimum material preconditions for a new culture constructed.

From polytechnical education and industrialization, Friedmann turned to Soviet advances and debates in science, philosophy, literature, art, and history in an effort to explain for his French audience those seemingly incomprehensible squabbles between "mechanist" and "idealist" Marxists, the rise and fall of the historian Pokrovsky, and the byzantine quarrels surrounding Soviet literature. Friedmann blamed the temptation among Soviet intellectuals to retreat into a comfortable, but acceptable, safe formalism on the political importance of intellectual debates, a tendency he thought might give rise to an increasing risk of intellectual disinterest in the real social and political problems confronting the Soviets. Friedmann attributed the heated Soviet debates about theory, and particularly philosophy, to the fact that idealism and mechanism mirrored the concrete reality of the USSR. The abstract philosophical struggles of the late 1920s represented a search for a practical method to transform the Soviet Union from a backward agrarian society, a transformation achievable neither by sheer will alone, nor by the simple application of massive quantities of labor or material, but requiring both.

Against this backdrop, Friedmann admitted and discussed the disturbing problems evident in the transformation from the czarist past toward an uncertain future. In comparison to the czarist pogroms and intolerance, Friedmann suggested that a confused and tortuous future opened to Soviet Jews, including the extreme but real possibility of total assimilation and the disappearance of the Jews as a distinct entity within the Soviet Union. Yet Friedmann did not dismiss the persistence of anti-Semitism and of traditional prejudices other ethnic and linguistic populations of the USSR did not confront.

Among the central problems confronting the Soviet transformation, Friedmann particularly feared that the legal rights of abortion and divorce, two early and popular reforms of the Bolsheviks, were being eroded and destroyed by an officially sanctioned campaign to inculcate a new cult of the family, although he mitigated his concerns by recalling personal contacts who had approached questions of love, sex, child rearing, and parental duty with a keen sense of individual and social responsibility.

More troublesome for Friedmann was the direction taken by the Soviet search for ideological cohesion in a new patriotism. By breaking the ideological power of the church, by demolishing the czarist state, and by demystifying the possession of knowledge through the expansion and transformation of education, many of the sinews binding together the sprawling Soviet Union had been torn away. At the same time, a conscious sense of difference separated the Soviet citizen, as member of a socialist society in formation, from the rest of the world, seen by the average Soviet as totally dominated by the capitalists. This sense of accomplishment and difference paradoxically fostered a form of nationalism and an attitude of superiority in a society that was seeking to transcend human distinctions.

Friedmann also tackled the disquieting growth of the cult of the chief, which he saw evident in the ritual invocation of Stalin's words, the proliferation of his portraits, and the unceasing tales of his personal intervention in every sphere of everyday life. While not ignoring the disturbing political ramifications of the cult, Friedmann argued that the shift to a policy of "socialism in one country," of a vision of Soviet society besieged by enemies, entailed an identification by individual citizens with the Party line, with the Party itself as the guide to the future. On a psychological level, Friedmann claimed, the identification of the individual with the Party was symbolized by an identification with the Party's general secretary, Stalin. Yet, while Friedmann admitted that this explanation was the most sensible for him, he viewed the cult as a break with the doctrine of Marx, of Engels, and of Lenin, a sort of "moral NEP."[33]

Friedmann's willingness to accept the cult of Stalin as a necessity of a historically specific moment had its clear limits. In particular, Friedmann expressed disappointment about Soviet failures in the realm of theory, a failure he directly linked to the emphasis on "elaborating the oeuvre of Lenin and Stalin(?), popularizing them."[34] After inserting that disbelieving question mark, Friedmann continued:

> The cult of Stalin—politically and socially justifiable—has certainly not had happy effects on the development of intellectual and artistic life. I have a great admiration for Stalin the statesman: I do not see the necessity of transforming him today into a philosopher, tomorrow into the theoretician of architecture, of mathematics, of dance, or of the theater. I am convinced, whatever certain overzealous officials might think, that he himself does not see the necessity either.[35]

Even more, Friedmann made no effort to avoid the question of Trotsky:

> The future historian, closely reading the theoretical writings of Stalin and those of Trotsky, will not be able to not see that the ends for both are identical. It will be a question above all of a schism over the means, "permanent revolution" or "socialism in one country," and of an opposition of temperaments where the consuming vanity of Trotsky played havoc.[36]

For Friedmann, the Soviet struggle to create socialism was a process embedded within conditions not of their own choice. The necessity of overcoming the material constraints inherited from the czars of war Communism with its images of immediate heroism, and of the NEP as the final program of an infallible Lenin, for Friedmann, had been replaced by the new necessity of patiently creating socialism in one country. Yet, paradoxically, this project of socialist construction in one country also required the worldwide participation and an effort to understand and to constructively criticize by all who supported the experiment:

> It is not a question of Paradise but better still one of a gigantic effort on Earth toward happiness and culture, raised against all the traps of people

and of things within the most backward country, in an epoch where grand capital, behind the mask of fascism, kindles around the world the most singularly skillful and cruel oppression. The USSR deserves to know what its friends in the West think of it. It even has need of knowing. Marxism, if it is not lucid and self-critical, is unfaithful to itself. Every flattery is a danger. The USSR, a regime I think has an unique solidity because it builds itself on the support of the largest of popular masses, is hence strong enough to, aside from praises, listen to friendly criticisms. The discarding of a certain mystical attitude in regarding the USSR will help make it possible to assess the interest in it, actually latent in many of the best of the West. It will serve, among other things, the cause of workers' unity in the democratic countries, France, England, the United States. It will not weaken the positions of the USSR, but, on the contrary, in making it better understood, strengthen it and sustain the indispensable current which should be established, for future profit, between bolshevism and western socialism.[37]

De la Sainte Russie à l'U.R.S.S. is unlike any other study of the early Soviet Union. Friedmann did not write a hymn of praise to Lenin's brilliance or to the historical development of the Bolsheviks, and downplayed without avoiding the conflicts between Trotsky, Stalin, and the other Bolshevik leaders. The key to understanding *De la Sainte Russie* can be found the structure Friedmann employed. The opening chapter on czarist Russia provides the concrete backdrop against which Friedmann sketched in the struggles to transform Russia into not simply an industrial but into a socialist society. This portrait of prerevolutionary Russia was essential to Friedmann's conception of the proper manner of studying human events, for the problems of prerevolutionary Russia were precisely those conditions directly given and inherited from the past within which men make their own history. Friedmann's conception of the *Annales* project, as embodied in *De la Sainte Russie*, provides a glaring contrast to the immobile world of his contemporary and fellow *annaliste* Fernand Braudel. Unlike the Braudellian paradigm, with its elevation of the conditions underlying human life to a position so dominant that human efforts and events were reduced to insignificance and virtually disappeared, Friedmann emphasized the human creative drama.

In the very opening lines of his review for *Etudes*, Henri du Passage made clear his criteria for judging Friedmann's work:

> M. Friedmann is a convinced Marxist. The USSR may therefore appear to him as, if not paradise realized, at least the promised land of his hopes.[38]

While willing to accept that what he termed Soviet "state capitalism" had at least improved the daily life of most, du Passage suggested greater continuity existed in Soviet adoration of Stalin, an adoration he viewed as a cynical but necessary substitution for the icons of religion. And in his closing lines du Passage returned to the themes closest to his heart:

> On religion, M. Friedmann has only several paragraphs concerning the "superstitions" of yesteryear and the discredit of the popes. Evidently, here, the work of the USSR appears to him entirely praiseworthy. And not for an instant does he even allow the hypothesis that to remove God from an entire people may constitute the worst of crimes.

In the July issue of *Esprit*, Georges Duveau reviewed Friedmann's *De la Sainte Russie* as part of a clump of eight books, including Trotsky's *Crimes of Stalin* and Victor Serge's *Destiny of a Revolution*. Thus, little space could be given to most of the books Duveau reviewed, and *De la Sainte Russie* received only a few lines:

> The Friedmann case is moving; Friedmann, Marxist pedagogue, wants to think well of the Soviet system. But this hyperinformed philosophe refuses to set any traps and at every instance when he pleads the Russian dossier, he defends it with a quiet style, he wants to convince with dignity. Few books are more susceptible than this one by Friedmann of serving the Soviet cause. With Friedmann one feels one is in good company. One is faced with a guide who tells us: "These people here fail often; all is not perfect in Russia; but in the end several things being built there merit sympathy."[39]

Still, in a brief closing line, Duveau, like du Passage, managed to weave in a barb, noting that Friedmann had "consecrated to the militarization of the

spirit in the Soviet Union a chapter of an extraordinary and of a involun-
tary virtuosity."

The responses by PCF intellectuals initiated what would become the
Friedmann affair. Jean Bruhat, long a colleague of Friedmann, reviewed *De
la Sainte Russie* first in *L'Humanité* of 21 April 1938, with excerpts in April's
Cahiers du Bolchevisme as well. Bruhat blasted at Friedmann's presumption to
judge the USSR in any fashion, scolding in unintentional imitation of du
Passage:

> Friedmann reports that in the USSR all is not perfect. Naturally! We have
> not said that the USSR was a paradise. The entire matter was, however,
> one for Soviet self-criticism and practice, not the opinionated judgments
> of some erring Frenchman.[40]

Only halfway through Bruhat's review did the essential point emerge: Friedmann had written some truly disconcerting pages on the Moscow trials and
on the Trotskyists. Whereas the trials led Friedmann to ask if the Party was
truly democratic and if the Trotskyists were truly guilty, Bruhat insisted
Trotsky and Bukharin were traitors, period—and he quoted Stalin as
authority. Even when Bruhat admitted, quite simply, that Friedmann was fully
aware of the USSR's place in history, he was unwilling to grant credence to
Friedmann's misgivings. Instead, Bruhat, in direct if less well-crafted imitation of Friedmann's own reviews of Gide, claimed that Friedmann

> takes a personal opinion (several times, a simple impression) for a uni-
> versal judgement. That is always the flipside to objectivity. That is to
> deform, without wishing it, reality. That is to forget, when one discusses
> of the USSR, that it should be studied not from an external vantage
> point, but from the interior, and that the personality of the author should
> disappear before the reality that he describes and explains. We should not
> imitate André Gide at all, even when it is a question of writing a sympa-
> thetic book on the USSR.[41]

After this old colleague's blast came another, from Paul Nizan in *Commune* of May 1938. Although many of the same points were scored at
Friedmann's expense, there was a tremendous difference in tone and

meaning in Nizan's review. Friedmann provided an excellent picture of "Holy Russia," Nizan began, and added that there were also "precise, informed, convincing chapters on several essential aspects of the Soviet reality. . . ."[42] At the end of a lengthy list of those areas Friedmann had gotten "right," Nizan paused to praise Friedmann for writing what Nizan called "some remarkable analyses of shock labor and of Stakhanovism, a subject on which too many were confused." Still, Nizan had misgivings:

> The testimony of Friedmann carries within the domains where he is expressly informed, where he has a specialist's competence. But he himself would not want me to not make at all several reservations which appear necessary to me: I know well that he expresses the willingness of serving the USSR by his criticisms themselves, but I ask myself if his genre of critique is not precisely of the type which risks injuring more subtly the cause that he desires to defend.[43]

Nizan alluded to his own *Chiens du Garde* published eight years earlier, suggesting

> . . . there is another type of criticism, that I will call the clerical critique, because it is proper to the cleric who judges himself authorized in general to give personal counsel to history and to assign a course to it. This critique is based on the feeling that the cleric has his right to reticence. He distributes therefore his warnings and establishes his proper tables of values; his mind [*esprit*], his tastes serve him as criteria in the lessons that he gives to history. Friedmann does not appear to me foreign to this costume; that which displeases him in the USSR, it is if one will, a certain moral style, a certain psychological distribution of shades and lights, that he would have distributed otherwise if he had been in charge of arranging the picture.[44]

Yet Nizan's criticisms were well nuanced and he faced the real issue—the confrontation of intellectual rigor and honesty with political considerations—squarely in the eye:

> Some readers may utilize many of the pages of the last part of Friedmann's book against the USSR, that's a fact. A fact that Friedmann regrets

like me: Because I do not doubt the authenticity of his intentions, but
these intentions themselves may be held at bay by a false perspective,
which is above all an error of the philosophic order. Philosophic, that is
to say political.[45]

As if these criticisms from two close friends were not sufficient,
Georges Politzer added fuel to the debate in a harsh review in *Cahiers du
Bolchevisme* in the May/June 1938 issue. Politzer began with a direct quotation from *Anti-Dühring*, Engels's effective discrediting of that hapless
German pendant, and made his comparison explicit, claiming that "just
like Dühring, Friedmann decrees that those who are not in agreement with
him, are not with the truth."[46] Unlike Bruhat or Nizan, Politzer would grant
Friedmann no credit whatsoever, even claiming that Friedmann ignored
prewar Russian economic development, especially large-scale industrialization and the development of the proletariat in Russia, in favor of a
lengthy (and, in Politzer's eyes, a suspiciously sympathetic) discussion of
the peasantry. According to Politzer:

> But what is most important, that is the method. At first look, Friedmann
> presents himself as a master of the school which distributes felicitations
> and blames. He has ideas on everything, from the rhythm of the five-
> year plans, through the teaching of higher mathematics and the pro-
> grams of street concerts, to abortion and Stakhanovism. In the name of
> these ideas, he approves and he disapproves in a very scholastic fashion,
> which does not prevent him from continually mocking some Soviet
> "popes." But if one looks a little closer, one realizes that there is some-
> thing else, many other things.[47]

Politzer claimed Friedmann manipulated or misunderstood his materials, using Soviet autocritiques only if they supported his views, over-
playing the significance of changes in political direction to suggest confusion about policy and the intrusion of politics into sociointellectual
spheres. Worse still, Friedmann ignored the importance of Lenin as
philosopher, thereby destroying the true picture of Lenin as a genius
linking theory and practice. Politzer focused in particular on Friedmann's
passing reference to *Materialism and Empirio-criticism*, which Friedmann

simply described as one of Lenin's early writings and limited to a polemic within the Russian socialist movement. For Politzer, Friedmann was guilty of minimalizing the philosophic oeuvre of Lenin, especially Politzer's personal favorite. Politzer devoted three printed pages to correct this perceived and odious falsification.

But perhaps, Politzer mused, Friedmann's errors might have a more simple origin:

> Friedmann has made for himself a certain conception of socialism. And seeing that the USSR is not constructing a Friedmannian socialism, he does not say that he is wrong and that he has made for himself an erroneous conception of socialism. This idea did not even occur to him. He thinks that it is the USSR which is wrong and that it is it which is deviating from socialism.[48]

Then Politzer realized the truth of Friedmann's errors lie in another direction. Friedmann's misgivings about the cult of Stalin were incomprehensible, Politzer thought, until one recognized that "moral NEP" and "revolutionary pause" as concepts formulated by Trotsky:

> Here, we have the true face of Friedmann's objectivity. That Stalin is the guide of the peoples toward the progress and peace definitively assured by socialism, that is a fact that precisely all lucid men may report and comprehend in examining his [Stalin's] work. That Trotsky is an agent of the Gestapo, that is a fact especially that the Moscow trials have thrown enough light on. What Friedmann writes, that is a deformation of facts which is in the end to make an apology for Trotsky at the precise moment when before all honest men, he risks being forever branded.[49]

Politzer's lengthy diatribe wound on, as he piled invective atop accusation in an effort to discredit Friedmann and *De la Sainte Russie*. He finally concluded that real French intellectuals, those heirs of the Enlightenment and the Encyclopedia Politzer was writing so extensively about, would know Friedmann for what he was.

What remarkable parallels and symmetry linked the two sets of criticism! Friedmann, the recognized French specialist on Soviet industrialization and labor, was on one interpretive level caught in a crossfire between two ideological competitors. Religiously inclined critics associated with the nonconformist movements pounced on his limited discussions of the trials and of the cult of Stalin to denounce him for not pushing further, while Communist reviewers blasted him for writing too much on exactly the same issues. To portray Friedmann as naive, Bruhat wrote that no one ever claimed the USSR was paradise, while du Passage, with the same intention, suggested that if Friedmann had not found paradise, he had at least glimpsed the promised land! For one side, Friedmann's work would subtly shift the reader into sympathy with the Soviet experiment, while the other foresaw an equally subtle undermining of confidence and faith.

The Communist response to Friedmann's *De la Sainte Russie à l'U.R.S.S.* marked a crucial turning point in French intellectual and political discourse prior to the Second World War. The entire broadly leftist framework constructed since 1932 unraveled in the spring and summer of 1938. The merger of inquisitive scholarship and political enthusiasm which had led to the introduction of Marxist theory into French universities and to support for the antifascist Popular Front was eroding. At issue was the application of Marxist theory to the study of the practices of the Soviets.

The responses of the Communist critiques were, frankly, bizarre. All three—Bruhat, Nizan, and Politzer—were among Friedmann's closest friends and collaborators for nearly two decades. The similarities of their three pieces suggest a concerted program of criticism covering specific points, and perhaps these three reviewers were chosen precisely because of their known affiliation with Friedmann. Bruhat and especially Nizan were willing to admit that Friedmann was not totally wrong, although only Nizan worded that point strongly and clearly for all to see. Indeed, in light of Politzer's review, Nizan's milder criticisms and softer presentation appears as a defense of Friedmann, an intelligent colleague who got many facts right, made some shrewd analyses on important matters, but badly handled some key issues despite his good intentions.

But Politzer's review was an unnecessarily violent and unrealistic caricature of what Friedmann had in fact written. Denying Friedmann's specialized knowledge of the USSR, denying what Friedmann had actually written in order to create gaps or substitute innuendos, and ultimately denying Friedmann any place on the Left, Politzer fabricated a nonexistent book which was alternately a blustering fraud, a naive compendium of errors, and a subtle subversion offered by a fascist-Trotskyist wrecker! While stunning in their audacity, Politzer's charges could not successfully persuade anyone of Friedmann's supposed heresies and ignorances.

The underlying reasons for such an assault are clear. The French Popular Front was in full decline, as the Socialists and Communists edged apart and the center of power moved to the right wing of the Radical Party. With the increasing international tensions caused by German rearmament and the Anschluss, by the lingering death of the Spanish Republic, and by the extravagant adventures of the Italian fascists, war appeared inevitable. The reviews of Bruhat, Nizan, and especially Politzer reflected the increasing isolation of the Communists and their need to clarify loyalties and priorities.

In response to the Communist critiques, a third category of responses to *De la Sainte Russie à l'U.R.S.S.* began to appear in the early fall of 1938. This trend—best represented by Jean Cassou, Jacques Soustelle, and Lucien Febvre—was composed of left-leaning scholars and intellectuals who were supporters of Popular Front unity, and who found themselves being squeezed between the demands of intellectual and ethical honesty on one hand and of political expediency and orthodoxy on the other. The Friedmann affair was at the center of the reshuffling of French intellectual life as politics and scholarship parted company.

Jean Cassou, reviewing *De la Sainte Russie* for September's *Europe*, immediately contradicted Bruhat and Politzer's claims of bias, but also nimbly responded to du Passage and to Bruhat in their own imagery, claiming:

> Making of the USSR neither a paradise nor a hell, he displays it as it is: a portion of the earth, and where is taking place at this moment an extraordinary social action. It is on this level that the study helps to disperse the prejudices, the errors, the ignorances, and that sort of obscure horror and panic which control so many minds before the novelty of human creations.[50]

That same month in *Annales d'histoire économique et sociale*, Lucien Febvre expressed his particular pleasure in Friedmann's work:

> Supple, nuanced, living, at equal distance from the blind apology and the
> denigrating critique—inspired without doubt by a very active sympathy
> for the USSR and its realizations, but dictated by a great concern for objec-
> tive reporting—it has the merits of being the work of a man who is not at
> all given to harvesting, in the course of a rapid ramble, some "visions" of
> Russia appropriate to give credence—I mean in the eyes of the simples—
> to some conclusions at once picturesque and theoretic on the USSR.[51]

Febvre noted that much of Friedmann's material had been personally collected and studied by the author in the course of his research from 1932 to
1936. For Febvre, the key to defending Friedmann lay in extolling his
integrity, for example when Febvre noted that "the responses of M. Friedmann, always nuanced and instructive, bear witness to a vigorous effort to
look things in the face without willingly abusing them through partisanship."[52]

Jacques Soustelle, another *Annales* associate, defended his friend in the
same manner but with even stronger language in *Nouvelle Revue Française*
during October. For Soustelle, the matter was quite simple, and his every
word was directed at Politzer:

> [I]f the work of Friedmann holds and attracts, it's above all because it is
> serious, that it is the result of an extensive and prolonged contact with
> Soviet reality; it is moreover that it is constructed on the theme that is
> announced in the title: the confrontation of czarist Russia and of the
> Soviet Union.[53]

More than any other reviewer, Soustelle demonstrated an accurate understanding of exactly what Friedmann's criteria for judgement were, noting
in particular Friedmann's analysis of the Soviet polytechnical education
system and his interest in the organization of labor as the keys to comprehending both Soviet goals and Friedmann's methodology. Does it really
need to be said, Soustelle asked, that Friedmann was not only a keen
observer but also deeply, sincerely sympathetic to the Soviet cause?

The responses provoked by Friedmann's *De la Sainte Russie* were not
simply indicative of the state of the politicized intellectual debates of the
late 1930s, for in a very crucial sense Friedmann's work was not only the key
to political debate in 1938, it was the debate itself. The published responses

to Friedmann document the existence of three irreducible discursive positions. Those who defined themselves in religious terms focused primarily on the state of belief in the Soviet Union and used that single issue to distinguish themselves from the Popular Front. Communist reviewers mirrored that position by maintaining an unconditional and unquestioning defense of the Soviet Union. Finally, adherents of the broader Popular Front concept sought to preserve both their intellectual and ethical integrity while struggling against the reduction of French political discourse to simplistic positions about the distant USSR. There was not—and never has been—a scholarly debate about *De la Sainte Russie*, only its absorption into a political topography specific to the late 1930s. As the unity of the Popular Front collapsed, Friedmann and his work served as the demarcation line for sorting out the various leftist factions once again.

Soustelle was not the only one surprised that anyone doubted Friedmann's commitment as an *engagé* intellectual. The published reviews were only the discernible skirmishes of the Friedmann affair. Just outside the public world of journals and newspapers, a large and not particularly private discussion about the merits of *De la Sainte Russie* and of the Communist critiques took place. Romain Rolland, Henri Wallon, Paul Langevin, Francis Jourdain, and numerous others besieged Thorez from March through December 1938, demanding that Friedmann be allowed to defend himself against the critiques of Politzer. From the correspondence between Friedmann and his supporters, it is certain the Friedmann himself had repeated meetings with Thorez, who had thoroughly read the hotly debated book. There were also indications of a possible quarrel between Jacques Duclos and Thorez, and suggestions of a growing split within the ranks of Party intellectuals. Indicative both of Thorez's willingness to retain the loyalty of intellectuals as well as of Friedmann's importance, he offered to allow Friedmann to publish a response, accompanied by Thorez's own commentary, and hence close the affair.[54] And while grappling with this issue, Thorez was similarly playing the role of ideological arbitrator in the matter of Lefebvre's writings—again because of Politzer's exclusionary denunciations.

But the September 1938 Munich crisis immediately shifted priorities and anxieties. When the Friedmann affair was never officially or fully resolved, the enthusiasms and loyalties for the ideals of the Popular Front increasingly seeped away, leaving a confused, disorganized, and cynical French Left to face the crises of 1939 and 1940.

But what of Friedmann's unpublished reply? For years, a copy remained among his personal papers, testimony to the importance he attached to both *De la Sainte Russie* and to the controversy. Written prior to 10 July 1938, it was delivered to Thorez ten days later. In his defense, Friedman provided a detailed reply to Politzer totaling roughly thirty-two typed, double-spaced pages.

From the onset, Friedmann distinguished between his critics, noting that Politzer's savaging differed tremendously in tone and conclusion from other Communist reviewers who, "while making some reservations on certain points, remained on the plane of a cordial discussion, as Bruhat said, 'between friends of the same cause.'"[55] On the other hand, Friedmann noted,

> Politzer's critique consists, among other procedures, of stating a one-sided assertion, next, of mangling the texts, of detaching from here and there the words placed by him within quotation marks, and drowned within his commentaries to make the author say . . . what Politzer would have him say.[56]

For the bulk of his response, Friedmann tenaciously answered all of Politzer's complaints in detail. Again and again, Friedmann could point that the supposed omissions and oddities bemoaned by Politzer—on the writings of Lenin or Stalin, regarding the roles of the peasantry or the clergy, and so on—were in fact discussed on specific pages of *De la Sainte Russie*. In explaining his favorable comments about Bukharin, Friedmann avoided pronouncing on his innocence or guilt, and instead simply traced the writing of *De la Sainte Russie*: written in the spring of 1937, revised, delivered to the Gallimard editors on 15 October, the proofs corrected in the last days of 1937, and the book released on the first of March 1938. Given this history of the text, Friedmann asked, how could he or anyone possibly have foreseen that Bukharin would be arrested and accused in the last days of February 1938?[57]

Yet Friedmann sensibly accepted that there were faults in his work: "that's very possible, it's even probable."[58] Still, despite any faults, Friedmann asked that his work be judged through verification of its facts and impacts, and not by deliberate perversions of what it meant. Wishing to not aggravate a debate "capable of delighting and serving the enemies of the great human cause which is the cause of all of us," Friedmann announced himself content to await the judgment of his Communist comrades.

In later years, Friedmann did blame himself for his "unpardonable naivete" regarding the Soviet camps, once telling Emmanuel LeRoy Ladurie that "I was a cuckold on the subject of the USSR."[59] To an extent, Friedmann would retrospectively shorten the duration of his ties with the Communists, claiming in 1970 "I had been, from 1930 until 1936, a disciplined 'fellow traveler,' militant not at the side of the party, but within the organizations to which it was tightly linked and that it practically controlled."[60] Again, in his memoirs, Friedmann wrote of *De la Sainte Russie à l'U.R.S.S.* that:

> [T]his book, prefaced by Francis Jourdain, was for the most part made as a defense and illustration of Soviet realities, such as I had been able to see them, but expressed, here and there, some reservations regarding the evolution of the regime and which contained a chapter on "the cult of the chief." Received with embarrassment and, above all, relatively spared by the PCF (I had then, accompanied by F. Jourdain, a long interview with Maurice Thorez who had closely read and annotated it), it was abruptly, at the start of June 1938, very probably on instructions coming from Moscow and despite the backing of Romain Rolland, Paul Langevin, Henri Wallon, the object of furious attacks in the Communist publications, *L'Humanité* in the lead. That was the end of my fellow traveling.[61]

Was the summer of 1938 in fact the end of Friedmann's fellow traveling? Certainly in the strictest sense, but although his involvement with Popular Front organizations sharply fell after mid-1938, Friedmann continued to work with a number of groups and journals on the Left, and in particular aided in the launching of *Volontaires*, a new, international, independent Marxist review. The PCF treated him badly, working to remove him from all his positions within Popular Front organizations and ending his editorial control over the well-received series "Socialisme et Culture." However, there is some evidence that, when the German occupation relegated past quarrels to the trash, Friedmann demonstrated his willingness to work, at least in a limited fashion, against a common foe with PCF militants.

Mobilized into the military medical service in the wake of the division of Poland, Friedmann began a diary which he kept from 6 September 1939 until 28 June 1940. In this remarkable document, published by Gallimard in late 1987, Friedmann candidly set down his often anguished thoughts concerning the entwined problems of the future of Man, of the Soviet Union, and of Marxism as a body of theory. These concerns were at the heart of Friedmann's *Journal de Guerre*, for on 13 September 1939, right after his mobilization, he wrote:

> [A]nd because I think that socialism remains in one manner or in another the necessity of the future, because more than ever I sense that a new civilization may only be a modern humanism based on technology and that this latter implies the rational organization of the world's resources, of a material and moral solidarity of nations, of a solution to class conflicts, I am going to try to comprehend, with a cool head (although with a bloody heart), the attitude, the conduct, the intentions of the USSR. The latter have played a very great role in my reflections, for so long in my hopes. I am going to try to comprehend, to judge the "realism" of Stalin, the mental attitude, the diverse mental attitudes of those who have performed their "gyration" [*tournant*] one more time, with him—after him.[62]

Through the tedious months of the *sitzkrieg*, as the fearful excitement of mobilization gave way to the apprehensive boredom of routine, Friedmann thought again and again of the future possibilities confronting humanity. In a long entry of 5 January 1940, Friedmann turned once more to the themes present in *La Crise du Progrès*:

> The Marxism of Marx and Engels is not tainted by the degradation of the Soviet experience. On the contrary: I am inclined to think that it will emerge strengthened in the end, beyond the psittacism, of the demagogy and of the intellectual sloth, of the disease of formula, of scholasticism spread among the Stalinist intellectuals. . . .
>
> There will come a time where one will cease to consider *Capital* and *Anti-Dühring* as closed works, as sacred texts good enough to be carved

into citations and surrounded by trenches. There will come a time where one will rediscover and respect—even within political action, propaganda, struggle—the humanism which is at the heart of the grandest doctrine of human liberation that the brain of man has ever conceived.[63]

Friedmann increasingly focused on the most essential, the most basic, and ultimately the most unanswerable problems of his search to understand. In seeking the foundations of Marxism in the context of early 1940, Friedmann returned to those very same dilemmas that he sought to answer in the early 1920s, which had led him to Marxism in the first place. His troubled thoughts emphasized the continuity within Friedmann's intellectual development for two decades.

In his postwar writings, Friedmann continued to explore the themes he had set out in the thirties. While less explicitly reliant on Marxist definitions and categories, Friedmann retained the concept of alienation at the center of his analyses, and, more crucially, set as his ultimate purpose for writing the transcendence, on a global scale, of the dehumanization and mass alienation of industrial societies. His hopeful search for liberating potentials of, and his repeated warnings about stunting pitfalls within, the organization of industrial societies was ever-present in his writings, *Problèmes humaines du machinisme industriel*, *Où va le travail humain?*, *Le Travail en miettes*, and *Sept Etudes sur l'Homme et la Technique*. Expanding the breadth of his search for the bases for universal human integration, Friedmann turned, like many others, to the study of mass communications, with his major writings on the subject anthologized as *Ces merveilleux instruments* after his death. That Friedmann continued to share his preoccupations with his contemporaries can be best illustrated by the two volumes of *Traité de Sociologie du Travail*, which Friedmann organized with that other searcher for social salvation, Pierre Naville.[64] In the hope of locating a solution within a previously ignored avenue, Friedmann scrutinized the new state and society of Israel, employing the much same criteria he had applied in all his works, including *De la Sainte Russie à l'U.R.S.S.* The record of his observations, of his hopes and fears, was published as *Fin du peuple juif?* and touched off reactions nearly as heated as its predecessor of 1938.

In his final work, the 1970 *La Puissance et la Sagesse*, Friedmann underscored his efforts to extract a liberating remedy for human anguish from

Marxism. Commenting on his 1936 *Crise de la Progrès*, Georges Friedmann openly admitted his hopes and disappointments of the interwar years:

> Such was my faith. It was an idealized and spiritualized "Marxism." I placed all in it, including the multidimensional development of Man, of his humanization: faith in the plasticity of Man but also in the full strength of good institutions, economic and political, at last "responsive to Man," to make him better, to deliver to him all his potential, to bring him to full bloom. Like many others, possessed by this faith, I belonged to a Church which had its saints, its martyrs, its Holy Books, its Vulgate. I would discover, soon after, that it also had its Inquisition, its terror, its victims.[65]

Yet, Friedmann, despite and perhaps because of his disappointments, retained an even stronger, more confident faith in humanity throughout his life and his works.

NOTES

1. Georges-Philippe Friedmann, "Lénine, matérialiste militant," *L'Humanité* (22 October 1935). Regarding *The German Ideology*, Friedmann specifically referred to the new series *Arkhiv Marksa I Engel'sa* 1, no. 6 (1933); still he may have also seen that text when it was published in vol. 4 (1929) of the original *Arkhiv K. Marksa I F. Engel'sa*. Elsewhere, he cited a 1932 German edition, probably the *Marx-Engels Gesamtausgabe*, 1 Abteilung, Band 5, the German translation of the complete works being published by the Marx-Engels Institute. Marx's "Critique of the Philosophy of Right of Hegel" was another of the pieces Friedmann and the Philosophies had read in the third volume of *Arkhiv*, along with the other 1844 Manuscripts. In her important contribution "L'équilibre difficile. Georges Friedmann avant la sociologie du travail," to the Colloque Friedmann (October 1987, Brussels), Michela Nacci demonstrated that Friedmann's writings for *Annales* displayed similar textual and theoretical patterns.

2. Georges Friedmann, "Materialisme dialectique et action réciproque," *À la lumiere du Marxisme* (Paris: Editions Sociales Internationales, 1935), tome 1, based on conferences of the Commission scientifique du Cercle de la Russie neuve 1933–1934; also in *Commune*, no. 15 (15 November 1934). All quotations from the

copy in *Commune*, p. 229. See the commentaries on *À la Lumiere* of Lucien Febvre, "Techniques, sciences et marxisme," *Annales d'Histoire économique et sociale*, tome 7, no. 36 (30 November 1935); Léon Werth, "À la Lumiere du Marxisme," *Europe*, no. 154 (October 1935); Pierre Gérome, "Le Marxisme pénètre en France," *Europe*, no. 152 (August 1935); and Valentine Feldman, "Science et Marxisme," *Revue de Synthèse*, tome 12 (1936): 115–17. A second, shorter review by Feldman appeared in the Frankfurt School's *Zeitschrift für Sozialforschung*, vol. 5 (1936). There was a passing comment in René Maublanc, "Le Rayonnement du marxisme," *Cahiers du Bolchevisme* 13, no. 1–2 (15 January 1936): 92. A direct quote from Friedmann (*Monde* [26 September 1935]) immediately follows Maublanc's mention, and contrasts glaringly with Maublanc's ignoral of the efforts of Lefebvre, an official Party member.

3. Friedmann, "Materialisme Dialectique," p.231.

4. Ibid., p. 235.

5. Ibid., pp. 240–41.

6. Georges Friedmann, "Machine et Humanisme," *Europe*, no. 151 (July 1935): 441–42.

7. Ibid., p. 443.

8. Georges Friedmann, "Les Rapports de la Conscience des hommes et des conditions économiques," in *Cours du Marxisme, 2e année, 1936–1937* (Paris: Editions Centrale, 1937), p. 23.

9. Ibid., p. 24.

10. Ibid., p. 30.

11. Ibid.

12. Georges Friedmann, *La Puissance et Sagesse* (Paris: Gallimard, 1970), p. 258.

13. Georges Friedmann, *La Crise du Progrès* (Paris: Gallimard, 1936), p. 7. Reviews included those by Henri Lefebvre, "La Crise du Progrès," *Nouvelle Revue Française*, no. 275 (August 1936); Lucien Febvre, "Puissance et déclin d'une croyance," *Annales d'Histoire économique et sociale*, tome 9, no. 43 (31 January 1937); Alexandre Marc, "Morale, Sociologie, Droit," *Archives de Philosophie*, tome 13, Supplement bibliographique, no. 3 (1937): 14–15; and Henri Hertz, "Panorama des Livres," *Europe*, no. 176 (August 1937). Michela Nacci, in "L'équilibre difficile, Georges Friedmann avant la sociologie du travail," delivered to the Colloque Friedmann, Brussels, in October 1987, compares *La Crise du Progrès* to *The Destruction of Reason* by Georg Lukács, an accurate description which underscores the parallel between the work of Friedmann and the Philosophies to the unorthodox Marxists of Central Europe.

14. Friedmann, *Crise du progres*, p. 48.

15. Ibid., p. 140.

16. Ibid., p. 219.

17. Ibid., p. 221.

18. Ibid., p. 224.

19. Ibid., pp. xiii–xiv.

20. *Nouvelle Revue Française*, no. 284 (May 1937).

21. Georges Friedmann, *Problèmes du machinisme en U.R.S.S. et dans les pays capitalistes* (Paris: Editions Sociales Internationales, 1934). Reviews included one by Lucien Febvre, "Machinisme et civilisation," *Annales d'Histoire économique et sociale*, tome 6, no. 28 (31 July 1934).

22. Georges Friedmann, "Quelques traits de l'esprit nouveau en U.R.S.S.," in C. Bouglé et. al., *Inventaires* (Paris: Felix Alcan, 1936). Reviewed by R. Schröder, *Zeitschrift für Sozialforschung*, vol. 5 (1936); Lucien Febvre, "Inventaires," *Revue de Synthèse*, tome 11 (December 1936), and Marc Bloch, "Un Inventaire de Crises," *Annales d'Histoire économique et sociale*, tome 8, no. 42 (November 1936).

23. Georges Friedmann, "André Gide et l'U.R.S.S.," *Europe*, no. 169 (January 1937): 5; reprinted in *De la Sainte Russie à l'U.R.S.S.* (Paris, Gallimard, 1938).

24. Ibid., p. 16.

25. Ibid., p. 23.

26. Ibid., p. 27.

27. Friedmann's commentary on Gide's *Retouches à mon Retour de l'U.R.S.S.* (Paris: Gallimard, 1937) first appeared in *Dépêche de Toulouse* of 25 July 1937, and was reprinted in *De la Sainte Russie à l'U.R.S.S.*, from which I cite p. 265. *Retouches à mon Retour de l'U.R.S.S.* included Jef Last's letter to Friedmann from *Europe*, no. 170 (February 1937), along with Pierre Herbart's from *Vendredi* (29 January 1937).

28. Georges Friedmann, *De la Sainte Russie à l'U.R.S.S.*, pp. 17–18. This work is a true classic in the field of Soviet studies, yet remains both out of print and untranslated into English. Apparently, during the early 1970s, Friedmann planned to revise and reissue the book with the collaboration of Marc Ferro and Marie Thèrése Basse. I have been informed, however, that for the moment the project is discontinued.

29. Ibid., p. 48.

30. Ibid., p. 49.

31. Ibid., p. 81.

32. Ibid., p. 87.

33. Ibid., p. 218.

34. Ibid., p. 234.

35. Ibid., pp 234–35.

36. Ibid., p. 238.

37. Ibid., p. 239.

38. Henri du Passage, "De la Sainte-Russie à l'U.R.S.S.," *Etudes*, tome 236 (July–September 1938): 131–32.

39. Georges Duveau, "Les Problèmes Russes," *Esprit*, no. 70 (July 1938): 613–14.

40. Jean Bruhat, "De la Sainte-Russie à l'U.R.S.S.," *Cahiers du Bolchevisme* 15, no. 4 (April 1938): 88. Also printed in *L'Humanité* (29 April 1938).

41. Ibid.

42. Paul Nizan, "Friedmann: De la Sainte Russe à l'U.R.S.S.," *Commune*, no. 57 (May 1938): 1123.

43. Ibid., p. 1124.

44. Ibid.

45. Ibid., 1125.

46. Georges Politzer, "A propos d'un livre sur l'U.R.S.S.," *Cahiers du Bolchevisme* 15, no. 5/6 (May/June 1938): 171.

47. Ibid.

48. Ibid., p. 179.

49. Ibid., p. 186.

50. Jean Cassou, "De la Sainte Russie à l'U.R.S.S.," *Europe*, no. 189 (September 1938): 84.

51. Lucien Febvre, "De la Sainte-Russie à l'U.R.S.S.," *Annales d'Histoire économique et sociale*, tome 10, no. 53 (30 September 1938): 442.

52. Ibid., p. 445.

53. Jacques Soustelle, "De la Sainte-Russie à l'U.R.S.S.," *Nouvelle Revue Française*, no. 301 (October 1938): 670.

54. The sheer quantity of contemporary responses offers proof of the importance French intellectuals attached to *De la Sainte Russie* and *l'Affaire Friedmann*. For a broader overview of reviews of *De la Sainte Russie*, I enthusiastically recommend the work of Catherine Melnik-Duhamel, "L'Affaire Georges Friedmann: à propos de la publication de `De la Sainte Russie à l'U.R.S.S.'," Mémoire de Diplome d'Etudes approfondes d'Histoire contemporaine, Institut d'Etudes Politiques de Paris, 1984–1985, under the direction of Pierre Nora. Even more important, Melnik-Duhamel includes typescript copies of the letters written to and by Friedmann about the Affair and a copy of Friedmann's unpublished response. I am indebted to Mme. le Docteur Liliane Boccon-Gibod for providing me with a copy of Melnik-Duhamel's work.

55. Georges Friedmann, "A propos d'un livre sur l'U.R.S.S.," in ibid., annex 3, p. 232.

56. Ibid.

57. Ibid., p. 253.

58. Ibid., p. 258.

59. Emmanuel LeRoy-Ladurie, *Paris-Montpellier* (Paris: Gallimard, 1982), p. 41.

60. Friedmann, *Puissance et la Sagesse*, p. 272 n.

61. Ibid.

62. Georges Friedmann, *Journal de Guerre, 1939–1940* (Paris: Gallimard, 1987); prefaces by Edgar Morin and Alain Touraine, text established and annotated by Marie-Thèrése Basse and Christian Bachelier, p. 47.

63. Ibid., p. 133.

64. Georges Friedmann, with Pierre Naville, *Traité de sociologie du travail*, 2 vols. (Paris: Armand Colin, 1961 and 1962).

65. Friedmann, *Puissance et la Sagesse*, p. 275.

Chapter 7

Lefebvre, Guterman, and the Critique of Everyday Life

After the failure of *Avant-Poste*, Lefebvre and Guterman continued their program of dissecting everyday life. While completing their major work, *La Conscience mystifiée*, they also translated, edited and introduced three important texts: *Morceaux Choisis de Karl Marx*, Lenin's *Cahiers sur la dialectique de Hegel*, and *Morceaux Choisis de Hegel*. The latter two volumes were completed in New York during 1935 and 1936, respectively, as indicated in the introductions to each. All four of the above titles were released through Editions Gallimard, the most prestigious French publisher, and hence guaranteed an extensive circulation. The introduction to each volume reflected the preliminary studies of Guterman and Lefebvre as they prepared *La Conscience mystifiée*, and therefore provides a vantage point from which to reconstruct the development of the theoretical framework they then implemented. These introductions are testimony to their comprehension of what Marxism "really is," an understanding so distinctive that, in the France of the 1930s, one could label it unique or, in political terms, heretical. Since they were absorbing the works of Marx, Lenin, and Hegel simultaneously, the chronological order in which the three volumes were published can be set aside and the order Hegel, Marx, Lenin adopted.

Within a year of its release, the *Morceaux Choisis de Hegel* had appeared in three printings. This remarkable record was certainly due to the "Hegel Renaissance" associated with Alexandre Kojève's lectures (1933–1939) as well as the growing interest in Marxist theory.[1] Unlike the more diffuse literary interest in Hegel during the twenties, Lefebvre and Guterman bluntly traced the revival of the thirties to current political passions. Both fascism and communism found theoretical justifications in Hegel's writings—the former in his emphasis on the State and the Nation, the latter from his method and his influence on Marx. In fact, Lefebvre and Guterman distinguished three political characteristics within Hegel:

> There is a reactionary Hegel—a liberal Hegel—a progressive and even revolutionary Hegel. But there are not, properly speaking, liberal, reactionary or revolutionary works or fragments. These three characteristics—expressed with more or less clarity or success—interpenetrate one another, traversing the entire organism of his oeuvre in a living disorder.[2]

Each of these political characterizations rested upon a specific logic. The liberal logic extractable from Hegel emphasized the reabsorption of the contradictions into an abstracted unity, without reconciliation or negation. This liberal logic paralleled the political life found in parliamentary democracies and constitutional monarchies, and served to legitimate the fragmentation of class interests in the name of the status quo. In the second, or fascist, logic, the opposition and conflict of contradictions were given preeminence, resolved not in an abstracted unity but in the subordination of antagonisms to some form of Absolute. For example, the fascist synthesis left the isolated individual defenseless when confronted with subsuming categories like the National Spirit or the State. The struggle of contradictions remained unresolved, while the synthesis immobilized the subordinated elements within an artificially closed and static conception of totality.

For Lefebvre and Guterman only the third, revolutionary logic could resolve the struggle of the contradictions, not by eluding nor exasperating those contradictions but through overcoming them. True resolution lay in the negation of the negation, the dialectical supersession (*aufheben*) which simultaneously destroys, preserves, and transcends contradictions. Lefebvre and Guterman argued that this logic permeated Marx's thought and made Marxism into a fruitful methodological system.

The second concept from Hegel that Lefebvre and Guterman linked to Marxism was that of totality. In completing the work of the French Encyclopedists, Hegel had grasped the isolated and fragmented categories of empirical knowledge as parts of an ever-greater whole. Hegel was thus "the Philosophe," the systemizer of his time, and not a metaphysician but a realist who understood and explained the reality of his times. This conceptualization of totality marked the glory and the limits of Hegel's work. By resolving contradictions within the Absolute Idea, Hegel had withdrawn knowledge from the ever changing realities of life. Yet the tensions between mind and life remained and continued their historical development, making the existence of an Absolute limit of knowledge impossible. The contradictions between Mind and Matter became infinitely prolonged, and the limits at which Absolute Knowledge existed infinitely withdrawn.

Marx and Engels stripped the religious elements from the Hegelian dialectique, incorporated social relations and practice, and in that famous phrase, rescued the precious kernel from the shell. Yet, in the end,

> ... neither Marx, nor Engels, nor their followers have yet provided a complete discussion of the dialectical method and the problems posed by the separation between this method and Hegelian idealism.[3]

When considered within their historical context, several remarkable elements emerge from these comments. At a time when Hegel was officially being cast as a forefather of fascism and Hegelian-Marxists within the Soviet Union forced into silence, Lefebvre and Guterman offered more than a partial rehabilitation. They claimed one could make valuable methodological extractions from Hegel's works, and tied Marx more directly to Hegel than was usually the case. Moreover, they asserted that not only was Hegelian thought necessarily and methodologically open-ended, but that Marxism was equally—and as necessarily—incomplete and uncompletable. Incidentally, it is very probable that this position, like most of those adopted by Lefebvre and Guterman, should be considered as testimony to the intellectual freedoms existing within the Parti Communiste Française during the 1930s, particularly when the lack of similar freedom of theoretical expression within other Communist Parties during the same era is taken into account.

Guterman and Lefebvre had considerably less control over the textual presentation and selection over *Morceaux Choisis de Karl Marx*. Paul Nizan edited and presented the first half, "Marx philosophe," while the second, entitled "Marx economist," was prepared by Jacques Duret. Despite their coordination of the entire project, Lefebvre and Guterman were effectively restricted to the writing of the introduction to the collection.[5] The bulk of this essay was a straightforward intellectual biography which, if nothing else, demonstrated the detailed knowledge of Marx's writings they had. But the themes of their Hegel again were present, if differently worded. Political concerns again justified the reading of Marx:

> "[T]od dem Marxismus"—"Death to Marxism."... This password of the Hitlerists can be read even on the walls of hamlets in Germany, and the most isolated peasant of Franconia or Bavaria knows already what will soon be known to the peasant of Brittany or the Dauphine: that Marxism is one of the forces engaged in the greatest struggles of history.[5]

The *Morceaux Choisis* was designed as an introduction to this badly understood system of thought, for those searching "sincerely" for a doctrine.[6]

Lefebvre and Guterman traced the emergence of Marxism, or of dialectical materialism, as a distinctive method and *Weltanschauung*, to the period of philosophic quarrels during which Marx broke with the Young Hegelians. Lefebvre and Guterman believed Marxism essentially was formed prior to the writing of the *Communist Manifesto*. Lefebvre and Guterman distinguished between the political and the philosophical elements within Marxism and, in an argument reminiscent of Lukács's *History and Class Consciousness*, emphasized that this internal duality of method and ideology within Marxism had been ignored too long. Against those political priests who turned Marx's writings into Scripture and his meaning into ideological pronouncements, Lefebvre and Guterman argued

> ...dialectical materialism is not a "system." The idea of a deductive and closed system is contrary to dialectical materialism, it denounces the falseness of metaphysical constructs, it demands specific analyses within each field, and finally and above all it unifies thought for its expression in practice. Marxism develops itself as a function of revolutionary practice: Within his works Marx only developed certain aspects of his immense doctrine, a necessary function of political practice.[7]

Nor was Marxism a sterile scholasticism, but the unification of thought with sensual practice. Lefebvre and Guterman described this unification in clearly Hegelian terms:

> This will of transformation, integration of practice and all of life within thought, this insoluble unity of action and knowledge makes dialectical materialism more than a philosophy. Philosophy supersedes itself: It becomes revolutionary.[8]

Lefebvre and Guterman reiterated the same point, "Marxism develops itself," over and again, and clearly preferred method as the standard of orthodoxy. The entire method hinged on human alienation in the world, a thus-far unresolved circumstance which, when applied to political economy, led to Marx's theoretical penetration of appearance and his analyses of commodity fetishism, of money and of capital. Marx provided the methodological principles for investigating the immense mystification of capitalist social relations, but "in the end, dialectical materialism cannot remain stationary. Immobilized, this doctrine of the development of the world and of society loses all meaning and becomes the most empty of scholasticisms. Marxism is only true when progressing."[9]

Lefebvre and Guterman provided a rapid double example of how this internal development takes place in their introduction to Lenin's 1914 reading of Hegel's *Science of Logic*, written during his Swiss exile:

> Lenin developed... one of the grand ideas of Marx [and] Engels. Classical philosophy had not completed its work; this work can only be continued by the representatives of the revolutionary proletariat; it will continue into the society without class. These [Lenin's] notebooks display at the same time the movement of Marxist-Leninist thought—and the authentic essence of Hegelian thought.[10]

Prefiguring Louis Althusser, Lefebvre and Guterman argued "we must read Lenin as he himself read Hegel," by adopting Lenin's method of reading. This "method" was simultaneously internal and external: internal in that Lenin as reader was confronting the progression of the *Science of Logic* itself; external in the sense that Lenin approached the text fully aware of his preconceived positions, positions against which he then measured Hegel. In other words, Lenin approached Hegel in same manner that Hegel approached skepticism, stoicism, and the various other philosophical systems representing historical moments: seeking the openings and the possibilities inherent within each system, and then attempting to develop those openings. Lenin therefore sought to locate the precise points where Hegel had reached his logical limits, and those remaining open to further development, to exploitation, and to transcendence.

Since, as Lefebvre and Guterman noted, Lenin was not one to engage in purely abstract exercises or to privilege action over thought, his study of Hegel was implicitly purposeful. He found "that the moment where the solution, the superior unity [i.e., the negation of the negation] seemed to be withdrawing itself, is sometimes the same moment in which it draws near."[11] And, in the late months of 1914, nothing seemed more distant than the proletarian revolution. Lenin's critical reading was a creative act, the forging of a theoretical tool Lenin would apply in revolutionary practice.

Not only had Lefebvre and Guterman partially (albeit critically) rehabilitated Hegel, and made Hegel's thought an integral part of Marx's method and doctrine—they had brought both into the theory and practice of Lenin.

This rapid presentation of Lenin's reading and transformation of Hegel was completed within the first seven pages of the introduction. In the remaining one hundred and twenty-eight, Lefebvre and Guterman presented their own systematic and detailed model of Marxist method. They tried to pinpoint exactly where Marxism was closed, where problems remained unresolved, where openings and possibilities began. In short, they applied the lessons they had learned from Marxism to Marxism.

To orient their readers, Lefebvre and Guterman outlined the problems they believed to be confronting "revolutionary philosophy." Their table (expressly "approximate," "provisional," and with the questions "artificially separated") conveys the open-endedness of their Marxism.[12] At the very end of their list, after what they labeled the "already elaborated aspects of dialectical materialism" and the "problems on which the founders of Marxism have given precise indications, but which have become revived as a functioning of philosophic actuality," Guterman and Lefebvre almost apologetically added a short category, the "open problems, perspectives of the development of dialectical thought." These appeared to be the insignificant questions of the "social critique of the categories of thought" and the "theory of human 'alienation' and of the integration of the elements of Man," but in fact Lefebvre and Guterman smuggled into this outline of Marxism those problems and questions which lay at the heart of their project.

In keeping with the methods outlined in Lenin's discontinuous text and in order to clarify matters for their readers, Lefebvre and Guterman supplied clarifications on each of these points. Yet clearly, they believed the key to dialectical thought to be entirely in the open problem of alienation.

For Hegel, alienation was an internal differentiation of consciousness, of the Idea become estranged from and exterior to itself. In the materialist conception of Guterman and Lefebvre, consciousness was embedded within natural and social realities, forming a unity of reciprocal determinations and contradictions. Their Marxism became a theory of the conditions of consciousness and not a reduction of consciousness to material or economic causes. According to Guterman and Lefebvre, human beings become free through comprehending these conditions and then transforming them through social practices. Lefebvre and Guterman reiterated these arguments against the inclusion of any form of Absolute within Marxism, which led them to a series of positions clearly deviant from "orthodox" Marxism. They argued that at any moment all knowledge has its limits and that therefore the creation of theoretical totalities from such knowledge necessarily produced partial truths:

> Knowledge is movement. Each of its moments is a whole. Each truth is a partial truth, relative and absolute at the time. The ensemble of partial and contradictory truths at a given moment is still a partial truth. Approximation, limitation, contradiction do not signify falseness.... The totality of the movement is true. At each particular point, one may and must grasp toward the totality of thought and the totality of things.[13]

Consciousness is therefore always limited, be it the consciousness of an individual, a class, or an epoch. Within this limitation resides the possibility of ideologic illusion and of error, of mystification. Yet this situation is in fact the most true condition of consciousness. Consciousness becomes true in triumphing over error, in moving from ignorance to truth, and in enlarging the spheres of reality it can know and transform.

In this formulation, there can be no end to the reciprocal development of consciousness and material reality, of the expansion of human liberty as expressed by and in human practices. Lefebvre and Guterman believed Marxism's contributions lay in the determination of the precise concrete and reciprocal relationships between "being" and "thought," and in its emphasis on the unity of theory and practice. Thus, Marxism itself will be self-superseding (*aufheben, depasser*) as part of the self-critical and revolutionary practice it requires. Not to do so would be fatal.

Lefebvre and Guterman clarified two key definitions they had already employed in *Avant-Poste*. Alienation, for them, occurred when consciousness reached the limits it could achieve at a specific moment, when consciousness confronted realities it is insufficiently developed to express or comprehend. The human aspirations to transcend these limitations became detached from human practices, sublimated and transposed into mysterious and apparently unknowable forms (such as magic, religion, and so on). Parallel to Hegel and Marx's formulations, human consciousness became internally divided from itself and posited its desires as an external. Such situations gave rise to the "unhappy consciousness," the inquietude plaguing French intellectuals after the Great War.

The adoption of pseudosolutions such as religion and mysticism perpetuated a false communion and prolonged the rupture of consciousness and practice. Social institutions, all the products of human activity, and the immediate historical totality became fetishized, immobilized, and oppressive. This antagonistic and unchanging reality was mystified. For Lefebvre and Guterman, only by recovering the historical development of both consciousness and reality as coupled in the resumption of praxis (as the unity of comprehension and transformation) could demystify such a reality. Marx's critique of political economy served as a model for the supersession of contemporary mystified reality, and suggested the possibility of unceasing human development without further alienation. The unified "subject-object" of this nonalienated human would be the "Total Man." The unity of the individual and the social, "the appropriation by man of nature and of his proper nature," Lefebvre and Guterman insisted, was not simply a metaphor but rather the self-critical and concrete resolution of all classical philosophy.

In retracing the progression of dialectical thought through Hegel, Marx, and Lenin, Lefebvre and Guterman delineated their own project.

Throughout the 1930s, Lefebvre and Guterman emphasized that the immediate and major problem requiring clarification was that of alienation, the undeveloped theme running throughout dialectical materialism:

> Within a given civilization, upon the basis of acts repeated billions of times (practical, technical and social acts, like the acts of buying and selling today), customs, ideologic interpretations, cultures and lifestyles erect themselves. The materialist analysis of these styles has progressed very little.[14]

This project corresponded to the "open problem" of the social critique of the categories of thought listed on their table of revolutionary philosophy. *La Conscience mystifiée* was their attempt to fill this gap.

Written during 1933–1935, *La Conscience mystifiée* was originally conceived as the first of five volumes. The others (*La Conscience privée, Critique de la vie quotidienne, La Science des ideologies,* and *Materialisme et Culture*) were only partially prepared and never published. But the ambitious project these titles represented was continued by Lefebvre in his postwar writings. *La Conscience mystifiée* thus stands as an early "critique of everyday life"—*critique de la vie quotidienne*—which Lefebvre elaborated over the next five decades. However, because of the specific context within which it was written, this text also stands as a memorial to the intense political debates within the France of the 1930s.

Throughout La *Conscience mystifiée,* Lefebvre and Guterman continued to work out the implications of their distinctive understanding of Marxism. Writing in the mid-thirties, they felt a great deal of tact and discernment was required of revolutionary philosophy

> precisely because we are in a revolutionary epoch, and because the stakes involved are no longer this or that limited problem but all of culture and civilization. Are we going to destroy without discrimination exactly what we should save, our wealth of tomorrow?[15]

The future was indeed the prize for Lefebvre and Guterman. Capitalism, having extended itself around the world, had reached the limits of its capacity and was becoming destructive. The forces of production had outstripped the forms of production, and one or the other must necessarily be destroyed. For Lefebvre and Guterman, the stock market crash and the wholesale waste of the products of human labor indicated that the forces of production were being sacrificed in order to preserve the forms of capitalism. In part, this demolition was intended to turn back the potential for revolutionary transformation. Lefebvre and Guterman were well within contemporary orthodoxy when arguing that only Marxist theory joined to revolutionary practice could overthrow the outdated and now destructive forms of capitalism while preserving and furthering the potential locked within the forces of production.

Guterman and Lefebvre argued that traditional philosophy was unequal to this task of demystification. Fragmented into specializations parallel to those found in the industrial division of labor, intellectuals had retreated into abstractions and idealism. Following the Great War, intellectuals found themselves unable to grasp the rapid transformations in the world about them and sought individual solutions in pure spirituality, in narcissism, and in the "discovery" of intuition and psychology. This abdication by bourgeois intellectuals was the "Crise de l'Esprit" heralded by Paul Valéry, which Lefebvre and Guterman now thought led only to "onanistic mysticism" and self-satisfaction of the intellect: self-destructive, paranoid, impotent.[16] This pursuit of "pure passions," of "art for art's sake," and of "intimate being" was the very cul-de-sac Lefebvre, Guterman, and the Philosophies admitted to having explored—and escaped—between 1924 and 1928. After the bordellos, the brawls, the ceaseless debates and disappointed hopes, they had turned to Marxism as the theory best explaining the causes of their inquiétude. In one stroke Guterman and Lefebvre succinctly accounted for their previous positions, performed a terse autocritique, and relegated those who failed to make the same transition to the political and intellectual wasteland!

Lefebvre and Guterman saw their work as accomplishing two specific tasks. The first was nothing less than the revival of dialectical materialism itself:

Marxists—save Lenin—have left Marxism shrouded in mystification. The most vast doctrine, which can envelop and supersede others, has appeared the most summary.[17]

Their resurrection of Marxism allowed them to undertake the second task, a critique of contemporary mystified realities. They portrayed this demystification of daily life as an emancipatory overthrowing of a limited bourgeois humanism in the name of a more universal revolutionary humanism.

Lefebvre and Guterman now reserved the term "mystification" for those specific moments in historical development when all the preconditions for a revolutionary supersession of a given society have been met. Yet, in part due to the ideological power of the dominant class and in part due to the insufficient growth of self-consciousness among the dominated, the revolutionary moment is not recognized and carried through. Shrouded in myths, the social status quo continued to be reproduced. Escape appeared only in unachievable utopias, in the sour contemplations of the "unhappy consciousness," or in an anarchistic self-destructive revolt.

Two fundamental social elements are preserved and suffer under this mystification. The first is private consciousness, left to face incomprehensible social forces in an atomized and isolated state. Attempts to recapture human dignity based on the individual, like that of Emmanuel Mounier and his doctrine of *personnisme*, marked only the existence of mystification and a retreat into an interior spirituality and asceticism. Since analysis of the private individual consciousness was to be the content of the promised second volume in Lefebvre and Guterman's series, their treatment of the topic in *La Conscience mystifiée* was brief.

The second category, that of *la conscience du forum*, they explored in more detail. Social consciousness and individual private consciousness had been divided as part of the development of capitalism, as reflected in bourgeois philosophy. Although they asserted that dialectical materialism provided the theoretical tool for reunifying both elements, Lefebvre and Guterman sensibly restricted themselves to an analysis of the public aspects of contemporary consciousness.

They perceived several major forms of mystification in the contemporary world. The dominating falsehood was that of nationalism. The myth of the nation-state, originally a revolutionary creation forged in the struggles against the absolutist monarchies, had assumed almost magical connotations for the masses. In an age when capitalism had developed into an international system and when the material conditions for a cultural unification of all humanity appeared inevitable, the nation-state was perpetu-

ated as the personification of abstract ideals. Instead of the universaliza-
tion of human consciousness on a global scale, the particularities of false
categories—race, language, and fragmented national cultures—were substituted by cynical capitalists and manipulated by fascist demagogues. The
opposition of nation-state against nation-state provided an appearance of
dynamic movement where in fact there was none. Before this greater, collective entity, the individual private consciousness could only retreat into
seclusion—or march along.

Lefebvre and Guterman found youth to be particularly vulnerable to the
effects of mystification. Simultaneously confronting social and biological
maturity, the young ran up against, and frequently rejected, the world of
seemingly meaningless hierarchies and unknown regulations, the educational
and occupational rituals of demanding and forcing compliance. Rejection led
to isolated revolts only superficially attacking the social order, which were in
fact condoned by society. With timely repentance and fatherly intervention,
the young could be brought back into "the machine" they came to identify
with. However, because of its mishmash constellation of myths (race, nation,
action, the rights of youth, sacrifice), Lefebvre and Guterman argued that fascism had a strong appeal for youth. By providing a social role at once
accepted and oppositional, and by substituting the leader for the authoritarian
father, fascism seemed the collective resolution of the problems of the youth.
The social role reserved for youth under fascism may have been without substance, and the father's authority never approached the severity of the
leader's. But fascism "saved" the young—from discovering the margins of
capitalist society and from turning toward a revolutionary overthrow of the
entire social edifice. The sincere idealism of youth was allowed a socially safe
outlet while insecurities inherent in maturation were assuaged.

These youthful idealists evolved into deceived and pessimistic adults.
A daily life centering around family, labor, social ritual, and personal isolation became a meaningless existence. Boredom and minor worries,
habits, vices, and hopelessness replaced the apparently false and unrealizable ideals of youth. The pursuit of universal ideals dissolved into the pursuit of individual gain, and the desire for personal immortality submerged
into an identification with the fate of an abstracted collective.

Following Marx's own comments, Lefebvre and Guterman argued that
the bourgeoisie itself was susceptible to these same processes, since their

devotion to profit proved incapable of solving individual essential human desires. Behind a superficial facade of tolerance and diversity, bourgeois culture fragmented into multiplicity of distinct spheres, each only monotonously mirroring the others. Culture decayed into mere diversion and compensation. With the dilution of bourgeois culture and its diffusion throughout society there existed elements from which systematic, cross-class mystifications could be constructed. The steady increase of social contradictions and tensions sped the decomposition of bourgeois culture and rendered it increasingly incapable of camouflaging the alienation of man from man, and man from himself.

This formulation by Lefebvre and Guterman was similar to Gramsci's concept of cultural hegemony. For if the dominant class was to retain its powers, then it must convince both itself and the dominated that only they knew not simply the solutions to immediate problems, but the "real" problems as well. The "defense of French culture" or the "salvation of the German race" masqueraded for the real issue, the overthrow of capitalism. In order to move beyond the verbal battles and empty formulas of journalists and *petits penseurs*, Lefebvre and Guterman stated the necessity of first recognizing the existence of pervasive mystifications, followed by the detailed analysis of the roots of alienated consciousness. In brief, they advocated that others engage in the same project they had undertaken.

If Lefebvre and Guterman had ended their text at this point, their work would still rank as one of the better theoretical works to come out of France during the 1930s. The breadth and depth of their analyses far outstripped the usual polemics of French intellectual and political discourse. The positions they presented were clearly Popular Frontist, in their attempt to appeal to a broad audience including sectors of the bourgeoisie and intelligentsia.

Yet Guterman and Lefebvre added two further elements, setting their work apart from those of their contemporaries. In the closing fifteen pages they return to the themes worked out in the introduction to Lenin's *Cahiers*. Since all knowledge was limited and determined by specific conditions, it could be either transcended or mystified. This statement applied to Marxism itself, for if Marxism wished to remain dynamic, it could not ever be completed. Nor could consciousness be reduced to a material or economic base. Either position—closure or reduction—transformed Marxism into a dogmatic mysticism like any other. Yet Marxists—save Lenin,

Lefebvre and Guterman hastily added—simply appropriated the partial truths available in Marx's economic writings without developing the methods embedded in his philosophic works.

The reverse would be equally true. The boundary between knowledge and mystification provided the realm manipulated by the fascists, who offered sleights of hand and falsehoods in place of critical knowledge. This theme woven throughout *La Conscience mystifiée* made the work one of antifascist demystification. However, since consciousness seeking to extend itself would always call mystification into question, mystification and demystification could conceivably proceed in an endless dialectic. Within the immediate context of fascism, Lefebvre and Guterman argued that the perpetuation of mystification and the contrived preservation of the forms of capitalism could be indefinitely prolonged. However, it was inevitable that this barbarism could be questioned, demystified, and superseded.

Reviewing *La Conscience mystifiée* in the professional *Archives de Philosophie*, Alexandre Marc began his commentary by stating:

> Materialist philosophy is in decline. After having apparently expressed the most daring conquests of *l'esprit*, Marxism reveals itself deficient and even reactionary. Living thought diverts itself everywhere with the materialist illusion. The latter no longer possesses the offensive spirit, it can only defend itself.[18]

Yet Marc, one of the *non-conformistes des années trente* who found his truth elsewhere, did not specifically link this polemical charge to *La Conscience mystifiée* or to either of the two other works critiqued in the same review, one of which was Friedmann's *Crise du Progrès*, discussed previously. About the work of Lefebvre and Guterman, he simply noted they

> denounce the decadence of bourgeois culture, and bring to light the vanity of the majority of myths nourishing the blindness of the masses. Most often we can only agree with the authors, praising their insight. But when they conclude "the age of gigantic mystifications is not over. It is up to us to penetrate into each of their particular manifestations with dialectical lucidity," we need not refrain ourselves from thinking of the gigantic mystification of Marxism.

In *Nouvelle Revue Française,* an equally brief review appeared over the name of René Etiemble.[19] For Etiemble, *La Conscience mystifiée* was an "effective contribution" avoiding loss of direction in byzantine theoretical discussion. Readers would discover "the theory of mystification at times stifled under the pressure of other things in the works of Marx." Finally, if Lefebvre and Guterman appeared "sometimes harsh, if they condemn without appeal those who still seek to grasp pure ideas, if the concern with form moves them less than that of efficacy, this is because they are playing neither at thinking nor at writing." Like Marc, Etiemble was virtually disinterested in what Lefebvre and Guterman actually wrote about, but rather entranced by the fact they did not flatter intellectual narcissism. "Those who prefer to be dupes," he concluded, should avoid this book.

Two prominent reviewers in two major periodicals both avoided a thorough discussion of *La Conscience mystifiée.* The reasons why emerge during an examination of two further pieces. *Commune,* journal of the Popular Front organization Association des écrivains et artistes révolutionnaires, carried a review signed H. Chassagne.[20] In fact the review was written by Charles Hainchelin, whose underrecognized role as a PCF militant and as one of the few French Communists thoroughly familiar with Marx's writings was noted in chapter 4. "A book to read, to think about, to criticize," Hainchelin began, "a revolutionary book which has above all the merit of being the first on these problems in France." Lefebvre and Guterman's major contribution was their attempt to give the notion of mystified consciousness a critical edge. Yet it was precisely in that attempt Hainchelin located the principal faults of the book:

> ...insufficient analyses of the real foundations of consciousness (but as the next volume promises to be a general theory of the conditions of mystification, one can extend them credit); too great an extension of the ideas of mystification and of fetishism; omissions regarding the inequalities of the diverse forms of social consciousness, et cetera....

Certainly, Hainchelin thought, the future volumes would avoid these problems "especially if the authors write less superficially, one might say less literally." Then their work would become a testimonial to its times, as well as a display of a knowledge of Marx's writings "rare in France." But,

Hainchelin added in parentheses, "in this regard we reproach their willingness, along with the majority of French comrades, to attach more importance to Marxism-in-formation—prior to 1847—than to formed Marxism."

Jean Grenier, that persistent observer of the Philosophies, provided the most interesting review in *Esprit*. Like Hainchelin, Grenier recognized that the writing of *La Conscience mystifiée* required a thorough immersion into Marx's works, and then demonstrated his own knowledge of such matters by providing a lengthy and detailed summary of Marx's early texts for those lacking the background. He thought that Lefebvre and Guterman's familiarity with Marx's writings enabled them to write a "masterpiece of intelligent propaganda, demonstrating how superficial (or malintentioned) minds have mistakenly presented Marxist propaganda as produced by semiliterates or pretentious ignoramuses who have only read *la petit Larousse révolutionnaire*."[21]

Within *La Conscience mystifiée*, Grenier located three levels of thought: an account of Marx's ideas, the adaption of those ideas to suit current reality, and a profession of faith. The second most disturbed Grenier, for Lefebvre and Guterman employed Marx's theories so well, leaving no problems unresolved, that "all is explained, and we cannot doubt the truth of this explanation since we see it conforms to the texts of Marx cited at the end of the volume." While recognizing their reliance on Marx's early writings was part of an effort to create a humanist Marxism distinct from the orthodox emphasis on political economy, Grenier felt that Lefebvre and Guterman occasionally provided explanations too summary if they were to successfully recruit "*plus d'esprits*." In the end, Grenier best understood their profession of faith and their mysticism, as indicated by their use of numerous citations from the great literary and philosophical figures—Nietzsche, Stendhal, Baudelaire, Dostoyevsky, Lawrence—who best expressed the metaphysical anguish of modern life. For Grenier it was "this messianism, which reappears in each age and which here takes the form of a romantic materialism, makes us more than sympathetic to its arguments."

These few reviews offer several glimpses into the world of French intellectuals in 1936. The most curious point is that these four reviews were among the very few critiques published. The previous and the following publications of the Philosophies had been reviewed rather widely, but silence greeted *La Conscience mystifiée*. In part, this lack of discussion may have been due to the state of Marxist theory in France. Grenier and Hainchelin were unusually well versed in Marx's writings. Although each have misgivings about *La Conscience mystifiée*, they also knew exactly what Lefebvre and Guterman were attempting.

The reviews of Marc and Etiemble indicated the crucial problem. The Catholic nonconformist Marc began his commentary with a proclamation of the decline of Marxism, but did not link *La Conscience mystifiée*, or the other works he discussed, to that decline. Indeed, with the exception of his parting comment regarding the mystifying power of Marxism, his review was essentially praise. René Etiemble provided no substantial comments on the contents of the work. A Popular Front sympathizer, Etiemble aligned himself with Lefebvre and Guterman against "those who would remain dupes." Written in the years just prior to the formation of the Popular Front, and released only months before its official formation, *La Conscience mystifiée* was received as yet another verbal salvo within a polarized and politically divided intellectual community.

Grenier's review was perhaps the most important. He comprehended the efforts of Lefebvre and Guterman in part because of his knowledge of Marxism, of the Philosophies, and of postwar *inquiétude*. But in part Grenier, also a nonconformist Catholic, shared their preoccupations with social and political change. His comments on the mysticism within Marxism and *La Conscience mystifiée* underlined the continuity within the thought of Lefebvre and Guterman since 1924. His willingness to discuss and even accept this work was also indicative of the ongoing effort at reconciliation between French Communists and Catholics, the famous *main tendu* of the Popular Front era.[22] Grenier knew precisely what the stakes were in *La Conscience mystifiée*, as his pun on *plus d'esprits*—meaning "more souls" as well as "more minds"—suggested. His comments appeared under the appropriate title "La Pensée Engagée."

Hainchelin's review was equally interesting, for it is the only one to appear in either a PCF or Popular Frontist periodical. Hainchelin was in an uncomfortable position, since while he was one of the few with a substantial knowledge of Marxist theory within the Party, he was also obliged to uphold the orthodox emphasis on political economy. Hence he treads a narrow line, listing a number of general criticisms while praising *La Con-science mystifiée* as a flawed but pioneering work which should be continued. Hainchelin's comments also are strikingly similar to those of Louis Althusser and others during the 1950s and 1960s, and suggest that the "humanist" versus "scientific" debates within French Marxism need to be reexamined as part of a larger historical context. Fortunately, during the thirties the PCF could and did allow for greater theoretical diversity within its ranks, and the debates on the early texts (and the expulsions of Lefebvre and Garaudy) are unthinkable outside of a cold war scenario. Unfortunately, Hainchelin provided no further details about that "majority of French comrades" who immersed themselves in Marx's early writings!

La Conscience mystifiée was clearly etched with the preoccupations of the specific time when it was written. The aspirations of the Popular Front and the efforts to theoretically comprehend fascism mark it as surely as the now-obscure debates Lefebvre and Guterman touched on in their text. But *La Conscience mystifiée* also belongs within a larger context from which it is often omitted, that of "unorthodox" or "Western" Marxism. Several classics of this genre furnish guidelines for fixing *La Conscience mystifiée* within this larger tradition. George Lukács's *History and Class Consciousness*, Karl Korsch's *Marxism and Philosophy*, and Theodore Adorno and Max Horkheimer's *Dialectic of Enlightenment* all have striking resemblances to Lefebvre and Guterman's *La Conscience mystifiée*, on even the most superficial level. All four were long out of print, while enjoying reputations as underground classics. All were reprinted as part of the growing search for alternatives to the official "dia-mat," with its emphasis on political economy which began during the late 1950s. In fact, Lefebvre and the Arguments group would be responsible for the translation and publication of the works of Lukács and the Frankfurt Critical Theorists in France.

Each of these works represents a specific moment in the history of twentieth-century Marxism. Lukács and Korsch released their works as the postwar revolutionary movement had begun to subside. In retrospect, there is a poignant irony about their emphases on revolutionary consciousness, since in their specific context it was the material reality that precluded the success of the revolutionary movement. On the other extreme, Hork-heimer and Adorno wrote their *Dialectic of Enlightenment* in the gloomiest days of the struggle against fascism and while living in exile in a society they ill fitted. Their critique of the decay of Reason into myth and domination was meant to apply to all industrial societies. *La Conscience mystifiée* falls squarely between both poles, most obviously chronologically. Although fascism appeared to be in retreat in France and Spain when the work was released, it is useful to recall that Lefebvre and Guterman were writing during the Nazi consolidation of power, during the repressions of the conservative republic in Spain, and with the riots of 6 February 1934 as an indication of the strength of the French Right. *La Conscience mystifiée* captured that brief period of Popular Front enthusiasm and hope, when it seemed that opinion could be swayed by argument. Yet this enthusiasm was tempered by sober reflection on the strength of tradition and of fascism, and ultimately the emphasis is thrown back on the individual reader, who must choose how to act.

Moreover, all of the authors engaged in extensive efforts to reinsert Marxist theory into and as part of the history of philosophy. (One should note, however, that Lukács and Korsch, like Lefebvre and Guterman, relied more heavily on the importance of Hegelian dialectics for Marxism than did Horkheimer and Adorno.) All of the studies are "dialectical" but with distinct emphases. Lefebvre and Guterman drew on a knowledge of Marx's early texts unavailable to Korsch and Lukács at the time they wrote. Like Lukács, Korsch, and Gramsci, who allowed for ideological deviation from class determinations, Lefebvre and Guterman deemphasized the economic determinations of consciousness. Thus their work was more Hegelian, since revolutionary consciousness could emerge across class divisions, and more Marxist, since "the Revolution" was supposed to liberate everyone, including the bourgeoisie from itself.

The position of Lefebvre and Guterman can be best be summed up in the phrase coined by Romain Rolland, but made most famous by the other major Marxist theorist of these years, Antonio Gramsci: "Optimism of the will, pessimism of the mind." Lefebvre and Guterman, while granting the probability of continued mystification, allowed for a revolutionary demystification by members of all social classes at any time. For Horkheimer and Adorno, who relied more heavily on Kant than Hegel and who were faced with an extremely bleak world, the reduction of all culture to the same monotony and repetition precluded transcendent practice or conceptualization. The very mystification Lefebvre and Guterman sought to undermine became the inescapable reality of Horkheimer and Adorno. By leaving no space for a reversal, Horkheimer and Adorno essentially signaled an end of dialectical movement in barbarism. The open-ended dialectic of Lefebvre and Guterman holds out the optimistic possibility of liberation, even in the midst of the most barbarous times.

By the late thirties, Guterman was firmly established in the United States, where he became "one of the few real international representatives of Western Marxism."[22] Lefebvre continued the project they had begun. His first solo works, *Nationalisme contre les Nations* and *Hitler au Pouvoir*, continued the themes of *La Conscience mystifiée*. The best known of all of Lefebvre's works from this period is his *Materialisme dialectique* of 1939. Although only Lefebvre's name is on the title page, two early fragments appeared in *Nouvelle Revue Française* during 1934, linking this work directly to the collaborative enterprise with Guterman.[24]

Since this study is regarded as one of the common coins, scholars have generally brushed past it with only brief commentary. Yet *La Materialisme dialectique* can be reexamined as a continuation of the trajectory traced above. Moreover, it is necessary to restate the arguments of *Materialisme dialectique* because Lefebvre's works are less commonly studied, in North America at least, than is usually asserted.

Lefebvre found Marx preoccupied with the concept of alienation throughout his writings. Lefebvre divided Marx's thought into two periods of development. The first, historical materialism, was developed between 1843 and 1859. During this phase, Lefebvre viewed Marx as rejecting Hegel's dialectical method but retaining the concept of alienation. Marx's highest achievement during this period was the unification of idealism and materialism in the *German Ideology*. The second phase of Marx's mature dialectical materialism Lefebvre traced to the first complimentary mention Marx had for Hegel, in a letter to Engels in 1858. From that point on, Lefebvre perceived the reintegration of the dialectical method into Marx's work as a tool Marx used to concretely analyze the causes of alienation. The fruits of this reconstructed methodology were *The Critique of Political Economy* and *Capital* itself.

As in the works summarized above, Lefebvre emphasized the perpetual dialectical movement of knowledge, the concept of totality, and that of alienation. Distinct from the theory of knowledge that he and

Guterman were developing, Lefebvre underscored, albeit abstractly, the processes of living by which man is self-creative. By focusing on the concepts of alienation and of totality, Lefebvre, following *The German Ideology*, posited the possibility of "the Total Man" as both subject and object of Becoming. This dealienated subject "is not the inevitable outcome of human prehistory, it cannot be produced by economic fatalism, not by some mysterious finality of history, not by a decree of 'society.' "[25] The themes of Lefebvre's earliest essays reemerged in his major theoretical writings of the 1930s.

Crucially, Lefebvre privileged neither material existence over the ideal (that is, over consciousness) nor the ideal over the material. Instead, after granting that one must exist materially before one can think, Lefebvre left the ideal and the material coexisting in tense opposition to each other. Not only did this formulation presuppose a Hegel-like movement of knowledge, but it also shifted Marxism away from materialist determinism and placed creative ability back into the consciousness—and will—of man. At the same time, consciousness was limited by the material conditions of a given historical moment and could transform those conditions only within a specific range of possibilities.

Ironically, about a month after the release of *Materialisme dialectique*, the infamous "theoretical sections" from the *Short Course of the History of the CPSU* were reprinted in *Cahiers du Communisme*. This crude exposition of Marxist theory inaugurated the official end of theoretical diversity within the PCF. The outlawing of the PCF in the wake of the Hitler-Stalin pact, followed by the declaration of war in September 1939 and the Nazi occupation, further precluded contemporary discussion of Lefebvre's work.

Yet Lefebvre's open totality lacked a motivating agent, a will to create and transform. Without the introduction of a source of human self-creative effort, Lefebvre's Marxism would sooner or later be forced to rely on either an idealist Absolute or a materialist determinism. It was in part to fill this lacuna that Lefebvre wrote his *Nietzsche*, published in early 1939.[26] The championing of Nietzsche by a Communist intellectual at this particular moment was certainly unusual. Not only had Nietzsche been usurped by National Socialism, but French supporters of fascism had also adopted Nietzsche as their prophet: Drieu la Rochelle even subtitled his *Socialisme fasciste* with the antagonism *Marx contre Nietzsche*. Moreover, the leading ideologists of the Communist movement, including George Lukács, not only left these claims undisputed, but condemned Nietzsche as a protofascist. In their introduction to Lenin's *Cahiers*, Lefebvre and Guterman had themselves written "to the formula of Nietzsche, 'Man must be surmounted,' Marxism responds, 'It is Man which surmounts.' "[27]

Lefebvre's ostensible reason for writing was to defend and to reclaim Nietzsche from the far Right, a motive endearing him to the German emigre community in Paris. In fact, barely four pages at the end of Lefebvre's 165-page introduction (the remaining pages of selected Nietzsche texts total barely 136!) directly dealt with the fascist claims to Nietzsche. These few brief pages tacked on at the very end of the introduction simply draw a vague balance sheet. Lefebvre conceded that some elements of Nietzsche's writings could be manipulated into a fascist ideology: his emphasis on heroism, on history as myth, and in particular on the combination of pessimism and tragedy. These elements Lefebvre believed "tainted" by Nietzsche's early ardor for Wagner, who Lefebvre directly linked to fascist ideology. Conversely, Lefebvre viewed the bulk of Nietzsche's writings as carrying an antifascist message. He singled out the concept of overcoming (*überwinden*) as a critical imperative destructive of fascist ideology. When Nietzsche's critique of the state, of nationalism, and of herd-like mass consciousness were taken into account, the antifascist elements outweighed those open to manipulation.

In particular, Lefebvre denied the fascist claims to the concept of *übermensch*, which Lefebvre equated with the Marxist concept of dealienated human existence, the "Total Man." Like the "Total Man," the *übermensch* represents the refusion of consciousness and being. Moreover, Lefebvre adopted the Nietzschean project of the total revalorization of values, of a perpetual critique of given social reality, and of consciousness at a given moment. Lefebvre's *Nietzsche* represented his first clear effort to forge a synthesis of the Hegelian-Marxist framework he had already articulated with elements of Nietzsche's thought.

Hence, Lefebvre's synthesis of Hegel, Marx, and Nietzsche was neither "idealist" nor "self-inverting" in the usual perjorative senses those labels have within Marxist debates. Instead, Lefebvre's fusion offered an "open totality" not reducible to the standard and rather sterile formulations serving to mark, in a very real Foucauldian sense, Marxist political theorists. Moreover, Lefebvre's continuing efforts to grapple with Pascal were evident, for if historical development is not inevitable as the official doctrine of dialectical materialism insisted, then one in effect "wagers" on one's understanding of the world and one's choice of actions. In underscoring the sensual practice of self-consciousness and self-overcoming, Lefebvre not only drew on the texts of Hegel and the early Marx, but also from Nietzsche's concepts of *übermensch* and *überwinden*. However, at this point in his intellectual development, Lefebvre had not yet examined the differences between the Hegelian-Marxist concept of *aufheben* and Nietzsche's *überwinden*, the compatibility of the "Total Man" with the *übermensch*. Furthermore, while an open totality provides an excellent vantage point for a penetrating social and cultural criticism, particularly by throwing out inevitable historical determinism, it places a tremendous urgency on human choices and actions in the present.

Throughout his postwar writings, Lefebvre continued to explore the concepts of "Total Man/*übermensch*," and in particular sought to further the Nietzschean project of a transvaluation of values. The critical imperative implied in this project added an existential complement to the open historical totality accessible through the Hegelian-Marxist dialectic. In his more recent writings, for example *Hegel-Marx-Nietzsche* and *La Fin de la Histoire*, Lefebvre carefully differentiated between the concepts of the three theorists, and described them as a mutually complementary triad, each contributing specific elements to an all-embracing critique of modern life. The writing of that critique is, of course, Lefebvre's life project. For Lefebvre, Hegel provided a historical framework for the analysis of the development of consciousness. Marx supplied the means for criticizing the industrial organization of society and the fetishization of the state. Nietzsche, the poetic prophet of the "Total Man," had made the transvaluation of social values and the perpetual critique of culture imperative, thus reintegrating into the flow of history that creative human element of which Marx dreamed.[28]

Even with these theoretical elements, Lefebvre still lacked a basic element for forging a revolutionary philosophy. The three critiques could explain how and why a revolution might be possible and necessary, but could not explain how total revolution came about as an event. On the level of the *événementielle*, the elements of Hegel, Marx, and Nietzsche woven together only explained in hindsight why an event occurred by referring to its pre-conditions. What remained undefined was the *spontanéité fondamentale* that made the revolution and brought the critical project to fruition.

To overcome this deficiency Lefebvre expanded his synthesis to incorporate Nietzsche's later formulations of the Dionysian, that sublimated expression of the will to power engaged in an ongoing revaluation of life. Lefebvre transformed the Dionysian into a *fête révolutionnaire*, as first presented in his *Proclamation de la Commune* of 1965. Lefebvre compared the Paris Commune to "Tragedy and Drama [which] are bloody festivals, at the hearts of which the defeat, the sacrifice and the death of the *héros surhumain* who defied destiny are accomplished."[29] The brief existence of the commune represented both absolute tragedy and Promethean drama in festival form, played without the slightest frivolity, accompanied by a unique fundamental will to change the world, even at the price of voluntary self-sacrifice. The commune's attempt to overcome alienation, to inaugurate history as lived and dominated by men, forced open a new horizon of possibilities for the future, "announced and prepared" the victory of the Soviet revolution as well as those more successful festivals Lefebvre believes still possible—and necessary.

With his *Everyday Life in the Modern World* (*La Vie quotidienne dans le Monde moderne*), which appeared in early 1968, Lefebvre applied to contemporary French society the same critical framework derived from Hegel, Marx, and Nietzsche he employed in studying the commune. Lefebvre again advocated the revolutionary festival, the experimental and total recreation of Man and the world, as the only possible solution to alienation in modern everyday life. The importance of Lefebvre's argument is given added weight when one recalls that Danny Cohn-Bendit and the sociology students of Nanterre—Lefebvre's students—were those who set off the explosion of May/June 1968. Lefebvre's open dialectic—with its emphasis on the human creation of the future—linked to Nietzsche's project of transvaluation and his concept of Dionysian fête—was designed to serve more than merely heuristic analytic purposes, and remains a project to be realized despite fading memories of May/June. Yet, paradoxically, Lefebvre's search for the ultimate demystifying theory remains both valid—and unachievable. The mystical pursuit of Absolutes of the Philosophies is perpetuated within Lefebvre's Marxism.

The period between the publication of *La Conscience mystifiée* and *Nietzsche* was thus the crucial phase of Lefebvre's intellectual development. This same time frame marked the decay of Lefebvre's relationships with the Philosophies. The common project with Guterman became impossible due to the distances involved. Morhange and Friedmann faded from Lefebvre's life as each pursued his own preoccupations. Nizan did review the *Nietzsche* in *Ce Soir*, and the improved relations between the two continued.[30]

Politzer greeted *La Conscience mystifiée* with derision, claiming "there's no mystified consciousness, there are only mystifiers," implying that Lefebvre fit this category.[31] The publication of *Nietzsche* led to a final loud confrontation in the Boulevard Saint-Michel. Lefebvre was accused of compromising with the fascists and even adopting their ideological positions, of confusing the workers, and of speaking of things which only *"le dirigeant politique, le chef"* had the right to speak.[31] To expose these errors, Politzer planned to print two articles to warn of Lefebvre's dangerous influence.

They were never published. Lefebvre credited Maurice Thorez for intervening and killing the articles at the presses of *L'Humanité*. Thorez wrote a lengthy letter to Lefebvre about the *Nietzsche*, indicating he had read the work and approved of its lack of dogmatism.[33] This personal intervention, made in the immediate aftermath of the Friedmann affair, calmed the matter for the moment, but underscored again both Thorez's role as mediator within the Party and the fact that Lefebvre's major writings during the thirties were ignored by the Party's major periodicals. Nizan's isolated review of *Nietzsche* is even more impressive given this silence and the undercurrent of sectarian debate. Since *Materialisme dialectique* appeared just prior to the announcement of the Hitler-Stalin pact, and quickly followed by the outlawing of the PCF and the mobilization for war, it is not surprising that this particular work was not widely reviewed.

However, two contemporary commentaries do exist. In the February 1940 issue of *Esprit*, Emmanuel Mounier described Lefebvre as *l'esprit le plus libre*—the most free-spirited and the most open minded—of the young postwar Marxists, who avoided the conformism imposed on and by communist intellectuals of the late thirties.[34] In an essay dated 1940, another familiar political maverick, Pierre Naville, denounced Lefebvre's position as meaningless idealism and as representative of a dangerous theoretical tendency within Marxism.[35] These final judgments before the onslaught of war came from the only appropriate sources: a nonconformist Catholic suffering from la *mal du siècle*, and a former Surrealist and Communist searching for the Revolution.

NOTES

1. Please see n. 38 to chap. 2.

2. Henri Lefebvre and Norbert Guterman, introduction to *Morceaux Choisis de Hegel* (Paris: Gallimard, 1938); all citations from 3d ed., 1939. The usually caustic reviewer for *Nouvelle Revue Française,* Jean Guérin, wrote "Il était délicat, et peut-être n'était-il pas opportun, de presenter de fragments de la pensée la moins aphoristique du monde. Lefebvre et Guterman s'y sont exercés avec une extrême application, et de l'intelligence," in no. 313 (October 1939): 672.

3. Ibid., p. 11.

4. Lefebvre later wrote of his dissatisfaction with Nizan's arrangement of the texts, *La Somme et le Reste* (1959; reprint, Paris: Bélibaste, 1973), tome 1, p. 45. An anthology of Lenin's texts was also planned, and a contract signed with Gallimard, according to Pascal Ory, *Paul Nizan, Destin d'un revolte* (Paris: Ramsay, 1980), p. 127, citing a contract in the possession of Mme. Nizan.

5. Henri Lefebvre and Norbert Guterman, introduction to *Morceaux Choisis de Karl Marx* (Paris: Gallimard, 1934), p. 7. All citations from original edition.

6. Although disliking anthologies on principle, Lucien Febvre found *Morceaux Choisis de Karl Marx* both intelligent and useful. His review is an excellent example of his interest in Marxism and his early antifascism. Note in particular his comment: "There is one certainty: that the intellectual appearance of Marx's works makes encountering them difficult, even disagreeable, for the masses. There is another fact no less certain: that harmful Marxists have played the same twist on Marxism as was played by long-winded, vulgar and colloquial preachers...." Febvre, "Pour rectifier un connaissance elementaire du marxisme," *Annales d'histoire economique et social,* tome 8, no. 41 (September 1936): 507.

In *Revue de Synthèse* Valentine Feldman wrote "the authentic thought of Marx is rendered accessible to the public, without commentary, thanks to an intelligent choice of texts" by Nizan and Duret (tome 13 [February–December 1937]: 163).

The only mention in the PCF press I have located is the isolated sentence in Rene Maublanc's "Le Rayonnement du Marxisme," *Cahiers du Bolchevisme* 13, no. 1/2 (15 January 1936): "Last year Editions Gallimard published *Morceaux choisis de*

Marx which contains many unedited and precious texts for the study of dialectical materialism." This lack of attention by the Party press will be discussed further below.

7. Lefebvre and Guterman, *Morceaux Choisis de Karl Marx*, p. 17.

8. Ibid., p. 29.

9. Ibid., p. 30.

10. V. I. Lenin, *Cahiers sur la dialectique de Hegel* (Paris: Gallimard, 1938; nouvelle edition revue, Gallimard, 1967). All citations from the 1967 edition. The original translation was apparently made from the *Leninskij Sbornik*, vol. 9 (1929); the text is available in English as vol. 38 of Lenin's *Collected Works* (Moscow: Progress, 1976). Jean Luc wrote that Hainchelin did the translation, see "Socialisme et Culture," *Europe*, no. 170 (February 1937): 250, n. 1.

Quote from Lefebvre and Guterman, introduction to *Cahiers*, p. 14. I cannot confirm nor refute the possibility of Guterman and Lefebvre having read issue 12 (1930) of the *Sbornik*, which contained the remainder of Lenin's "philosophic notebooks." See my "Leninskij Sbornik (Part I)" bibliography in *Studies in Soviet Thought* 32 (1986).

In his important *Lenin, Hegel, and Western Marxism* (Urbana and Chicago: University of Illinois, 1995), Kevin Anderson adds several dimensions to my present discussion, first by rigorously analyzing Lenin's writings on Hegel, and second by thoroughly exploring the broader international discussions of Lenin's philosophical writings from the twenties until the death of Stalin, and from then through the present. Anderson evaluates the work of Lefebvre and Guterman (pp. 186–93) as well as Lefebvre's later writings on Lenin as philosopher (pp. 193–97 and 211–16). I am indebted to Anderson for his encouragement and for generosity.

11. Lefebvre and Guterman, introduction to *Cahiers*, p. 9.

12. Ibid., p. 19.

13. Ibid., pp. 61–62.

14. Ibid., p. 72.

15. Henri Lefebvre and Norbert Guterman, *La Conscience mystifiée* (Paris: Gallimard, 1936; reprint, Paris: Le Sycomore, 1979). All citations from 1936 edition (p. 20).

It is evident that *La Conscience mystifiée* remained one of Lefebvre's personal favorites. A full chapter is devoted to this book in *La Somme et le Reste*, tome 2, chap. 9, and additional discussion in *Les Temps des Méprises* (Paris: Stock, 1975), as well as in an interview published in *Nouvelle Critique*, "Une vie pour penser et porter la lutte de classes à la théorie," no. 306, ns# 102 (June 1979). See also the joint preface to the new edition by Guterman and Lefebvre. On the fate of the volume dedicated to "La Conscience privée," see *La Somme et le Reste*, tome 2, chap. 17.

16. Lefebvre and Guterman, *Conscience mystifiée*, p. 15-19.

17. Ibid., p. 259.

18. Alexandre Marc, "Lefebvre and Guterman: La Conscience mystifiée; Friedmann: La Crise du progres; Fernandez: L'Homme est-il humain?" *Archives de Philosophie*, tome 13, supplement bibliographique no. 1 (1937): 14–15. On Marc's importance during the 1930s, see Jean Loubet del Bayle, *Les Non-conformistes des années trente* (Paris: Editions du Seuil, 1969).

19. René Etiemble, "Lefebvre and Guterman: La Conscience mystifiée," *Nouvelle Revue Française*, no. 270 (March 1936): 439–40.

20. "H. Chassagne" [Charles Hainchelin], "Lefebvre and Guterman: La Conscience mystifiée," *Commune*, no. 32 (April 1936): 1005–1006. On Hainchelin, see chap. 4 and n. 51 to that chapter.

21. Jean Grenier, "La Pensée engagée," *Esprit*, no. 42 (March 1936): 959–64.

22. On the historiography regarding Communist-Catholic relations in France, see n. 25 to chap. 5.

23. Russell Jacoby, *Dialectic of Defeat: Contours of Western Marxism* (London: Cambridge University, 1981), p. 109. Jacoby's paragraph on *La Conscience mystifiée* is the most glowing (and I believe the longest published) discussion of that work I have uncovered. He is particularly gracious to Guterman. While noting Lefebvre's comment that Lukács was not specifically mentioned in *La Conscience mystifiée* because he and Guterman knew of Lukács' heresies, Jacoby cites a private letter from Guterman dated 12 October 1979, in which Guterman recalls they were unfamiliar with Lukács's work (p. 182, n. 22). Guterman confirmed this point in our conversations. However, Lefebvre and Guterman certainly knew who Lukács was and had a fairly clear idea of his ideas were. It is probable they read several of his shorter pieces, for example, the review contained in *Arkhiv Marksa-Engel'sa*, no. 3—the issue with the 1844 manuscripts.

24. Henri Lefebvre, *Le Materialisme dialectique*, trans. John Sturrock (1939; reprint, London: Cape, 1968). On Lefebvre's misadventures while writing the work, see *La Somme et le Reste*, tome 1, pp. 45–47. The fragments were published as "Qu'est-ce que la Dialectique?" in *Nouvelle Revue Française*, no. 264 (September 1935), and no. 265 (October 1935). All citations in text from Sturrock's excellent translation.

25. Lefebvre, *Materialisme dialectique*, p. 164.

26. Henri Lefebvre, *Nietzsche* (Paris: Editions Sociales Internationales, 1939). The German exiles fêted Lefebvre: See *Commune*, no. 66 (February 1939), and Heinrich Mann's "L'Allemagne eternelle" in the following issue.

Guterman was also influenced by Nietzsche, as his earliest contributions to *Philosophies* show. During two of our interviews (July 1982 and April 1984), he mischievously recalled how, too literally following Zarathustra's advice, he once carried a riding crop to an adolescent rendezvous! Also, he claimed that he had a hand in the preparation of the Nietzsche anthology, although his name does not appear on the cover (personal communication, 8 May 1982).

27. Lefebvre and Guterman, introduction to *Cahiers*, p. 85.

28. Henri Lefebvre, *Hegel Marx Neitzsche ou Le Royaume des Ombres* (Paris: Casterman, 1975), pp. 9–12; Lefebvre, *La Fin de l'Histoire* (Paris: Editions du Minuit, 1970), pp. 12–17. In his preface to Presence et l'Absence (Paris: Casterman, 1980), p. 7, Lefebvre wrote that the major texts on his work table were *The Gay Science*, the *Geneology of Morales, Grundrisse*, and the *Phenomenology*. On Lefebvre's use of Nietzsche, see Pierre Boudot's *Nietzsche et l'au-delà de la liberté: Nietzsche et le ecrivains français 1930 à 1960* (Paris: Aubier Montaigne, 1960); Kurt Meyer's *Henri Lefebvre, Ein Romantischer Revolutionär* (Vienna: EuropaVerlag, 1973); and the recent *Transvaluations: Nietzsche in France 1872–1972* by Douglas Smith (Oxford: Clarendon Press, 1996), especially pp. 81–88. I have not been able to consult Louis Pinto's *Les Neuveux de Zarathoustr: la reception de Nietzsche en France* (Paris: n.p., 1995), but I wish to thank the subscribers of the H-France Listserve for bringing that work to my attention during February 1997. For an overview of the explosion of works on Nietzsche, see Allan Megill, "Historicizing Nietzsche? Paradoxes and Lessons of a Hard Case," *Journal of Modern History* 68, no. 1 (March 1996). Christopher E. Forth shared chapters of his "Zarathustra in Paris: The Nietzsche Vogue in French Intellectual Life, 1891–1914," which deepened my understanding of the background to Lefebvre's work.

29. Henri Lefebvre, *La Proclamation de la Commune* (Paris: Gallimard, 1965), pp. 21–22.

30. Paul Nizan, "H. Mann: Nietzsche; H. Lefebvre: Nietzsche," *Ce Soir* (1 June 1939): 2. Jean Guérin gave mixed praise in *Nouvelle Revue Française:* "L'explication de Nietzsche par la dialectique hégélienne ne va pas loin. Mais les morceaux sont, ici, remarquablement choisis," no. 312 (September 1939): 527.

31. Lefebvre, *La Somme et le Reste*, tome 2, p. 458.

32. Lefebvre, *Temps des Méprises*, p. 76.

33. Lefebvre, *La Somme et le Reste*, tome 2, p. 479; see also tome 1, p. 47, and *Temps du Méprises*, pp. 74–76.

34. Emmanuel Mounier, "H. Lefebvre: Matérialisme dialectique," *Esprit*, no. 89 (February 1940): 316–17.

35. Pierre Naville, "Materialisme dialectique," in *Psychologie, Marxisme, Materialisme*, 2d rev. ed. (Paris: Rivière, 1948), especially pp. 221–23.

Epilogue

With the signing of the Hitler-Stalin pact in August 1939 and the opening of hostilities in Poland, the French found their established lives turned topsy-turvy. The Communist Party was outlawed, along with a wide range of opposition publications. Between mobilization and the confusion of the German invasion in 1940, individuals tried to sort out and reorient their beliefs.

Nizan broke from the Communist Party almost immediately. From the front, he continued to correspond with publishers and friends, as shown by his published letters to Henriette Nizan. During the invasion of France, Nizan was killed, and his manuscript of *Les soirées du Somosierra* lost.[1] As early as 1940, his memory was anathema to the Communists: His novels fell out of print, and he served only as a foil "traitor" against which to play Politzer as the model militant. With the republication of his works beginning in 1960 interest in Nizan, the vigorous corpse, has continued to grow rapidly.

Politzer was mobilized as an instructor of the *École militaire* in Paris, and during the frantic days of the invasion, Politzer is credited as the messenger who carried Communist proposals for the defense of Paris to the French government.[2] Long before the 1941 Nazi invasion of the Soviet Union, Politzer, with Jacques Decour and Jacques Solomon, engaged in a variety of resistance activities on behalf of the PCF. They launched several clandestine periodicals during the first eighteen months of the occupation. The first of these was *Université Libre*, the organ of an organization begun in September 1940 at the direction of Jacques Duclos. *Université Libre* began to circulate as early as November 1940, and survived throughout the occupation, its number 102 appearing during the Battle for Paris.[3]

Another venture was *Pensée Libre*, which first appeared dated February/March 1941. Its first issue carried Politzer's "L'obscurantisme au XXe siècle," itself a short draft of his clandestine pamphlet "Révolution et Contre-révolution au XXe siècles."[4] In these, Politzer continued to expose the myths of racism and mystical nationalism which he had denounced in the prewar years in the name of philosophical rationalism. A second issue appeared before the police closed in and arrested Georges and Maï Politzer, Solomon and his wife, and others in the spring of 1942. Cursing his torturers, Georges Politzer was shot with the men on 23 May 1942. The women vanished into concentration camps, and few returned. Just before his death, Politzer was allowed a final brief visit with his wife, who described their last meeting in a letter:

> He was sublime. Never had his face shone with such luminosity. A radiant calm flowed from him, and his whole manner was impressive, even for his executioners.
>
> He spoke to me of his happiness at giving his life for his Party and for France. He was especially content that he would be dying on French soil. You know how important that was for him.[5]

The double loss of Nizan and Politzer led to an odd reincarnation for each. Nizan was vilified, caricaturized in the novels and polemics of Communist writers, and slid into comparative obscurity before his resurrection by Sartre and others two decades after his death. Politzer was iconized as the perfect militant, loyal and dedicated unto death. Yet the French government long delayed recognizing his role as a resistant, a dishonor attributable to the beginnings of the cold war and the ghettoization of the PCF. While many of Politzer's writings have been anthologized, the bulk remain uncollected, in particular those dealing with political economy, his specialty as advisor to the Central Committee. Yet Politzer remains firmly established—and very justifiably so—within the Valhalla of Party heroes, while Nizan was long ignored. Still, Nizan and Politzer have become inextricably entangled so that even their mutual friend Jean-Paul Sartre never quite separated the one from the other, as shown by his schziophrenic characters Brunet/Schneider in *Les Chemins de la liberté*.

Friedmann was particularly active in the Resistance, working with a variety of overlapping networks such as the circle at the Musée de l'Homme, Libérer et fédérer, and apparently with both the Gaullists and the Communists. Based out of Toulouse, Friedmann joined Jean Cassou, Paul Eluard, Louis Aragon, Pierre Seghers, Jean Guéhenno, and other important intellectuals in bringing out *Cahiers de Liberation*. Friedmann's antifascist dedication earned him the Legion of Honor with Rosette.[6]

After the war, Friedmann returned to academic life. When Lucien Febvre retired, it appeared that his joint heirs would be Friedmann and Fernand Braudel. Director of studies at the École practique des Hautes Etudes, a founder and later director of the Centre d'etudes des communications de masse, Friedmann was a central figure in the education of many of today's leading French scholars. Yet, while remaining on the editorial board of *Annales: Economies, Sociétés, Civilisations* and one of the moving forces in the famous "Annales" school of historical investigation, Friedmann slowly moved to the periphery of the movement and is scandalously ignored by historiographers entranced with the Braudellian era. An editor of the innovative periodicals *Critique* and *Communications*, a tremendously productive and active scholar, and always a respected colleague, Friedmann produced studies of labor, technology and social communication systems that have become established cornerstones of intellectual life worldwide. His death in 1977 took from the world a generous and gentle man at a time when both virtues were in short supply.

Accompanied as it was by a public denunciation to the French police, the *Revue marxiste* affair literally saved his life, as Guterman later viewed it. By being forced out of Europe, he avoided Auschwitz and the terrible fate that claimed a younger brother and other family members remaining in Poland. In New York, Guterman continued working with *New Republic*, where his efforts caught the eye of English critic T. C. Wilson, who described Guterman as the most intelligent critic writing for American reviews, and where Kenneth Burke thought him "one of the most ingenious men" he had ever met.[7] Guterman's major efforts went into translating novels and scholarly works, ultimately topping over one hundred titles. The New York-based Frankfurt School theorists learned of his presence, probably from Friedmann, and invited Guterman to join their sessions, thus solidifying the ties between the projects of the Philosophies and the Frankfurt School theorists. Guterman wrote a lengthy review on political propaganda for the Institute's *Studies in Philosophy and Social Science*, and coauthored of *Prophets of Deceit* with Leo Lowenthal as part of the Institute's famous Studies in Authority series.[8] These activities led to Lefebvre's description of Guterman as "one of the most brilliant Marxists in the United States."[9] Older quarrels were laid to rest, for when Henriette Nizan arrived in New York in late 1940, the first face she recognized, "...exactly on the corner of Central Park South and Fifth Ave...," was Guterman's.[10]

During 1951, Guterman was named in an espionage case being pursued by the Federal Bureau of Investigation. Following a thorough background check, the FBI interviewed Guterman twice in early 1955. Uncertain just what to make of a man who openly admitted past connections with the French Communists and who calmly admired Leon Trotsky's literary criticism and intellectual brilliance, the FBI repeatedly urged that Guterman be brought before a federal grand jury. On 17 January 1957, Guterman appeared before a grand jury in New York, after which the FBI closed its six-year search for lack of the slightest evidence of wrongdoing.[11]

Lefebvre and Guterman continued to keep up their contacts as best as possible after the war, reissuing *La Conscience mystifiée* in 1979, and arranging for Guterman's translation of Lefebvre's *Sociology of Marx*. Lefebvre compared his friend's life to that of the Hasidim: "He doesn't like to have that said," Lefebvre confided, "but he has attained the contemplative wisdom of that celebrated sect."[12] Guterman died just short of his eighty-fifth birthday, in the fall of 1984.

With the occupation, Lefebvre found himself in Toulouse as well. His works were banned and destroyed, his teaching position revoked, and even his personal papers and notes lost, but Lefebvre survived to write for the PCF paper *Patriote* and serve as an artistic director in Toulouse for Radiodiffusion française, a position he lost in 1949, two years after the removal of the Communists from the French government at the onset of the cold war.

In the immediate postwar era, Lefebvre occupied an uneasy position as both the most prominent and the most unorthodox intellectual of the Parti Communiste. After retreating somewhat into literary criticism, much as Lukács had, Lefebvre saw the destalinization program proclaimed by Khrushchev in 1956 as essential to the continuing vitality of Marxism. After repeated warnings and arguments, Lefebvre was expelled from the Party in 1958. Central to his expulsion was the "Humanist-Hegelian" versus "Scientific-Structuralist" Marxisms debate of the mid-fifties, which pitted Lefebvre against Louis Althusser in a replay of the Politzer quarrels of 1938–1939. Lefebvre's influence continued to grow among the gauchist groups like *Arguments* and the *Internationale situationniste*, among the rebellious students of Nanterre (and across the world) during the 1960s, as well as among scholars. His continuing productivity and political independence were best described by Perry Anderson, who, after decrying the tendency of European theorists to reject Marxism for versions of liberalism and outright conservativism, paid homage to

> at least one exception, of signal honor, [who] stands out against the general shift of positions in these years. The oldest living survivor of the Western Marxist tradition I discussed, Henri Lefebvre, neither bent nor turned in his eighth decade, continuing to produce imperturbable and original work on subjects typically ignored by much of the Left.[13]

Lefebvre died in mid-1991, the last survivor of the circle.

It is regrettable but necessary to record that Lefebvre and Friedmann argued bitterly during the postwar years, and their friendship died in political polemics. However, each mentions the other in their respective biographic writings, not always with rancor. In fact, the tone approaches that mixture of remembered anger and unforgotten comradery with which one recalls lost friends.

In 1940, Morhange was removed from his teaching post by Vichy, and worked in a factory, where he organized a resistance triangle. His clandestine work led to his election as vice president of the Committee of Liberation of the Hautes-Pyréneés. After the Liberation, he was reintegrated into the French educational system with a post in Tarbes. At the end of his career, Morhange was teaching at the prestigious lycée Condorcet in Paris, obviously well beloved by his students.

During the last years of his life, he accepted the comparison between himself and the biblical Job, the poet of desire and doubt, of everyman.[14] And, as if to underscore the continuity and collectivity of the Philosophies project, Morhange in 1959 described poetry as a method of dealienating life, as "*poésie de la vie quotidienne purement concrète*"—poetry of daily life—purely concrete.[15] He died in 1972, shortly after reaching his seventy-first year.

NOTES

1. Nizan's letters home have been published as "Correspondance de guerre" in *Paul Nizan, Intellectuel communiste,* ed. Jean-Jacques Brochier (Paris: Maspero, 1967), tome 2. See Nizan's only reference to Politzer in his letter of 20 December 1939, p. 122.

2. Politzer's role in the Resistance is indisputable, and accepted by writers examining this period regardless of personal politics. See Roland Gaucher, *Histoire secrète du Parti Communiste* (Paris: Albin Michel, 1974), pp. 294–95; Jacques Milhau, "Georges Politzer ou la Raison militante," *Cahiers de l'Institut Maurice Thorez,* no. 27 (May–June 1972): 87; Germaine Willard, "XXXe anniversaire: Jacques Decour—Georges Politzer—Jacques Solomon," *Pensée,* no. 163 (May–June 1972): 117; Pierre Seghers, *La Résistance et ses poètes* (Paris: Editions Seghers, 1974); Henri Noguères, *Histoire de la Résistance en France* (Paris: Robert Laffont, 1967), tome 1; *Les Actes du Colloque les Femmes dans la Résistance* (Paris: Editions du Rocher, 1977); Philippe Robrieux, *Histoire Intérieure du Parti Communiste* (Paris: Fayard, 1980), tome 1 (1920–1945).

3. Seghers, *Résistance et ses poètes,* pp. 103–106.

4. Politzer, "Obscurantisme au XXe siècle" and "Révolution et contre-révolution au XXe siècles" in *Ecrits II: Les Fondements de la Psychologie* (Paris: Editions Sociales, 1969). The opening editorial of *Pensée Libre* is contained in Seghers, *Résistance et ses poètes.*

5. Cited by Georges Cogniot in his preface to *Elementary Principles of Philosophy,* trans. B. L. Morris (New York: International, 1976), p. xiv. There is a large Party hagiology surrounding Politzer's activities, some of which is listed below. The most insightful commentary is that of François Hinker in *Cahiers du Communisme* 48, no. 6 (June 1972).

Louis Althusser provided a few passing comments on "Politzer's inspired errors" in *Reading Capital*, trans. B. Brewster (London: NLB, 1970), p. 39, n. 18, and the odd comment that "Politzer is the Feuerbach of our time," p. 138, n. 28. Lucien Séve went further and suggested that Politzer rediscovered in his own fashion the impasse of the "1844 Manuscripts" and, like Marx, turned from the science of human individuality to the science of objective social relations. I have argued in chapter 3 that Politzer's reading of Lenin, especially of *Materialism and Empirio-criticism*, is the key to his development, not the "1844 Manuscripts," and believe the comments by Althusser and Séve were inspired by the "humanist versus scientific" debates within the Party. See both Séve's "Politzer et Nous," *Cahiers de l'Institut Maurice Thorez*, no. 27 (May–July 1972); and *Marxism and the Theory of Human Personality* (London: Lawrence and Wishart, 1975), pp. 35–38. Séve also provides comments in his *Man in Marxist Theory and the Psychology of Personality*, trans. J. McGreal (Atlantic Highlands, N.J.: Humanities, 1978), especially pp. 57, 299–311. The discrepancy between the positions of Séve and Althusser is easily resolved: As Althusser reminded his audience, previous readers of Marx (except Lenin) had "read" *Capital* incorrectly, therefore Politzer could not be compared to Marx (or Althusser) but only to a talented and "wrong" forerunner!

In 1946, a "Trotskyist" suggested instead that "Politzer exchanged his genius for a Party card," which seems to go too far in the opposite direction (from "Roland," "Georges Politzer ou le destin d'Ugolin," in *Octobre* [October 1946], as cited in Laurent Alexandre, "Freud et Politzer: Le Travail d'un rêve," *Europe*, no. 539 [March 1974]: 67). On this piece see also Jean Kanapa, "Georges Politzer et la Calomnie," *Pensée*, no. 10 (1947): 106–109. See Pierre Naville's "Itinéraire de Georges Politzer," in *Psychologie, Marxisme, Matérialisme*, 2d ed. (Paris: Rivière, 1948).

According to Robrieux, *Histoire Intérieure du Parti Communiste*, tome 2 (1945–1972), p. 269, the young Michel Politzer once sent a photo of himself as a child posing with his father to Stalin as a gift. This inane detail does raise the point, however, that the only published photograph of Politzer I am aware of is in *Cahiers de l'Institut Maurice Thorez*, no. 27 (May–July 1972).

Previously uncited pieces concerning Politzer include: Pierre Bruno, "Psychanalyse et matérialisme," *Nouvelle Critique*, no. 97 (1976); Georges Chomarat, "Georges Politzer, aujourd'hui: Le Sens d'un sacrifice," *Pensée*, no. 98 (July–August 1961); Maurice Dayan, "La Dialectique du Comportement," *Etudes Philosophiques* 22, no. 3 (July–September 1967), and 22, no. 4 (October–December 1967); Jean Florence, "Propos sur les Fondements de la Psychologie," *Revue Philosophique de Louvain* 68, no. 4 (1970); Terry Kupers, "Historical Materialism and Scientific Psychology," *Science and Society* 37, no. 1 (spring 1973); Victor Lafitte, "Georges Politzer et la Psychanalyse," *Cahiers du Centre d'Etudes et de Recherches Marxistes*, no. 83 (*Psychanalyse et Marxisme III*, 1970); G. Lanteri-Laura, "Nizan et Politzer Quarante Ans Après," *Critique* 24: 255–56 (August–September 1968); Michel Legrand, "L'Inconscient et la Psychanalyse," *Revue Philosophique de Louvain* 76, no. 3 (1978) and his "L'Objet empirique de la psychanalyse," *Revue Philosophique de Louvain* 78, no. 2 (1980).

See also Michel Marairaz, "Inflation, déflation, reflation: la position de Georges Politzer," *Cahiers de l'Institut Maurice Thorez*, no. 31, ns# 3 (April–June 1973); Bernard Michaux, M.-H. Lavallard, and P. Fuchsman, "G. Politzer et la nécessité de la bataille ideologique," *Cahiers du Communisme*, 48, no. 6 (June 1972); Bernard Michaux, "La Psychanalyse: Psychologie Utiopique?" *Europe*, no. 539 (March 1974); Jacques Milhau, "Georges Politzer ou la Raison Militante," *Cahiers de l'Institut Maurice Thorez*, no. 27 (May–July 1972), and "Georges Politzer ou le Retour Philosophique," *Pensée*, no. 205 (May–June 1979), both also in Milhau, *Chroniques philosophiques* (Paris: Editions Sociales, 1972); Bernard Muldworf, "Georges Politzer et la Psychanalyse," *Cahiers du Centre d'Etudes et de Recherches Marxistes*, no. 83 (*Psychanalyse et Marxisme III*, 1970); Rodolphe Roelens, "Une Recherche psychologique méconnue: Le Courant «Dramatique» de Georges Politzer à aujourd'hui," *Pensée*, no. 103 (May–June 1962); André Richel, "Contributions à la discussion," *Cahiers du Centre d'Etudes et de Recherches Marxistes*, no. 84 (*Psychanalyse et Marxisme III*, 1970); Bernard Toboul, "Ecrits de Politzer," *Cahiers du Communisme* (January 1970); D. Voutsinas, "Psychologie abstrait et Psychologie concrète. En relisant Georges Politzer," *Bulletin de Psychologie*, no. 2 (1967); N. B. Zavadskaia, "Georges Politzer et la crise de la psychologie," *Nouvelle Critique*, no. 19 (September–October 1950); "G. Politzer: 'Le Bergsonisme' et 'Révolution et Contre-Révolution au XXe siècle,'" *Cahiers du Communisme* 24, no. 3–4 (March–April 1947); and "G. Politzer: Principes élémentaires de Philosophie," *Cahiers du Communisme* 23, no. 7 (July 1946).

6. On Friedmann's role in the Resistance, see Seghers, *La Résistance et ses poètes*; Noguères, *Histoire de la Résistance en France*, tome 1; H. R. Kedward, *Resistance in Vichy France* (London: Oxford University, 1978); and Frida Knight's memoir, *The French Resistance 1940–1944* (London: Lawrence and Wishart, 1975). In *End of the Jewish People?* (Garden City, N.Y.: Doubleday Anchor, 1968), Friedmann mentions his use of the pseudonym "Gaston Fromentin" and other variants using the same initials (p. 11). For Friedmann's attempts to grapple with the French Communists and the policies of the USSR, see the excerpts from his wartime writings in *Sagesse*

et Puissance, pp. 149–51, 249–53, and 358–63, and his moving *Journal du Guerre* (Paris: Gallimard, 1987).

7. T. C. Wilson, "American Letters," *Life and Letters Today* 16, no. 8 (summer 1936); Kenneth Burke, personal communication, 10 May 1986.

8. On the Frankfurt School in New York and *Prophets of Deceit* see Martin Jay's *The Dialectical Imagination* (Boston: Little, Brown, 1973), pp. 235, 237–38. Guterman, personal communication, 16 May 1982. There is, of course, a massive literature on the Frankfurt School, but two recent pieces are of particular interest. See the contributions to the panel on Lukács at the American Association of Slavic Studies (November 1984) published in *Studies in Soviet Thought* 31, no. 1 (January 1986). And see the multi-issue discussion of "The Social Philosophy of the Frankfurt School" in *Soviet Studies in Philosophy*, running from vol. 23, no. 4 (summer 1985) through vol. 24, no. 4 (spring 1986). In particular, note the article by V. I. Garadzha, " 'Critical Theory' and Christian Theology," in vol. 24, no. 3 (winter 1985–86). See also John J. Neumaier, "The Frankfurt School in Soviet Eyes," *The Philosophical Forum* 17, no. 4 (summer 1985).

9. Henri Lefebvre, *L'Existentialisme* (Paris: Editions du Sagittaire, 1946), p. 23. To which Guterman sarcastically rejoined, "It's not difficult to be the best Marxist in the U.S.!" Personal communication, 16 May 1982.

10. Annie Cohen-Solal and Henriette Nizan, *Paul Nizan, Communiste Impossible* (Paris: Grosset, 1980), p. 87; Guterman, personal communication, 8 May 1982.

11. Guterman first came to the FBI's attention in 1949, when a source sent copies of *Prophets of Deceit* to the Bureau's headquarters in Washington, D.C., and received a note of thanks from J. Edgar Hoover (dated 30 November 1949). Guterman's name next appeared as a contact or acquaintance of an individual being investigated by the FBI Baltimore Office in May 1951, in a Detroit Office memo of October, and again in a memo from the U.S. Legat in Mexico during November. Initially, there was some confusion as to just which individual the bureau wanted, until Norbert Guterman of New York emerged as the most likely candidate. Despite the fact that a six-year investigation uncovered no evidence of espionage or other subversive activities by Guterman, the investigation was kept open and even pressed until the assistant U.S. attorney, John D. Roeder, advised closing the case after Guterman's grand jury appearance. Guterman's bureau file is #100–384556, and I extend my appreciation to the bureau's FOI/PA Office and staff for providing most of the relevant pages to me. All told, I have received 213 pages of an apparent total of 343.

12. Henri Lefebvre, *Temps des méprises* (Paris: Stock, 1975), pp. 137–38.

13. Perry Anderson, *In the Tracks of Historical Materialism* (Chicago: University of Chicago, 1984), p. 30. Also Anderson's comments in *Considerations on Western Marxism* (London: NLB, 1976), where he placed Lefebvre in the "second" generation of Western marxists and claims Lefebvre was the only French Communist intellectual to achieve "both a relatively high level and volume of written output" in the midst of the general Stalinist ossification (pp. 27, 35–36).

14. Pierre Morhange and Luc Boltansky, "Ce qui m'engage," *Action poétique*, no. 18 (October 1962): 8–9; originally published in *Paris—Lettres*, no. 32 (December 1959).

15. Morhange and Boltansky, *Action poétique*, p. 11. This issue contains photos of Morhange (circa 1960), and the famous group photo of the *équipe Revue marxiste*.

Conclusions

In their attempts to resolve the postwar cultural crises, the Philosophies circle revealed themselves as representative of their generation's need to comprehend the world and to find meaning in apparent chaos. The confusion of poetry and philosophy in their review *Philosophies* exactly matched the symptoms of Valéry's description of the *crise de l'esprit*, while their search for answers in a mysticism and in an ethics demonstrate that they were already pursuing the solution to the *nouvelle mal du siècle* later advocated by Arland. From the origins of the group in 1924 and throughout its evolutions, contemporaries closely scrutinized the efforts of the Philosophies and took those attempts seriously. In their 1925–1926 transition to *Esprit*—marked by political commitment and the search for a method—the Philosophies were a full decade or more in advance of most French intellectuals: While many would follow their example during the Popular Front era, others remained with Sartre on the sidelines, only to belatedly "discover" similar solutions much later.

For Lefebvre, Friedmann, and most of the circle, the *Revue marxiste* experiences of 1929 were critical. Their political commitment and their philosophical searches fused, as their immersion into Marx's early writings provided them with the conceptual keys they sought and the French Communist Party seemingly offered substance and structure within which to work. This commitment endured despite the *Revue marxiste* affair, as

245

demonstrated by their collective and individual efforts throughout the 1930s and, for some, beyond.

The "Priest and Jester" schema suggested by Kolakowski can be applied to the Philosophies in various ways. All were jesters, critical of their France, yet remained "on the fringes" of polite society and never totally separated from it. All unceasingly questioned the values and the structure of the world they inhabited, in pursuit of more perfect human communities and of more perfect knowledge.

Yet within the emerging microcosm of the Parti Communiste Français, Politzer became what Kolakowski termed a "priest." His sudden and dramatic conversion to a Marxism of the most simplistic form, his dogmatic adherence to changes in Comintern and Soviet policies, and his self-appointed, even eager, willingness to serve as inquisitor, suggest Politzer had found some "truth," some solution to his personal and the collective interwar crisis—and he looked no further.

Nizan poses a more complicated case: A late arrival to the Philosophies, he displayed far greater critical independence and intelligence than Politzer, even when serving as a defender of the Party's faith. Nizan's defenses of Friedmann and Lefebvre against Politzer are indicative of this ambivalence within his life as a militant. Nizan's break with the Party in 1939 suggests he never completely relinquished his critical abilities, his doubts, or his search for a solution to his inquietude. His early death leaves forever open the question of where Nizan might have turned next.

Each of the other Philosophies clearly remained "jesters" in his own fashion. Morhange remained on the periphery, of the Party as well as within the French educational system, his visibility fading, perhaps, with time as he chose to remain unnoticed and undisturbed. But Morhange's poetry inspired others, in great part because of his efforts to reveal and criticize the concrete daily life surrounding him. Guterman slowly isolated himself, withdrawing into a small circle of new friends and coworkers in New York, leading Lefebvre to compare his life to the contemplative seclusion of the Hasidim. Although slightly exaggerated, Lefebvre's suggestion does have value, especially when one recalls (as Lefebvre did not) Morhange's description of the early Philosophies, of their monastic lives and warrior spirits, and of their search for absolutes in mysticism.

In the works of Georges Friedmann, the initial Philosophies project continued but was elevated to a theoretical level far more sophisticated than most French intellectual efforts of the interwar era. Retaining the ethical and critical criteria he set out in his earliest writings as well as in *Crise du Progrès*, Friedmann turned to the methods of a historicized sociology, as he employed in *De la Sainte Russe à l'U.R.S.S.* as well as in *Annales* and his other works. Friedmann's fusion of Marxist concepts and analyses, although later less explicit, with his determination to live an ethical life and his faith in the possibility of human progress, provided him with the methods and the criteria for judging the world and himself. He achieved those goals, throughout his life and works displaying not simply keen critical abilities but also a rare sympathetic understanding of humanity.

Of all the Philosophies, Henri Lefebvre most clearly remained the jester, constantly critical of the world and of the various spheres—political, professional, and personal—he moved within. While the theoretical emphases and preoccupations of Friedmann and Lefebvre (working with Guterman and later alone) remained identical, their published writings indicate they diverged along complementary and parallel paths. In general, Lefebvre focused on more abstract theory and textual analysis, on philosophy properly speaking, as shown by the Hegel, Marx, Lenin, and Nietzsche anthologies, and by his later works. However, in Lefebvre's search for a resolution of the interwar *crise de l'esprit* there is something remarkable and unique. Like others marked by that era who sought a solution to the need for certainty, Lefebvre ransacked every imaginable system of thought and method before weaving together elements of Hegel, Marx, Lenin, Nietzsche, and others. Yet what Lefebvre ultimately constructed was an incomplete and uncompletable, self-critical method, even more than Friedmann's. In transcending the *crise de l'esprit*, Lefebvre in fact never totally solved its contradictions but instead preserved its anxieties and its imperative desperate search for absolutes at the centerpiece of his project.

Reconstructing the history of the Philosophies displays the multifaceted search and creativity of the interwar era. At the same time, understanding the specific events and impacts of those years required reconstructing the historical context that conditioned their efforts. This process often entailed revision as well, particularly when examining their relationships to the Parti Communiste and its evolutions, although the same can be said for the development of French psychology and even more broadly the development of French thought as well as Marxist theory in the twentieth century. The small Philosophies circle was at the center of the crucial events and problems of the interwar era, and retracing its history allows for a greater understanding of that troubled time.

When taking up the tools of their craft, historians are actually preoccupied with something other than the past. In attempting to comprehend the past, historians also seek to understand their present. Look again at Valéry's description of the *crise de l'esprit*, at the postwar loss of certainty and direction which sparked those desperate searches for absolutes and meaning. There is something disturbingly contemporary in his list of the symptoms of that crisis, for, on a global scale, has not the closing third of the century witnessed a new outbreak of the same problems? Behind the various and innumerable religious revivals, in the resurgence of nationalisms, and in the persistence of ideologies many thought discredited, lie the same anxieties, anguish, and fears. And in their trendy proliferation of fashionable new theories, new schools of thought, or new searches for minuscule methods, intellectuals are displaying the same bewilderment and confusion that Valéry, Arland, the Philosophies, and so many others described.

Whether Lefebvre, Friedmann, and the Philosophies found the answers necessary to resolve their crisis can and should be debated. But it cannot be doubted that they were asking the same questions so urgently needing to be answered today.

Bibliography

I. SELECTED WRITINGS OF THE PHILOSOPHIES

For reasons of space, I have listed only the most essential writings of the Philosophies. For a more thorough compilation, please refer to the dissertation version of this study (University of Wisonsin at Madison, 1986). Fairly complete bibliographies exist for several of the Philosophies. For Georges Friedmann's writings see the listing by Marie-Thèrése Basse in *Une Nouvelle Culture? Hommage à Georges Friedmann* (Paris: Gallimard, 1973). Although useful, the bibliography found in Kurt Meyer, *Henri Lefebvre, Ein Romantischer revolutionär* (Vienna: EuropaVerlag, 1973), became outdated due to Lefebvre's output until his death in 1991. Since most of Paul Nizan's writings have little direct relevance for this study, readers should consult the bibliographies found in *Pour une nouvelle culture*, edited by Susan Sulieman (Paris: Grasset, 1971), and in Jacqueline Leiner, *Le Destin littéraire de Paul Nizan* (Paris: Klincksieck, 1970). For Morhange, Nikiprowetzky's study in *Le Sentiment lui-même* (Honfleur, Editions Oswald, 1966) and the bibliography in *Action Poétique* no. 18 (1962) are fairly complete, but lack Morhange's last or posthumously published works. Titles are listed first alphabetically by author and then in chronological order of publication.

Friedmann, Georges-Philippe. "Comment l'Etat bourgeois fabrique ses intellectuels." *Clarté*, no. 59 (1924).

————. "Quelques Jeunes." *Clarté*, no. 65 (1924).

————. "Le Forum." *Clarté*, no. 70 (January 1925).

————. "L'Inquiétude de Marcel Arland: à propos d'une nouvelle mystique."
Europe, no. 28 (April 1925).

————. "Une direction dans la Nouvelle Génération." *Europe*, no. 29 (May 1925).

————. "Notes prises en Toscane fasciste." *Europe*, no. 36 (December 1925).

————. "Ils sonts perdu la partie èternelle d'eux-mêmes." *Esprit*, no. 1 (May 1926).

————. "Austro-Marxisme et religion." *Revue Marxiste*, no. 1 (February 1929).

————. *Votre tour viendra*. Paris: Gallimard, 1930.

————. *Ville qui n'a pas de fin!* Paris: Gallimard, 1931.

————. "P. Nizan: Aden Arabie." *Cahiers du Sud*, no. 132 (July 1931).

————. *L'Adieu*. Paris: Gallimard, 1932.

————. "Message à l'A.E.A.R.," in *Ceux qui ont choisi*. Paris: Editions de l'A.E.A.R., 1933.

————. "H. Daniel-Rops: Le Monde sans âme." *Zeitschrift für Sozialforschung*, vol. 2
1933.

————. *Problèmes du machinisme en U.R.S.S. et dans les pays capitalistes*. Paris: Editions
Sociales Internationales, 1934.

————. "Matérialisme dialectique et action réciproque." *Commune*, no.15
(November 1934). Also in *A la Lumière du Marxisme*, tome 1. Paris: Editions
Sociales Internationales, 1935.

————. "Organisation économique et Machinisme." *Annales d'Histoire économique et
sociale*, tome 6, no. 30 (November 1934).

————. "Aspects de la philosophie marxiste." *Monde* (9 May 1935, 6 June 1935,
and 5 September 1935).

————. "Machinisme et humanisme." *Europe*, no. 151 (July 1935).

————. "Progrès du marxisme en France." *Monde* (26 September 1935).

————. "Lénine, matérialiste militant." *L'Humanité* (22 October 1935).

————. *La Crise du Progrès*. Paris: Gallimard, 1936.

————. "Quelques traits de l'Esprit nouveau en U.R.S.S." in C. Bouglé, *Inventaires:
La Crise sociale et les Ideologies nationales*. Paris: Alcan, 1936. A fragment previously published as "Travail et communion en U.R.S.S." *Europe*, no. 153 (September 1935).

————. "La Lumière du Marxisme." *L'Humanité* (15 March 1936).

————. "Un aspect du mouvement stakhanoviste." *Annales d'Histoire économique et
sociale*, tome 8, no. 38 (March 1936).

———. "A propos de la sociologie allemande contemporaine." *Commune*, no 34 (June 1936).

———. "Les Rapports de la conscience des hommes et des conditions économiques." in *Cours du Marxisme* (2ᵉ année, 1936–1937). Paris: Editions centrale, 1937.

———. "La Crise du progrès et l'humanisme nouveau." *Bulletin de l'Union pour la Vérité*, no. 3 (December 1936), no. 4 (January 1937).

———. "Vers la culture des masses (en U.R.S.S.)." *L'Internationale de l'Enseignement* (1936).

———. "André Gide et l'U.R.S.S." *Europe*, no. 169 (January 1937). Also in *De la Sante Russie à l'U.R.S.S.*

———. "Règression idèologique du Fascisme." *Clarté*, no. 6 (January 1937).

———. "Tèmoignage (sur l'Espagne et l'Europe)." *Clarté*, no. 12 (July–August 1937).

———. "Descartes, prince des temps modernes." *Europe*, no. 175 (July 1937). Also in Maxime LeRoy et al. *Descartes*. Paris: Rieder, 1937.

———. "Le Roman de l'Espagne (L'Espoir d'André Malraux)." *L'Humanité* (29 January 1938).

———. "Psychotechnique industrielle et sciences sociales." In *Les Convergences des sciences sociales et l'esprit international*. Paris: Editions Paul Hartmann, 1938.

———. *De la Sainte Russie à l'U.R.S.S.* Paris: Gallimard, 1938. An extract was published in *Europe*, no. 182 (February 1938).

———. "Esquisse de quelques problèmes." *Europe*, no. 185 (May 1938). In *L'Homme, la technique, et la nature*, Paris: Rieder, 1938.

———. "L'U.R.S.S. et le drame tchécoslovaque." *Europe*, no. 193 (January 1939).

———. "Ceux qui vinrent trop tôt." *Europe*, no. 199 (July 1939).

———. *Leibniz et Spinoza*. Paris: Gallimard, 1946.

———. *Problèmes humains du machinisme industriel*. Paris: Gallimard, 1946. Eng. trans., Glencoe, Ill.: Free Press, 1955.

———. "Forces Morales et valeurs permanentes." In *L'Heure du Choix*, edited by C. Aveline, J. Cassou, L. Martin-Chauffer, G. Friedmann, and Vercors. Paris: Editions de Minuit, 1947.

———. *Où va le travail humain?* Paris: Gallimard, 1950.

———. *Humanisme du travail et humanités*. Paris: A. Colin, 1950.

———. *Le Travail en miettes*. Paris: Gallimard, 1956. Eng. trans., New York: Free Press, 1961.

———. *Fin du peuple juif?* Paris: Gallimard, 1965. Eng. trans., New York: Doubleday, 1967.

————. *Sept Etudes sur l'homme et la technique.* Paris: Gonthier, 1966.

————. *La Puissance et la Sagesse.* Paris: Gallimard, 1970.

————. *Ces merveilleux instruments.* Paris: Denoël, 1979.

————. *Journal de Guerre 1939–1940.* Paris: Gallimard, 1987.

Friedmann, Georges-Philippe, with Pierre Naville. *Traité de Sociologie du Travail.* 2 vols. Paris: A. Colin, 1961, 1962.

Guterman, Norbert, "B. Russell: Les Problèmes de la Philosophie." *Philosophies,* no. 1 (March 1924).

————. "J. Cocteau: Thomas l'Imposteur." *Philosophies,* no. 1 (March 1924).

————. "M. Proust: La Prisonneriere, Sodome et Gomorrhe III." *Philosophies,* no. 2 (May 1924).

————. "C. Spiess: Ainsi Parlait l'Homme." *Philosophies,* no. 2 (May 1924).

————. "A. Gide, Souvenirs de la Cour d'Assises." *Philosophies,* no. 3 (September 1924).

————. "La Théorie de la Connaissance selon Léon Brunschvicg." *Philosophies,* no. 3 (September 1924).

————. "Rétrospection sur Ecce Homo, de Frédéric Nietzsche." *Philosophies,* no 4 (November 1924).

————. "Christianisme, décadence et esprit juif." *Philosophies,* no. 4 (November 1924).

————. "La Fin d'une Histoire. Quelques notes sur le «Surréalisme» dans le sens que lui donne M. Breton." *Philosophies,* no. 4 (November 1924). Excerpted in *Révolution Surréaliste,* no. 2 (15 January 1925).

————. "A propos de M. Maritain." *Philosophies,* no. 5/6 (March 1925).

————. [Albert Mesnil, pseud.], "Avertissement à Marx." *Revue Marxiste,* no. 1 (February 1929).

————. "L'Ile de Bitche." *Cahiers du Sud,* no. 121 (May 1930).

————. "A. Gide: Feuillets." *Avant-Poste,* no. 1 (June 1933).

————. "P. Nizan: Chiens de Garde." *Avant-Poste,* no. 2 (August 1933).

————. "Why Cabinets Fall in France." *New Republic* 78, no. 15–16 (14 February 1934).

————. "The French Press and the Riots." *New Masses* (27 March 1934).

————. "Toward Marxist Criticism." *New Masses* (2 April 1935).

————. "Analysis of Communication." *New Masses* (16 April 1935).

————. "Frontiers of Credulity." *New Republic* 93, no. 49 (17 November 1937).

————. "Revolt in the Desert." *New Republic* 99, no. 185 (21 June 1939).

————. "French Story." *New Republic* 102, no. 614 (6 May 1940).

————. "Lee and Lee: Propaganda Analysis; Lavine and Wechsler: The Fine Art of Propaganda; Bartlett: Political Propaganda; Carr: Propaganda in International Politics; Chakotin: The Rape of the Masses; Taylor: The Strategy of Terror." *Studies in Philosophy and the Social Sciences,(Zeitschrift für Sozialforschung)*. Vol. 9 (1941).

Gutterman, Norbert, trans., *Le Nuage dans le Pantalon*, by V. Mayakovsky. Paris: Les Revues, 1930.

————. "Comment on fait un poème" by V. Mayakovsky. *Europe*, no. 127 (July 1933).

————. *The Alienation of Reason*, by Leszek Kolakowski. Garden City, New York: Doubleday, 1968.

————. *The Sociology of Marx*, by Henri Lefebvre. New York: Pantheon, 1968.

————. *42ᵉ Parallèle*, by John Dos Passos. Paris: Grasset, 1934. Reprint, Paris: Gallimard, 1977.

Guterman, Norbert, and Henri Lefebvre. "Individu et Classe." *Avant-Poste*, no. 1 (June 1933).

————. "La Mystification: notes pour une critique de la vie quotidienne." *Avant-Poste*, no. 2 (August 1933).

————. "Journal d'un Aryen." *Avant-Poste*, no. 3 (October–November 1933).

————. *Morceaux Choisis de Karl Marx*. Paris: Gallimard, 1934. Numerous reprintings.

————. *La Conscience mystifiée*. Paris: Gallimard, 1936. Reprint, Paris: Le Sycomore, 1979.

————. *Les Cahiers de Lénine sur la dialectique de Hegel*. Paris: Gallimard, 1938. Reprint, Gallimard, 1967. An extract of the introduction published as "Le problème de la conscience" in *Europe*, no. 175 (July 1937), and in M. LeRoy et al., *Descartes*. Paris: Rieder, 1937.

————. *Morceaux Choisis de Hegel*. Paris: Gallimard, 1938. Numerous reprintings.

Guterman, Norbert, and Leo Lowenthal. *Prophets of Deceit*. New York: Harper, 1949. 2d ed.; Palo Alto, Calif.: Pacific Books, 1970, with forward by H. Marcuse and M. Horkheimer.

Guterman, Norbert, and Pierre Morhange, trans. *Poèmes d'Ouvriers américains*. Paris: Les Revues, 1930. Reprint, Tarbes: Cercle des Lettres, 1948; Saint-Giron: Au Colporteur, 1951.

————. "A Vous, Nos maîtres encores," trans. by H. G. Weiss. *Avant-Poste*, no. 3 (October–November 1933).

Lefebvre, Henri. "Sur une note de M. Ramon Fernandez «les intermittences du coeur»." *Philosophies*, no. 2 (May 1924).

———. "Gide: Incidences." *Philosophies*, no. 3 (September 1924).

———. "Une Tentative métaphysique. La thése de M. Laville." *Philosophies*, no. 3 (September 1924).

———. "Fragment d'une Philosophie de la Conscience." *Philosophies*, no. 4 (November 1924).

———. "T. Tzara: 7 Manifestes dada." *Philosophies*, no. 4 (November. 1924).

———. "Positions d'attaque et de défense du nouveau mysticisme." *Philosophies*, no. 5/6 (March 1925).

———. "La Pensée et l'Esprit." *Esprit*, no. 1 (May 1926).

———. "Description de Ce Temps: Misére de M. Jacques Maritain." *Esprit*, no. 1 (May 1926).

———. "Description de Ce Temps: Notes pour le procès de la chrétiente," *Esprit*, no. 2 (May 1927).

———. "Reconnaissance à l'Unique." *Esprit*, no. 2 (May 1927).

———. Introduction to *La Liberté Humaine*, by Friedrich Schelling. Translated by G. Politzer. Paris: Rieder, "Collection Philosophie," 1926.

———. "Du Culte «L'Esprit» au Matérialisme dialectique." *Nouvelle Revue Française*, no. 231 (December 1932).

———. "La Fascisme en France." *Avant-Poste*, no. 1 (June 1933).

———. "A. Breton: Les Vases Communicant." *Avant-Poste*, no. 1 (June 1933).

———. "A propos du livre de L. F. Cèline." *Avant-Poste*, no. 1 (June 1933).

———. "Autocritique." *Avant-Poste*, no. 2 (August 1933).

———. "Echange de lettres avec L. F. Cèline." *Avant-Poste*, no. 2 (August 1933).

———. "Lettre d'un jeune à la jeunesse." *Avant-Poste*, no. 3 (October–November 1933).

———. "Le Karl Marx de M. Otto Ruhle." *Avant-Poste*, no. 3 (October–November 1933).

———. "B. Mussolini: Le Fascisme." *Avant-Poste*, no. 3 (October–November 1933).

———. "La Revue *Esprit*." *Avant-Poste*, no. 3 (October–November 1933).

———. "Qu'est-ce que la Dialectique?" *Nouvelle Revue Française*, no. 264 (September 1935) and no. 265 (October 1935).

———. "People's Front in France." *New Republic* 84, no. 235–237 (9 October 1935).

———. "France decides Europe's *Fate*." *New Republic* 86, no. 306–308 (22 April 1936).

———. "G. Friedmann: Crise du Progrès." *Nouvelle Revue Française*, no. 275 (August 1936).

———. "Essai sur les rapports de la Critique et le Roman." *Commune*, no. 48 (August 1937).

———. "P. Morhange et M. Matveev: Lettres de Lénine à sa famille." *Europe*, no. 177 (September 1937).

———. *Le Nationalisme contre les Nations*, preface by Paul Nizan. Paris: Editions Sociales Internationales, 1935. Reprint, Meridiens Klincksieck, 1988, with a preface by Michel Trebitsch.

———. "Affair of the Hooded Men." *New Republic* 93, no. 162–164 (15 December 1937).

———. "P. Nizan: Les Matérialistes de l'Antiquité; I. K. Lappol: Diderot; G. Friedmann: La Crise du Progrès." *Zeitschrift für Sozialforschung*, vol. 6 (1937).

———. *Hitler au Pouvoir: les enseignements de cinq années de fascisme en Allemagne.* Paris: Bureau d'Editions, 1938.

———. "Watch France!" *New Republic* 97, no. 226 (28 December 1938).

———. *Le Matérialisme dialectique.* Translated by J. Sturrock. Paris: Alcan, 1939. Numerous reprints and translations.

———. *Nietzsche.* Paris: Editions Sociales Internationales, 1939.

———. "Nietzsche et la fascisme hitlérien." *Commune*, no. 66 (February 1939).

———. [signed H. L.], "Georges Politzer." *Pensée*, no. 1 (1944).

———. *L'Existentialisme.* Paris: Editions du Sagittaire, 1946.

———. *Critique de la vie quotidienne.* Tome 1, Introduction. Paris: Grasset, 1947. Reprint, L'Arche, 1959. Translated by John Moore as *Critique of Everyday Life.* Vol. 1, Introduction, with a preface by Michel Trebitsch (London: Verso, 1991); Tome 2, *Fondement d'une sociologie de la quotidienneté.* Paris: L'Arche, 1961. Tome 3, *De la modernité au modernisme (Pour une métaphilosophie du quotidien)* (Paris: 1981).

———. *Pascal.* 2 volumes. Paris: Nagel, 1949, 1954.

———. "Georges Politzer et la Psychanalyse." *Raison, Cahiers de Psychopathologie* (1957).

———. "Vers un Romanticisme révolutionnaire." *Nouvelle Revue Française*, no. 58 (October 1957).

———. "Les Rapports de la Philosophie et de la Politique dans les premières oeuvres de Marx." *Revue de Métaphysique et de Morale* 63, no. 2–3 (April–September 1958).

———. *La Somme et le Reste*, 2 volumes. 1959. Reprint, Paris: Bélibaste, 1973.

———. *Introduction à la Modernité.* Paris: Editions de Minuit, 1962.

———. "Henri Lefebvre par lui-même." In *Les Philosophies Française d'aujourd'hui*, edited by G. Deledalle and D. Huisman. Paris: CDU, 1963.

———. *La Métaphilosophie.* Paris: Editions de Minuit, 1965.

———. *La Proclamation de la Commune.* Paris: Gallimard, 1965.

————. "1925." *Nouvelle Revue Française*, no. 172 (April 1967).

————. *Sociologie de Marx*. Paris: Presses Universitaires de France, 1968. Reprint, translated by N. Guterman. New York: Pantheon, 1968.

————. *La Vie quotidienne dans la Monde moderne*. Paris: Gallimard, 1968; Reprint, translated by S. Rabinovitch, New York: Penguin, 1971.

————. *La Fin de l'Histoire*. Paris: Editions de Minuit, 1970.

————. *Hegel Marx Nietzsche, ou le Royaume des Ombres*. Paris: Casterman, 1975.

————. *Les Temps des Méprises*. Paris: Stock, 1975.

————. *La Presence et l'Absence*. Paris: Casterman, 1980.

Lefebvre, Henri, and B. Bernardi, "Une Vie pour penser et porte la lutte de classes à la theorie: Entretien..." *Nouvelle Critique*, no. 306, ns #125 (June 1979).

Lefebvre, Henri, L. Goldmann, T. Tzara, et al., *Le Romanticisme révolutionnaire*. Paris: La Nef de Paris, 1958.

Lefebvre, Henri, and Leszek Kolakowski, "Evolution or Revolution." In *Reflexive Water: The Basic Concerns of Mankind*, edited by F. Elders. London: Souvenir, 1974.

Lefebvre, Henri, and M. Trebitsch, "Le Renouveau philosophique avorté des années Trente. Entretien." *Europe*, no. 683 (March 1986).

Morhange, Pierre. "Cinq fragments." *Philosophies*, no. 1 (March 1924).

————. [John Brown, pseud.], "Billet." *Philosophies*, no. 1 (March 1924).

————. "Jules Fabius (Fragment)." *Philosophies*, no. 2 (May 1924).

————. [John Brown, pseud.], "Billet." *Philosophies*, no. 2 (May 1924).

————. [John Brown, pseud.], "de Montherlant: Le Paradis a l'ombre des épées." *Philosophies*, no. 3 (September 1924).

————. [John Brown, pseud.], "Billet où l'on donne le «la»." *Philosophies*, no. 3 (September 1924).

————. "L. Lambelin: L'Imperialisme d'Israël." *Philosophies*, no. 3 (September 1924).

————. "M. Jacob: Visions infernales." *Philosophies*, no. 3 (September 1924).

————. "Jules Fabius (fragment)." *Philosophies*, no. 3 (September 1924).

————. "Réponse à l'enquête sur Rêves." *Disque Verte* 3, no. 2 (1925).

————. "Sagesse juive." *Revue Juive* (1925).

————. "Réponse à l'enquête sur Les Appels de l'Orient." *Cahiers du Mois*, no. 9/10 (February/March 1925).

————. "P. Eluard: Mourir de ne pas mourir." *Philosophies*, no. 5/6 (March 1925).

————. "Réponse à l'Appel aux Travailleurs intellectuels." *Clarté*, no. 76 (1925).

————. "Réponse." *Nouvelle Revue Française*, no. 141 (June 1925).

————. "La Présence (I)." *Esprit*, no. 1 (May 1926).

————. "Réponse à l'Enquête sur l'Anti-Poésie." *Cahiers Idealistes*, no. 14 (June 1926).

―――. "Réponse." *Nouvelle Revue Française*, no. 191 (August 1929).

―――. "Poème inédit." *Monde*, no. 68 (21 September 1929).

―――. "Poèmes du Mauvais Temps." *Cahiers du Sud*, no. 116 (November 1929).

―――. "Lettre." *Nouvelle Revue Française*, no. 198 (March 1930).

―――. "Gallia." *Europe*, no. 102 (June 1931).

―――. "La Vie est Unique." *Avant-Poste*, no. 1 (June 1933).

―――. "Finalement." *Avant-Poste*, no. 1 (June 1933).

―――. "Reportage à la portée de ma bourse." *Avant-Poste*, no. 2 (August 1933).

―――. "Reportage à la portée de ma bourse." *Avant-Poste*, no. 3 (October/November 1933).

―――. "NRF (1st oct.)." *Avant-Poste*, No. 3 (October/November 1933).

―――. *La Vie est Unique*. Paris: Gallimard, 1933.

―――. "Correspondance." *Nouvelle Revue Française*, no. 242 (November 1933).

―――. "Trois poèmes." In *Anthologie des poètes de la Nouvelle Revue Française*. Paris: Gallimard, 1936; 2d ed. 1959.

―――. "Air de flute improvise pour l'anniversaire de Henri Heine." *Europe*, no. 170 (February 1937).

―――. "Poèmes d'amour." *Europe*, no. 181 (January 1938).

―――. "Séparations." *Esprit*, no. 91 (April 1940).

―――. *Bouquet de poèmes pour mes amis de Bigorre*. Tarbes: Cercle des Lettres, 1948.

―――. *Autocritique*. Paris: Seghers, 1951.

―――. *Le Blessé*. Saint-Giron: Au Colpolteur, 1952.

―――. *La Robe*. Paris: Seghers, 1954.

―――. *Poèmes bref*. Columbes: Edition de la revue Strophes, 1965.

―――. *Le Sentiment lui-même*, with an introduction by V. Nikiprowetzky. Honfleur: Editions Pierre Jean Oswald, 1966.

Morhange, Pierre, and A. Breton, "Un Curieux Echange de lettres." *Nouvelle Revue Française*, no. 134 (September 1924). Breton's letter can also be found in *Journal Littéraire*, no. 26 (18 October 1924), and in Jose Pierre's anthology listed in section 2 of this bibliography.

Morhange, Pierre, and M. Matveev. *La Septième République*. Translated by Pilniak. Paris: Les Revues, 1929.

Morhange, Pierre, and M. Matveev, trans. *Lettres de Lénine à sa famille*. Paris: Rieder, 1936.

Morhange, Pierre, et al., "Hommage à Miguel de Unamuno." *Philosophies*, no. 1 (March 1924).

―――. "Votre méditation sur Dieu." *Philosophies*, no. 4 (November 1924).

Nizan, Paul Yves. *Pour une nouvelle culture.* Edited by Susan Sulieman. Paris: Grasset, 1971.

———. *Paul Nizan, intellectuel communiste.* Edited by Jean-Jacques Brochier. 2 volumes. Paris: Maspero, 1967.

———. "La Rationalisation." *Revue Marxiste,* no. 1 (February 1929) and no. 2 (March 1929).

———. "F. Arouet: Le Fin d'un parade philosophique." *Revue Marxiste,* no. 2 (March 1929).

———. "Organisation du 1er Congres de l'Internationale Communiste." *Revue Marxiste,* no. 6 (July 1929).

———. "N. Guterman and P. Morhange: Poémes d'Ouvriers americains." *Europe,* no. 94 (October 1930).

———. "G. Friedmann: Votre Tour viendra." *Europe,* no. 99 (March 1931).

———. *Aden-Arabie.* Paris: Rieder, 1931. Reprint, Maspero 1960; translated by J. Pinkham, New York and London: Monthly Review, 1968.

———. "Les Conséquences du refus." *Nouvelle Revue Française,* no. 231 (December 1932).

———. "Sur un certain Front unique." *Europe,* no. 121 (January 1933). Also in Sulieman.

———. *Les Chiens du Garde.* Paris: Rieder, 1932. Reprint, Maspero, 1960; translated by P. Fittingoff, New York and London: Monthly Review, 1971.

———. "Les enfants de la lumière." *Commune,* no. 3 (November 1933).

———. "Marx Philosophe." In *Karl Marx: Morceaux Choisis,* edited by N. Guterman and H. Lefebvre. Paris: Gallimard, 1934.

———. "Tendances actuelles de la philosophie." *L'Etudiant d'Avant-Garde,* no. 1 (1934).

———. Avant propos to *Le Nationalisme contre les Nations,* by H. Lefebvre. Paris: Editions Sociales Internationales, 1935.

———. "Sur l'Humanisme." *Europe,* no. 151 (July 1935).

———. *La Conspiration.* Paris: Gallimard, 1938. Reprint, Gallimard, 1973.

———. "G. Friedmann: De la Sainte Russie à l'U.R.S.S." *Commune,* no. 57 (May 1938).

———. "Les Livres: Nietzsche par H. Lefebvre, Nietzsche par H. Mann." *Ce Soir* (1 June 1939).

———. "Les Livres: La *Pensée.*" *Ce Soir* (15 June 1939).

Politzer, Georges. *Ecrits I: La Philosophie et les Mythes* and *Ecrits II: Les Fondements de la Psychologie.* Paris: Editions Sociales, 1969.

———. *La Liberté Humain.* Translated by F. Schelling. Paris: Rieder, "Collection Philosophie," 1926.

———. *Critique des fondements de la psychologie*, Tome 1. Paris: Rieder, 1928. Reprint, Presses universitaires de France, 1967.

———. [François Arouet, pseud.], *Le Bergsonisme. Une mystification philosophique.* Paris: Les Revues, 1929. Reprint, Editions Sociales, 1947; Jean-Jacques Pauvert, 1968.

———. [Félix Arnold, pseud.], "La Lutte pour le Matérialisme." *Revue Marxiste*, no. 1 (February 1929).

———. [F. A., pseud.], "La Lutte des classes en Angleterre." *Revue Marxiste*, no. 2 (March 1929).

———. [Félix Arnold, pseud.], "E. Vandervelde: Le Marxisme a-t-il fait faillite?" *Revue Marxiste*, no. 2 (March 1929).

———. [F. A., pseud.], "Marx: 18e Brumaire." *Revue Marxiste*, no. 2 (March 1929).

———. [Félix Arnold, pseud.], "Au-delà du Marxisme ou en deçà de la réalite." *Revue Marxiste*, no. 3 (April 1929).

———. [Félix Arnold, pseud.], "Oeuvres politiques de K. Marx." *Revue Marxiste*, no. 3 (April 1929).

———. [Félix Arnold, pseud.], "J. Benda: La Fin de l'Eternel." *Revue Marxiste*, no. 6 (July 1929).

———. "L'Unitè ideologique du Parti," *Cahiers du Bolchévisme* 12, no. 10/11 (15 May/1 June 1935).

———. "Leurs arguments et les nôtres." *Cahiers du Bolchévisme* 12, no. 17/18 (September 1935).

———. "Les Discussions sur le problème du Parti Unique." *Cahiers du Bolchévisme* 13, no. 1/2 (15 January 1936).

———. "A propos du programme du Rassemblement populaire." *Cahiers du Bolchévisme* 13, no. 3/4 (15 February 1936). Reprinted in *Nouvelle Critique*, no. 241, ns# 60 (1973).

———. "La Légende de la «Main de Moscou»." *Cahiers du Bolchévisme* 13, no. 6 (1 April 1936).

———. "L'Exécution du Programme du Rassemblement populaire." *Cahiers du Bolchévisme* 13, no. 10/11 (15 June 1936).

———. "L'Etat." In *Cours de Marxisme*, Première Année 1935–1936. Paris: Bureau d'Editions, 1937.

———. *Les Grandes Problèmes de la Philosophie Contemporaine.* Paris: Bureau d'Editions, 1938. Vol. 21 of *Les Cours de l'Université ouvriere de Paris*.

———. "A propos d'un livre sur l'U.R.S.S." *Cahiers du Bolchévisme* 15, no. 5/6 (May/June 1938).

———. "La Facture de Munich." *Cahiers du Bolchévisme* 15, no. 11 (November 1938).

———. *Principes élémentaires de philosophie.* Paris: Editions Sociales, 1975. Multiple editions, including an expanded *Principes fondamentaux de Philosophie* by Guy Besse and Maurice Caveing. Paris: Editions Sociales, 1954. The 1975 edition was translated as *Elementary Principles of Philosophy* by Barbara L. Morris. New York: International, 1976, 1978.

II. SECONDARY SOURCES

Anderson, Kevin. "Rubel's Marxology: a critique." *Capital and Class* 47 (summer 1992).

———. *Lenin, Hegel, and Western Marxism: A Critical Study.* Urbana and Chicago: University of Illinois, 1995.

Anderson, Perry. *Considerations on Western Marxism.* London: NLB, 1976.

———. *In the Tracks of Historical Materialism.* Chicago: University of Chicago, 1984.

Andreu, Pierre. "Les Idées politiques de la Jeunesse intellectuelle de 1927 à la guerre." *Revue des Travaux de l'Academie des Sciences morales et politiques* 110, no. 2 (1957).

———. *Le Rouge et le Blanc.* Paris: Table Ronde, 1977.

Aron, Raymond. *Marxismes imaginaires; d'une Sainte Famille à l'Autre.* Paris: Gallimard, 1970.

———. *The Committed Observer.* Translated by J. and M. McIntosh. Chicago: Regnery Gateway, 1983.

———. *Memoires.* Paris: Julliard, 1983.

Balakian, Anna. *Surrealism: The Road to the Absolute.* New York: Dutton, 1970.

Balmand, Pascal. "Les jeunes intellectuels de l'Esprit des années Trente: un phénomène de génération?" *Cahiers de l'Institut d'Histoire du Temps Present,* no. 6 (November 1987).

Bandyopadhyay, Pradeep. "The Many Faces of French Marxism." *Science and Society* 36, no. 2 (Summer 1972).

Barande, Ilse and Robert. *Histoire de la Psychanalyse en France.* Paris: Privat, 1975.

Barba, Gianni. "Bibliographische Notizen zum Werke von Henri Lefebvre." *Neuekritik,* no. 31 (August 1965).

Barber, John. "The Establishment of Intellectual Orthodoxy in the USSR 1928-1934." *Past and Present,* no. 83 (May 1979).

Baruk, Henri. *La Psychiatrie française de Pinel à nos jours.* Paris: PUF, 1967.

Basse, Marie-Thérèse. "Georges Friedmann: son itinéraire, son influence et quelques thèmes principaux de son oeuvre," *Sociologie du Sud-Est*, no. 26 (October–December 1980).

Bernard, Jean-Pierre A. *Le Partie Communiste Française et la question littéraire.* Grenoble: Presses Universitaires de Grenoble, 1972.

Bernard, Philippe, and Henri Dubief. *The Decline of the Third Republic 1914–1938.* New York: Cambridge University Press, 1985.

Bianquis, Geneviève. *Nietzsche en France, L'Influence de Nietzsche sur la Pensée française* Paris: Alcan, 1929.

Borel, Jacques. "Poésie et vérité de Pierre Morhange." *Europe*, no. 390 (October 1961).

———. "Hommage à Pierre Morhange." *Nouvelle Revue Française*, no. 237 (September 1972).

Boudot, Pierre. *Nietzsche et l'au-delà de la liberté: Nietzsche et les écrivains français 1930 à 1960.* Paris: Aubier Montaigne, 1960.

Breton, André. *Entretiens 1913–1952.* Paris: Gallimard, 1952.

Broadbent, P. N., and J. E. Flower. "The Intellectual and his Role in France between the Wars." *Journal of European Studies* 8, no. 4 (December 1978).

Bruhat, Jean. *Il n'est jamais trop tard.* Paris: Albin Michel, 1983.

Burkhard, Fred (Bud). "D. B. Rjazanov and the Marx-Engels Institute: Notes Toward Further Research," *Studies in Soviet Thought* 30, no. 1 (July 1985): 39–54, and the accompanying "Bibliographic Annex: The Periodicals of the Marx-Engels Institute," 75–88.

———. "Revealing Thoughts: French Post-War Cultural Disarray and the *Revue marxiste enquête* of 1929," *Contemporary European History* 2, no. 3 (November 1993): 225–41.

———. "Henriette Valet's *Mme. 60 bis:* French Social Realities and Literary Politics of the 1930s," *French Historical Studies* 18, no. 2 (fall 1993): 503–23.

———. "The *Revue marxiste* Affair: French Marxism and Communism in Transition Between the Wars," *Historical Reflections/Réflexions historiques* 20, no. 1 (winter 1994): 141–64.

Carbonell, Charles-Olivier, and Georges Livet, eds. *Au Berceau des Annales.* Toulouse: Institut d'Etudes politique, 1983.

Cardon, Claudin, and Germain Willard. "Des Intellectuels dans l'Action Antifasciste: L'Exemple du CVIA." *Cahiers de l'Institut Maurice Thorez* 33, ns# 5 (October/November 1973).

Caute, David. *Communism and the French Intellectuals 1914–1960.* New York: MacMillan, 1964.

————. *The Fellow-Travellers: A Postscript to the Enlightenment.* New York: MacMillan, 1973.

Cluny, Claude-Michel. "Une Voix de Notre Temps: Pierre Morhange et Le Sentiment lui-même." *La Quinzaine Littéraire* (15–28 February 1967).

Cohen, Mitchell. *The Wager of Lucien Goldmann: Tragedy, Dialectics, and a Hidden God.* Princeton: Princeton University Press, 1994.

Cohen-Solal, Annie, with Henriette Nizan. *Paul Nizan, Communiste impossible.* Paris: Grasset, 1980.

Collomb, Michel. "Américanisme et Anti-Américanisme dans la dans la littéature française de l'entre-deux-guerres." *Romantische Zeitschrift für Literaturgeschichte* 6 (1982).

Coutau-Begarie, Hervé. *Le Phenomene "Nouvelle Histoire," Strategie et ideologie.* Paris: Economica, 1983.

Crémieux, Benjamin. *Inquiétude et reconstruction.* Paris: Correa, 1931.

Daniel-Rops, Henri, [Henri Petriot]. *Notre Inquiétude.* 1927. Reprint, Paris: Academie Perrin, 1953.

Debray, Règis. *Teachers, Writers, Celebrities: The Intellectuals of Modern France.* Translated by David Macey. London: NLB, 1981.

Desjardins, Robert. *The Soviet Union through French Eyes.* New York: St. Martin's, 1988.

Dommanget, Maurice. *L'Introduction du Marxisme en France.* Lausanne: Rencontre, 1969.

Droz, Jacques, ed. *Histoire générale du socialisme.* Tome 3: 1919–1945; Tome 4; 1945 à nos jours. Paris: Presses Universitaires de France, 1978.

Duvignaud, Jean. "France: The Neo-Marxists." In *Revisionism,* edited by Leopold Labedz. London: Allen and Unwin, 1962.

Essertier, Daniel. *Philosophes et Savants Français du XXᵉ Siècle.* Tome 4: La Psychologie. Paris: Alcan, 1929.

Fauvet, Jacques. *Histoire du Parti Communiste Française.* 2 volumes. Paris: Fayard, 1964.

Ferlé, T. *Le Communisme en France.* Paris: Documentation Catholique, 1937.

Ferrarotti, Franco. *Toward the Social Production of the Sacred.* La Jolla, Calif.: N.p., 1977.

————. *Le Paradoxe du Sacre.* Bruxelles: Les Eperonniers, 1987.

Ferro, Marc. "Georges Friedmann, Historien de l'avenir," *Annales: Economies, Sociétés, Civilisations* 33, no. 2 (March/April 1978).

Fetscher, Iring. "Der Marxismus in Spiegel der französischen Philosophie." *Marxismusstudien,* no. 1 (*Schriften der Studiengemeinschaft der Evangelischen Akademien Tübingen,* no. 3) (1954).

Fohlen, Claude. *La France de l'Entre-deux-guerres.* Paris: Casterman, 1966.

Forbes, Jill, and Michael Kelly. *French Cultural Studies: an introduction.* Oxford: Oxford University Press, 1995.

Francioni, Mario, with M. A. Schepisi. *Storia della psicsanalisi francese: teorie e instituzioni freudiane.* Turin: P. Boringhieri, 1982.

Gelly, Jean-Francois. "A la Recherche de l'Unité organique: la démarche du Parti Communiste Français (1934–1938)." *Mouvement Sociale,* no. 121 (October–December 1982).

Gerbod, Paul. "L'Université et la Littérature en France de 1919 à 1939." *Revue d'Histoire moderne et contemporaine* 25, no. 1 (January–March 1978).

Gershman, Herbert S. *The Surrealist Revolution in France.* Ann Arbor: University of Michigan, 1969.

Gide, André. *Retour de l'U.R.S.S.* Paris: Gallimard, 1936.

———. *Retouches à mon Retour de l'U.R.S.S.* Paris: Gallimard, 1937.

Ginsbourg, Ariel. *Nizan.* Paris: Editions Universitaires, 1966.

Gombin, Richard. *The Origins of Modern Leftism.* Translated by M. K. Perl. London: Penguin, 1975.

Guillaume, Marc, ed. *L'Etat des Sciences sociales en France.* Paris: La Découverte, 1986.

Hess, Rémi. *Henri Lefebvre et l'aventure du siècle.* Paris: A. M. Métailié, 1988.

Hewitt, Nicholasm. *"Les Maladies du siècle." The Image of Malaise in French Fiction and Thought in the Inter-war Years.* Hull, U.K.: .Hull University Press, 1988.

Hirsh, Arthur. *The French New Left: An Intellectual History from Sartre to Gorz.* Boston: South End, 1981.

Ishashpour, Youssef. *Paul Nizan, Une Figure mythique et son temps.* Paris: Sycomore, 1980.

Jacob, Max. *Lettres à un amie; Correspondance avec Jean Grenier 1922-1937.* Cognac: Le Temps qu'il fait/Monti, 1982.

Jacoby, Russell. *Dialectics of Defeat: Contours of Western Marxism.* New York: Cambridge University, 1981.

Jay, Martin. *The Dialectical Imagination.* Boston: Little Brown, 1973.

———. *Marxism and Totality: The Adventures of a Concept from Lukács to Habermas.* Berkeley and Los Angeles: University of California, 1984.

Joravsky, David. *Soviet Marxism and Natural Science 1917-1932.* London: Routledge and Kegan Paul, 1961.

Judt, Tony. "A Clown in Regal Purple: Social History and the Historians." *History Workshop,* no. 7 (1979).

———. *Marxism and the French Left.* New York: Oxford University Press, 1985.

Kelly, Michael. *Modern French Marxism*. Baltimore: Johns Hopkins, 1982.

———. "Hegel in France to 1940: A Bibliographic Essay." *Journal of European Studies* 11, no. 1 (#41, March 1981). An expanded version appeared in pamphlet form, University of Birmingham Modern Languages Publications, 1992.

King, Adèle. *Paul Nizan, Ecrivain*. Paris: Didier, 1976.

Kleinspehn, Thomas. *Der verdrängte Alltag: Henri Lefebvre, marxistische Kritik des Alltagslebens*. Glessen: Focus-Verlag, 1975.

Knight, Frida. *The French Resistance 1940–1944*. London: Lawrence and Wishart, 1975.

Kolakowski, Leszek. *Toward a Marxist Humanism*. Translated by J. Z. Peel. New York: Grove, 1968.

———. *L'Esprit révolutionnaire et Marxisme—Utopie et Anti-Utopie*. Translated by. J. Dewitte. Paris: PUF, 1978.

———. *Main Currents of Marxism*. Volume 3. Translated by P. S. Falla. London: Oxford University, 1978.

Koyre, Alexandre, "Rapport sur l'état des études Hegeliennes en France." *Revue des Sciences humaines* 5, no. 2 (April–June 1931).

Kriegel, Annie. "Le Parti communiste français sous la Troisième République (1920–1939). Evolution de ses effectifs." *Revue Française de Science Politique* 16, no. 1 (Frbruary 1966).

LeGuennec, Nicole. "Le Parti Communiste Français et la guerre du Rif." *Mouvement Sociale*, no. 78 (January–March 1972).

Le Grignou, Brigitte. "Henri Lefebvre ou les miroirs de l'intellectuel engage." 2 volumes. Ph.D. thesis, Université de Rennes, 1985.

Leiner, Jacqueline. *Le Destin Littéraire de Paul Nizan*. Paris: Klincksieck, 1970.

LeRoy Ladurie, Emmanuel. *Paris-Montpellier*. Paris: Gallimard, 1982.

Lichtheim, George. *Marxism in Modern France*. New York: Columbia University, 1966.

———. *From Marx to Hegel*. New York: Seabury, 1974.

Lindenberg, Daniel. *Le Marxisme introuvable*. Paris: Calmann-Lévy, 1975.

———. *Les Années souterraines (1937–1947)*. Paris: La Découverte, 1990.

Loubet del Bayle, Jean-Louis. *Les Non-Conformistes des Années trente*. Paris: Editions du Seuil, 1969.

Löwy, Michael. *Dialectique et Révolution*. Paris: Editions Anthropos, 1973.

———. *George Lukács—From Romanticism to Bolshevism*. Translated by P. Camiller. London: NLB, 1979.

McLellan, David. *Marxism and Religion*. London: Macmillan, 1987.

Megill, Allan. "Historicizing Nietzsche? Paradoxes and Lessons of a Hard Case." *Journal of Modern History* 68, no. 1 (March 1996).

Melnik-Duhamel, Catherine. "L'Affaire Georges Friedmann: à propos de la publication de 'De la Sainte Russie à l'U.R.S.S.," Mémoire de Diplome d'Etudes Approfondes d'Histoire contemporaine, Institut d'Etudes Politiques de Paris, 1984–1985.

Menucci, Vittorio. "La Molla del Progresso in un Revisionista: Henri Lefebvre." *Rivista di Filosofia Neo-Scolastica* 62 (1970).

Meyer, Kurt. *Henri Lefebvre, Ein Romantischer Revolutionär.* Vienna: EuropaVerlag, 1973.

de Mijolla, Alain. "La Psychanalyse en France." In *Histoire de la Psychanalyse*, edited by R. Jaccard. Tome 2. Paris: Hachette, 1982.

Milhau, Jacques. *Chroniques philosophiques.* Paris: Editions Sociales, 1972.

Morin, Violette. "A Georges Friedmann." *Communications*, no. 28 (1978).

Morino, Lina. *La Nouvelle Revue Française dans l'Histoire des Lettres.* Paris: Gallimard, 1939.

Mortimer, Edward. *The Rise of the French Communist Party, 1920–1947.* London and Boston: Farber and Farber, 1984.

Mounin, Georges. "La poésie de Pierre Morhange." *Chorus*, no. 2/3 (July 1962).

Nadeau, Maurice. *History of Surrealism.* Translated by R. Howard. New York: MacMillan, 1965.

Nasaw, David. "From Inquiétude to Revolution." *Journal of Contemporary History* 11, no. 2–3 (April–July 1976).

Naville, Pierre. *Psychologie, Marxisme, Matérialisme.* 2d ed. Paris: Rivière, 1948.

———. *L'Entre-deux-guerres: la lutte des classes en France 1927–1929.* Paris: Etudes et Documentation internationales, 1975.

Nizan, Henriette, with Marie-José Jaubert. *Libres mémoires.* Paris: Editions Robert Laffont, 1989.

Nora, Pierre, ed. *Les Lieux de Memoire.* Paris: Gallimard, 1984.

———. *Essais d'Ego-histoire.* Paris: Gallimard, 1987.

Normand, Guessler. "Henri Barbusse and his *Monde* (1928–1935): Progeny of the *Clarté* Movement and the Review «*Clarté*»." *Journal of Contemporary History* 11, no. 2-3 (April–July 1976).

Ory, Pascal. *Nizan: Destin d'un révolte.* Paris: Ramsay, 1980.

———. "Une Culture nationale à son apogèe." In *Histoire des Français, XIXᵉ-XXᵉ siècles*, edited by Yves Lequin. Tome 3. Paris: Armand Colin, 1984.

Pierre, Jose, ed. *Tracts Surréalistes et Déclarations Collectives.* Tome 1. 1922–1939. Paris: Terrain Vague, nd.

Pitkethly, Lawrence. "Hegel in Modern France (1900–1950)." Ph.D. thesis, University of London [1978?].

Poster, Mark. *Existential Marxism in Postwar France: From Sartre to Althusser.* Princeton: Princeton University, 1975.

Racine-Furlaud, Nicole. "Les Écrivains communistes en France (1920–1936)." thèse 3e cycle, Université de Paris, 1963.

———. "L'Association des écrivains et artistes révolutionnaires." *Mouvement Sociale*, no. 54 (January–March 1966).

———. "The *Clarté* Movement in France 1919–1921." *Journal of Contemporary History* 2, no. 2 (April 1967).

———. "Le Parti Communiste Français devant les Problèmes ideologiques et culturels." *Cahiers de la Fondation Nationale des Sciences Politiques*, no. 175 (1969); *Le Communisme en France et Italie.* Paris: Armand Colin, 1969.

———. "Le Comité de Vigilance des Intellectuels Antifascistes (1934–1939). Antifascisme et pacificisme." *Mouvement Sociale*, no. 101 (October–December 1971).

Racine-Furland, Nicole, and Louis Bodin, eds. "Une Revue d'intellectuele communiste dans les années vingt: *Clarté* (1921–1928). *Revue Française de Science Politique* 17, no. 3 (June 1967).

———. *Le Parti Communiste Français pendant l'entre-deux-guerres.* Paris: Armand Colin, 1972.

———. "Du mouvement à la revue *Clarté:* jeunes intellectuels 'révolutionnaires' de la guerre et de l'après-guerre 1916–1925." *Cahiers de l'Institut d'Histoire du Temps Present*, no. 6 (November 1987).

Rearick, Charles, *The French in Love and War: Popular Culture in the Era of the World Wars.* New Haven: Yale University Press, 1997.

Redfern, W. D. *Paul Nizan: Committed Literature in a Conspiratorial World.* Princeton: Princeton University, 1972.

Rieuneau, Maurice. *Guerre et Révolution dans le Roman français de 1919 à 1939.* Paris: Klincksieck, 1974.

Robert, J.-L., et al. *Le PCF: étapes et problèmes 1920–1972.* Paris: Editions Sociales, 1981.

Robrieux, Philippe, *Histoire intérieure du Parti Communiste.* Tome 1. Paris: Fayard, 1980.

Roth, Jack J. *The Cult of Violence: Sorel and the Sorelians.* Berkeley and Los Angeles: University of California, 1980.

Roth, Michael S. *Knowing and History: Appropriations of Hegel in Twentieth-Century France.* Ithaca: Cornell University, 1988.

Roudinesco, Elisabeth. *La Bataille de cent ans: histoire de la psychologie en France.* Tome 1: 1885–1939. Paris: Ramsay, 1982.

Rubel, Maximilien. *Bibliographie des oeuvres de Karl Marx,* Paris: Rivière, 1956. *Supplement à la Bibliographie.* Paris: Rivière, 1960.

Salvadori, Roberto. *Hegel in Francia.* Bari: DeDonato, 1974.

Sanouillet, Michel. *Dada à Paris.* Paris: Pauvert, 1965.

Schalk, David L. *The Spectrum of Political Engagement.* Princeton: Princeton University, 1979.

Schmidt, Alfred. "Henri Lefebvre and Contemporary Interpretations of Marx." in *The Unknown Dimension: European Marxism since Lenin,* edited by D. Howard and K. E. Klare. New York: Basic, 1972.

Schrift, Alan D. *Nietzsche's French Legacy.* New York: Routledge, 1995.

Sève, Lucien. *La Philosophie française contemporaine et sa genèse de 1789 à nos jours.* Paris: Editions Sociales, 1962.

———. "Le Rôle du Parti Communiste français dans l'édition en France des classiques du Marxisme-Leninisme." In *La Fondation du Parti Communiste français et les pénétration des idées léninistes en France: Cinquante ans d'action communiste (1920–1970); compte rendu analytique du colloque scientifique.* Paris: Editions Sociales, 1971.

———. "Politzer et Nous." *Cahiers de l'Institut Maurice Thorez,* no. 27 (May–July 1972).

———. *Marxism and the Theory of Human Personality.* London: Lawrence and Wishart, 1975.

———. *Man in Marxist Theory and the Psychology of Personality.* Translated by J. McGreal. Atlantic Highlands N.J.: Humanities, 1978.

Short, Robert S. "The Political History of the Surrealist Movement in France, 1918–1940." Ph.D. thesis, University of Sussex, 1965.

———. "The Politics of Surrealism, 1920-1936." *Journal of Contemporary History* 1, no. 2 (April 1966).

———. "Paris Dada and Surrealism." *Journal of European Studies* 9, no. 1–2 (March–June 1979).

Siegel, Jerrold. *Bohemian Paris: Culture, Politics, and the Boundaries of Bourgeois Life 1830–1930.* New York: Elisabeth Sifton/Viking, 1986.

Smith, Douglas. *Transvaluations: Nietzsche in France 1872–1972.* Oxford: Clarendon Press, 1996.

Soubise, Louis. *Le Marxisme après Marx (1956–1965).* Paris: Aubier Montaigne, 1967.

Soucy, Robert. *French Fascism: The First Wave 1924–1933.* New Haven: Yale University Press, 1986.

———. *French Fascism: The Second Wave 1933–1939.* New Haven: Yale University Press, 1995.

Tartakowsky, Danielle, "Les Conditions de la pénétration du Marxisme en France." *Cahiers de l'Institut Maurice Thorez,* no. 28 (September–October 1972).

———. "Le Marxisme et les intellectuels de 1920 à 1935." *Pensée,* no. 205 (May/June 1979).

———. *Les Premiers Communists français: formation des cadres et bolchévisation.* Paris: Presses de la Fondation Nationale des Sciences Politiques, 1980.

Tartakowsky, Danielle, and Claude Prevost, "Les Intellectuels et le P.C.F. 1920–1940, Héritage et réalités nouvelles." *Cahiers de l'Institut Maurice Thorez,* no. 43, ns# 15 (January–March 1976).

Thibaudet, Albert. "Réflexions sur la Littérature: L'Idée de Génération." *Nouvelle Revue Française,* no. 90 (March 1921).

Thirion, André. *Revolutionaries without Revolution.* Translated by J. Neugroschel. London: Cassell, 1976.

Tison-Braun, Micheline. *La Crise de l'Humanisme.* Tome 2. Paris: Nizet, 1967.

Tonnet-LaCroix, Eliane. "Le Monde littéraire et le Surréalisme: Premières Réactions." *Melusine,* Tome 1 (1980).

Touchard, Jean. "L'Esprit des années 1930." In *Tendances politiques dans la vie française depuis 1789.* Paris: Hachette, 1960.

———. "Le Parti Communiste française et les intellectuels (1920-1939)." *Revue Française de Science Politique* 27, no. 3 (June 1967).

———. *La Gauche en France depuis 1900.* Paris: Editions du Seuil, 1977.

Trebitsch, Michel. "Le Renouveau philosophique avorté des années trente. Entretien avec Henri Lefebvre." *Europe,* no. 683 (March 1986).

———. "Les mésaventures du groupe Philosophies (1924–1933)." *Revue des Revues,* no. 3 (spring 1987).

———. "Le groupe 'Philosophies' de Max Jacob aux Surréalistes 1924–1925." *Cahiers de l'Institut d'Histoire du Temps Present,* no. 6 (November 1987).

———. "La mystique révolutionnaire dans les avant-gardes des années vingt," *Révolte et Société.* Actes du quartrieme Colloque d'histoire du Temps Present. Tome 1 (1989).

———. "Henri Lefebvre et la revue *Avant-Poste.* Une analyse marxiste marginale du fascisme," *Lendemains,* no. 57 (1990).

———. "Philosophie et marxisme dans les années trente: le marxisme critique d'Henri Lefebvre." *L'Engagement des intellectuels dans la France des années trente.* Montreal: Université du Quebec, 1990.

Winock, Michel. *Histoire politique de la Revue Esprit 1930–1950.* Paris: Editions du Seuil, 1975.

Wohl, Robert. *The Generation of 1914.* Cambridge: Harvard University, 1979.

Index

Academie matérialiste, 136, 150
Action française, 76, 96, 139
Adler, Alfred, 87
Adorno, Theodore, 138, 222–24
Alain, 145
Althusser, Louis, 15, 209, 222, 239, 240n. 5
Amis de l'U.R.S.S., 134
Anderson, Kevin, 231n. 10
Anderson, Perry, 239
Annales, 116–17, 166n. 68
Annales d' Histoire économique et sociale (*Annales: Economies, sociétés, civilisations*), 137, 138, 160n. 14, 179, 186, 193, 194, 237, 247
Année Psychologique, 93, 94, 96
Aragon, Louis, 42, 43, 114, 237
Archives de Philosophie, 93, 124, 218
Archives de Psychologie, 93
Archiv für die Geschichte des Sozialismus und der Arbeiterbewegung (*Grünberg Archiv*), 137

Arguments, 239
Arkhiv K. Marksa i F. Engel'sa, 107, 114
Arland, Marcel, 20–21, 22, 23, 44, 46, 66, 245
"Arnold, Félix," 77n. 4. *See also* Politzer, Georges
Arnold, V., 77n. 4
Aron, Raymond, 26, 137, 160n. 13
"Arouet, François," 82. *See also* Politzer, Georges
Association des Ecrivains et des Artistes Révolutionnaires (AEAR), 135, 140, 147, 150, 151, 219
Audard, Jean, 98–99
Avant-Poste, 140–49, 150, 156, 157, 161n. 22, 205, 212

Barbé, Henri, 112–13, 130n. 33, 135
Barbusse, Henri, 26, 36, 55n. 37, 110, 114, 123, 134, 135, 146
Barres, 66
Barsalou, André, 57n. 65

271

Bartoli, Jacques, 148, 149

Baudelaire, Charles , 220

Beauroy, Gabriel, 57n. 65

Beauvoir, Simone de, 28

Benveniste, Emile, 53n. 22 , 57n. 65

Bergson, Henri, 38, 55n. 51, 74, 81–84, 85, 87, 91, 95, 100nn. 3 & 10, 106, 136, 143, 150, 155

Berl, Emmanuel, 108, 138

Bernier, Jean, 51

Berr, Henri, 137

Bertram, Ernst, 38

Bifur, 123

Bischler, W., 93

Blake, William, 61

Bloch, Jean-Richard, 145

Bloch, Marc, 137

Blondel, Maurice, 25, 55n. 37, 68, 100n. 3

Blum, Leon, 110

Boccon-Gibod, Liliane, 10, 33n. 26, 203n. 54

Bogdanov, A. A., 97

Boucher, Maurice, 70

Bouglé, Celestine, 137, 153

Boutonnier, Paul, 106

Boutroux, Emile, 100n. 3

Braudel, Fernand, 137, 186–87, 237

Breton, André, 23, 42, 43, 70, 114, 118–19

"Brown, John," 23. *See also* Morhange, Pierre

Bruhat, Jean, 106, 117, 129n. 32, 188, 190, 192, 193

Brunschvicg, Leon, 36, 40, 44, 100n. 3, 138

Bukharin, N., 110, 120, 188, 196

Bulletin communiste, 109

Burke, Kenneth, 87, 101n. 20, 134, 237–38, 243n. 7

Cahiers de Liberation, 237

Cahiers du bolchévisme (later *Cahiers du Communisme*), 50, 109, 113, 117, 120, 121, 152, 188, 190, 225

Cahiers du Sud, 60, 61, 119, 150

Cahiers du mois, 48

Cassou, Jean, 193, 237

Caute, David, 13

"Caves, Jean," 35. *See also* Grenier, Jean

Ce Soir, 151, 229

Céline, Louis-Ferninand, 141, 146

Célor, André, 112–13, 130n. 33, 135

Cercle d'Etudes marxistes, 136

Cercle de la Russie Neuve, 134, 150

"Chassagne, H.," 219. *See also* Hainchelin, Charles

Chiappe, Jean, 50

Chalput, René, 55n. 37

Clarté, 36, 37, 40, 46, 47, 48, 49, 50–51, 65, 134, 137

Clarté (1926–1929), 72, 108

Clarté (1936–1939), 151

Cocteau, Jean, 35, 37, 40, 53n. 22, 108

Cognoit, Georges, 153

Cohen-Solal, Annie, 33n. 26, 115, 129n. 32

Cohn-Bendit, Danny, 228

Combat, 139

Comité de Vigilance des Intellectuels antifascistes (CVIA), 136

Commune, 98–99, 141, 147, 148, 151, 152, 170, 189, 219

Communications, 237

Correspondance, 49
Cowley, Malcolm, 134
Crastre, Victor, 72
Crémieux, Benjamin, 73, 124
Crevel, René, 35, 43, 48
Critique, 237
Curtis, Ernst Robert, 55n. 37

Dachkowski, 109
Daniel-Rops, Henri (Petriot, Henri), 22–23, 28, 47, 59
Deborin, Abram, 107, 114, 120
de Man, Henri, 97
Decour, Jacques, 235
Delteil, Joseph, 43
Descartes, René, 65, 82, 136, 150, 152, 154
Desson, André, 37, 40
Devenir social, 114, 117
Divorse, Fernand, 55n. 37
Doriot, Jacques, 50, 110, 121, 135
Dostoyevsky, 106, 220
Drieu la Rochelle, Pierre, 35, 37, 152, 225
Duclos, Jacques, 195, 236
Duret, Jacques, 208
du Gard, Martin, 141
Duveau, Georges, 187–88
Duvignaud, Jean, 14

Eastman, Max, 110
Ehrenburg, Ilya, 133
Eluard, Paul, 23, 42, 43, 48, 55nn. 36 & 37, 237
Engels, Friedrich, 14, 70, 72, 90, 107, 108, 113, 120, 133, 153, 169, 170, 171, 185, 190

Esprit: Cahiers (1926–1927), 44, 60, 61, 62, 64, 67, 70, 72, 73, 74, 76, 77n. 5, 94, 107, 115, 124, 148–49, 180, 245
Esprit (1932–), 139, 145, 147, 148–49, 156, 187, 220, 229
Etiemble, René, 219, 221
Etudes, 73, 94, 187
Europe, 26, 37, 75, 91, 95, 108, 139, 150, 151, 155, 156, 172, 179, 193

Febvre, Lucien, 137, 193–94, 230n. 6, 237
Federal Bureau of Investigation (FBI), 130–31n. 35, 157n. 2, 159n. 7, 238, 243n. 11
Fernandez, Ramon, 39
Flügel, J. C., 94
Ford, Henry, 175–76
Forti, Edgard, 38, 40
Frankfurt School, 15, 87, 108, 123, 126n. 7, 138, 160n. 13, 222, 238, 243n. 8
Freud, Sigmund, 24, 52n. 1, 84–87, 95, 97, 98, 99
Fréville, Jean, 106
Friedmann, Georges, 13, 14, 15, 16, 22, 24, 25–26, 52, 59, 60, 66, 67, 68, 69, 74, 75, 76, 87, 106, 115, 117, 122, 124, 134, 136–38, 148, 149, 151, 156, 160n. 14, 169–200, 218, 229, 245, 246–48; *Crise du Progrés*, 169, 174–77, 198, 200, 201n. 13, 218, 237, 247; *De la Sainte Russe à la U.R.S.S.*, 150, 172, 180–97, 199, 247
Fromm, Erich, 87

Garaudy, Roger, 222
George, Pierre, 153

"Gérard, Francis," 38. *See also* Rosenthal, Gérard
Gide, André, 66, 141, 177–80, 188
Giese, Fritz, 87, 88
Glaymann, Claude, 106, 116, 118, 123
Gorky, Maksim, 97, 178
Gramsci, Antonio, 72, 217, 222–23
Grand Jeu, 114
Green, Julien, 40
Grenier, Jean, 35, 38, 40, 74–75, 103n. 55, 148–49, 220, 221
Groupe d'Etudes matérialistes, 136
Groupe des Ecrivains Poletariens, 135
Grünberg, Carl, 137–38
Guéhenno, Jean, 237
Guerre Civile, 51
Guterman, Norbert, 10, 13, 14, 15, 16, 24, 28, 31n. 18, 39, 40, 41, 43, 52, 53n. 22, 55n. 51, 57n. 65, 60, 61, 76, 77n. 4, 106, 107, 115, 116, 118, 119, 122, 123, 124, 126n. 7, 130nn. 34 & 35, 133, 138, 140, 142–44, 147–50, 155, 157, 157n. 2, 159n. 7, 205–17, 224, 226, 229, 232n. 23, 237–38, 246
Hainchelin, Charles, 114, 150, 219–22
Harlaire, André, 37, 40
Hegel, George Wilhelm Friedrich, 14, 15, 16, 61, 62, 70, 71, 72, 76, 86, 98, 107, 108, 120, 138, 147, 171, 205–207, 209–12, 226, 227, 228
Heidegger, Martin, 69, 155, 176
Hésnard, André, 88, 95–96
Honnert, Robert, 37
Horkheimer, Max, 138, 222–24
L'Humanité, 49, 50, 51, 75, 112, 113, 118, 121, 151, 152, 170, 188, 197, 229

Humbert-Droz, Jules, 117, 130n. 33
Humeau, Edmond, 147–48
Husserl, 176
Hyppolite, Jean, 71

International Journal of Psycho-Analysis, 94
International Union of Revolutionary Writers, 134–35, 151
International Psycho-Analytic Association, 99
Internationale situationniste, 239
Izvestia, 110

Jacob, Max, 31n. 18, 35, 37, 38, 40–41, 42, 74
Jacoby, Russell, 232n. 23
Janet, Pierre, 88
Jeune Europe, 139
Jouhandeau, Marcel, 38
Jourdain, Francis, 195, 197
Jourdan, Henri, 38, 57n. 67

Kant, Immanuel, 14, 44, 84, 86, 93, 223
Kantor, J. R., 87
Kautsky, Karl, 110, 175
Kojéve, Alexandre, 71, 205
Kolakowski, Leszek, 15, 28–30, 246
Korsch, Karl, 72, 222–23
Koyré, Alexandre, 71

Lalou, René, 108
Langevin, Paul, 153, 195, 197
Lavelle, 41
Lawrence, D. H., 220
Lecache, Bernard, 145
LeCorbusier, 21

Lefebvre, Henri, 13, 14, 15, 16, 23, 24, 25, 28, 38–39, 41, 44–46, 51–52, 53n. 22, 55n. 67, 60, 61, 62, 67–69, 73, 74, 75, 105, 106, 109, 111, 115, 116, 118, 119, 120, 123, 124–25, 133, 134, 138–50, 157, 195, 205–17, 232n. 23, 238–39, 245, 246–48; *Cahiers sur la dialectique de Hegel*, 205, 209–12, 217, 226, 247; *Conscience mystifiée*, 157, 205, 213–24, 229, 231n. 15, 238, 247; *Materialisme dialectique*, 224–25, 229; *Morceaux Choisis de Hegel*, 205–207; *Morceaux Choisis de Karl Marx*, 205, 207–209, 247; *Nietzsche*, 150, 225–28, 229, 247

Lefranc, Georges, 14

Leibniz, 26, 136, 173

Lenin, Vladimir Ilych, 14, 72, 106, 107, 108, 109, 114, 120, 122, 173, 179, 185, 190–91, 196, 205, *Materialism and Empirio-criticism*, 97, 98, 99, 154, 170, 191; *Philosophic Notebooks on Hegel's Science of Logic*, 15, 98, 150, 169, 170, 171, 209–12, 217, 226, 231n. 10

Leonovich, M., 110

LeRoy Ladurie, Emmanuel, 197

Lesvignes, Marcel, 38–39

Lichtheim, George, 13, 17nn. 1 & 4

Ligue Communiste, 134

Lindenberg, Daniel, 14

Loewenstein, Roldolphe, 93

Lotte, Paul, 35

Lowenthal, Leo, 138, 238

Löwy, Michel, 34n. 39

Lubeck, Mathias, 55n. 37

Lukács, Georg, 69, 72, 201n. 13, 208, 222–23, 226, 232n. 23, 239

Lunacharsky, Anatole, 97, 126n. 7

Lustiger, Jean-Marie (Cardinal and Archbishop of Paris), 17n. 5

Lutte de Classes, 108–109, 110, 114, 133, 134

Mach, Ernst, 97

Malraux, André, 146–47

Mandelbrojt, Szolem, 24, 31n. 18, 41, 43

Marc, Alexandre, 124, 218, 221

Marcel, Gabriel, 55n. 37, 73, 75, 108, 154

Marcuse, Herbert, 138

Maritain, Jacques, 67

Marx, Karl, 14, 15, 47, 49, 70, 71, 72, 76, 90, 95, 109, 113, 120, 143–44, 147, 185, 205, 206, 226, 227, 228, 245; "Economic and Philosophic Manuscripts," 15, 98, 107, 108, 142, 169, 200n. 1

Marxism, 13, 14, 15, 16, 65, 67, 69, 70, 73, 75, 84, 91, 98, 105, 142, 150, 155, 157, 169–74, 179, 198–200, 205–18, 222–24

Marx-Engels Institute, 107, 114, 120, 126n. 7, 138

Massis, Henri, 47

Maulnier, Thierry, 147

Maurras, Charles, 96

Mauvais Temps, 106, 119

Melnik-Duhamel, Catherine, 203n. 54

Melora, Victor, 106

"Mesnil, Albert," 106. *See also* Guterman, Norbert

Meyers, Charles, 87

Michael, Georges, 37, 46–47, 49, 68
Minev, Stefan, 117, 120, 121, 130n. 33
Monde, 110, 123, 134, 179
Morhange, Pierre, 13, 14, 16, 23–24, 35–52, 55n. 36, 57n. 65, 60, 61, 62, 63–64, 66, 68, 74, 75–76, 87, 105, 106, 109, 110, 112, 115, 116, 118, 119, 122, 123, 133, 134, 140, 149, 155–57, 229, 239–40, 246
Morin, Edgar, 10, 14, 23
"Morris, Th. W.," 99. *See also* Politzer, Georges
Mounier, Eammanel, 139, 147, 148, 149, 215, 229
Muller, Maurice, 57n. 65
Münzenburg, Willi, 130n. 33

Nacci, Michela, 200n. 1, 201n. 13
Naville, Pierre, 72, 77n. 4, 108, 109, 114, 124, 133, 134, 199, 229–30
New Republic, 123, 134, 138, 159n. 7, 237
Nietzsche, Friedrich, 25, 32n. 25, 46, 49, 67, 84, 220, 226–29, 247
Nizan, Henriette (Alphen), 27, 33n. 26, 115, 129n. 32, 237, 238
Nizan, Paul-Yves, 13, 14, 16, 26, 27, 106, 115, 116, 118, 121, 123, 129n. 32, 134, 138, 139–40, 147–48, 149–51, 157n. 2, 189–90, 192, 193, 207, 229, 235–37, 246
Nora, Pierre, 10, 203n. 54
Nouvelle revue française, 19, 20, 37, 38, 39, 42, 44, 48, 73, 74, 94, 108, 119, 139–40, 147, 148, 155–56, 178, 194, 219, 224
Nouvelle revue marxiste, 124
Nouvelles littéraires, 48, 72, 94

Ordre nouveau, 139
Ory, Pascal, 10, 13

Parain, Charles, 155
Parisian Psychoanalytic Society, 92, 96
Parti Communiste français (PCF, French Communist Party), 14, 16, 49–52, 65, 72, 75–77, 87, 98, 99, 105, 106, 111–23, 133, 134–36, 140, 153, 157, 207, 225, 229, 235–37, 245, 246
Pascal, Blaise, 25, 32n. 25, 46, 67, 227
Passage, Henri du, 187
Pensée, Revue du Rationalisme moderne, 153–55, 166n. 68
Pensée libre, 236
Perretz, Martin, 159n. 7
Péri, Gabriel, 75–76
Perrot, Michelle, 17n. 5
Philosophies, 24, 35–52, 52n. 1, 55n. 51, 60, 67, 74, 107, 124, 141, 245
Pialat, Etienne, 93
Piatnitsky, Osip A., 111
Pichon, Edouard, 95–96
Piéron, Henri, 93, 94, 96
Pierre-Quint, Leon, 95, 96, 109, 145
Plans, 139
Plekhanov, G., 113, 114, 133
Pod Znamenem Marksizma, 110
Pokrovsky, 183
Polgar, Viktor, 32n. 20
Politzer, Georges, 13, 14, 16, 24–25, 28, 41, 43, 44, 47, 52, 60, 61, 62, 64–66, 68, 69, 70, 74, 75, 76, 77n. 4, 81–99, 109, 115–18, 119, 121, 123, 129n. 32, 133, 138, 148, 150, 151–55, 157, 165n. 60, 190–96, 229, 246; *Critique*

des fondements de la psychologie, 84–86, 91–92, 93–94; *Fin d'une parade philosophique*, 81–84, 92, 95

Politzer, Maï, 236

Pollock, Frederick, 138

Prévost, Jean, 91

Prinzhorn, Hans, 87–89

Proust, Marcel, 39, 143

Pushkin, Alexander, 110

Rank, Otto, 88

Ranki, Gyorgy, 32n. 20

Rappoport, Charles, 106, 107, 109, 110, 114, 117, 120, 121, 125n. 4

Reich, Wilmelm, 99

Révolution Surréaliste, 49, 50, 51, 72

Revue de la psychologie concrète, 77, 87–91, 93–97, 101n. 22, 106, 115, 117, 129n. 32

Revue des Pamphletaires, 40, 53n. 20, 61

Revue française de Psychanalyse, 93

Revue marxiste, 14, 15, 16, 51, 87, 105–25, 126n. 6, 129n. 32, 134, 135, 137, 142, 155, 157, 237, 245

Riazanov, David, 107, 109, 114, 120, 126n. 7, 133, 138

Rilke, 53n. 22

Rimbaud, Arthur, 49

Rivera, Primo de, 36

Rolland, Romain, 26, 195, 197

Rosenberg, Alfred, 154

Rosenthal, Gérard, 38, 108, 134

Rougemont, Denis de, 139, 140, 147

Roure, Lucien, 73, 94, 96

Russell, Bertrand, 133

Sartre, Jean-Paul, 21, 26, 69, 237, 245

Schelling, 14, 16, 46, 61, 62, 65, 70, 72, 76, 86, 108

Schwab, Raymond, 155–56

Schwob, Lucie, 55n. 37

Seghers, Pierre, 237

Serge, Victor, 141, 187

Séve, Lucien, 240n. 5

Short, Robert S., 57n. 66, 58nn. 71 & 73

Solomon, Jacques, 153, 235–36

Sorel, Georges, 47

Soupault, Philippe, 35, 43

Soustelle, Jacques, 137, 193, 194, 195

Souvarine, Boris, 109, 121

Spinoza, 26, 48, 66, 136, 171, 173

Stalin, Joseph, 72, 110, 120, 185, 186, 187, 188, 191, 192, 196

Stendhal, 220

Szombati, Béla, 32n. 20

Tarlé, E., 108, 109

Tayor, Frederick, 175–76

Terray, Emannual, 14

Thibaudet, Albert, 38, 40, 48, 74, 108

Thirion, André, 114, 115, 121

Thomas, Norman, 110

Thorez, Maurice, 50, 57n. 66, 76, 112, 121, 122, 135–36, 165n. 60, 195, 196, 229

Trebitsch, Michel, 32n. 25, 129n. 32

Touraine, Alain, 10, 14

Tribune marxiste, 124

Trotsky, Leon, 75, 106, 109, 110, 112, 114, 126n. 7, 133, 134, 185, 186, 187, 188, 191

Tzara, Tristan, 43, 53n. 22

Unamuno, Miguel, 36, 37, 141

Université libre, 236

Vaillant-Couturier, Paul, 75–76, 112, 114, 121, 135
Valéry, Paul, 19–20, 21, 23, 35, 46, 65, 143, 214, 245, 248
Valet, Henriette, 140, 146
Valois, Georges, 27
Variétés, 115
Vérité, 134
Vestnik Kommunisticheskoi Akademii, 114
Vitrac, Roger, 42
Volontaires, 197

Wahl, Jean, 61, 70–71, 94, 154–55
Wallon, Henri, 153, 155, 195, 197
Weber, Jean, 38
Weitling, Wilhelm, 129n. 30
Wilson, T. C., 237
Wittfögel, Karl, 108

"Yankel," 118. *See also* Glayman, Claude

Zeitschrift für Sozialforschung, 138
Zetkin, Clara, 110
Zimmerman, Jean-Paul, 57n. 65